'This text provides a welcome and comprehensive look at the circumstances of refugees, and in so doing, argues effectively that education is an essential pathway into their resettlement, flourishing and future opportunities.'

Susan Barber, Senior Lecturer in Education, Simon Fraser University, Canada

'This is a very timely and internationally significant book on refugee education. It is moving, informative and academically robust. It is an inspirational book that highlights optimism over despair and offers ways forward for schools. This is a must-read book for all involved in refugee education.'

Ian Thompson, Associate Professor of Education, University of Oxford, UK

'Bringing together the lived experiences of refugee students with practical theory, the authors brilliantly illuminate the difference schools can make, as sites of recognition, belonging and ultimately healing, in the lives of young people who have experienced too much of the world's cruelty. A must read for anyone interested in inclusive education, refugee studies or social and global justice.'

Wayne Veck, Reader in Education, University of Winchester, UK

REFUGEE EDUCATION

In the last five years, more child refugees have made perilous journeys into Europe than at any point since the Second World War. Once refugee children begin to establish their new lives, education becomes a priority. However, access to high-quality inclusive education can be challenging and is a social justice issue for schools, policymakers and for the research community. Underpinned by strong theoretical framings and based on socially just principles, this book provides a detailed exploration into this ethically charged, emotive and complex subject.

Refugee Education offers an interdisciplinary perspective to critical debates and public discourse about the topic, contextualized by the voices of young refugees and those seeking to support them in and out of education. Shaped by practitioners, the book develops an inclusive model of education for refugee children based on the concepts of safety, belonging and success, and presents practical tools for planning and operationalizing the ethics of inclusive education.

This book includes a wide range of case study examples which reveal the positive outcomes that are possible, given the right inputs. It is essential reading for teachers, senior leaders and policymakers as well as academic researchers in education, social policy, migration and refugee studies.

Joanna McIntyre is Associate Professor of Education at The University of Nottingham, UK.

Fran Abrams is Chief Executive of the Education Media Centre charity, which is devoted to raising the profile of good evidence about education. She is a journalist and the author of five earlier books on education, social policy and social history.

REFUGEE EDUCATION

Theorising Practice in Schools

Joanna McIntyre and Fran Abrams

LONDON AND NEW YORK

First published 2021
by Routledge
2 Park Square, Milton Park, Abingdon, Oxon OX14 4RN

and by Routledge
52 Vanderbilt Avenue, New York, NY 10017

Routledge is an imprint of the Taylor & Francis Group, an informa business

British Library Cataloguing-in-Publication Data
A catalogue record for this book is available from the British Library

Library of Congress Cataloging-in-Publication Data
Names: McIntyre, Joanna (Associate professor of education), author. | Abrams, Fran, 1963- author.
Title: Refugee education: Theorising Practice in Schools / Joanna McIntyre and Fran Abrams.
Description: Abingdon, Oxon ; New York, NY : Routledge, 2021. | Includes bibliographical references and index. | Identifiers: LCCN 2020038748 | ISBN 9780367208653 (hardback) | ISBN 9780367208660 (paperback) | ISBN 9780429263811 (ebook)
Subjects: LCSH: Refugee children--Education--Europe. | Inclusive education--Europe.
Classification: LCC LC3736.A2 M35 2021 | DDC 371.826/914--dc23
LC record available at https://lccn.loc.gov/2020038748

ISBN: 978-0-367-20865-3 (hbk)
ISBN: 978-0-367-20866-0 (pbk)
ISBN: 978-0-429-26381-1 (ebk)

Typeset in Interstate
by SPi Global, India

'Now every day is better than the year before, every day I am learning something- education is the only way'

Ammar, aged 16

CONTENTS

FIGURES

ACKNOWLEDGEMENTS

I am deeply grateful to the many people I have encountered during the writing of this book who have willingly engaged in conversations about the topic of refugee education. They might not have known it at the time, but they have all in different ways shaped my thinking for the content of this text. I am particularly grateful to colleagues in the School of Education, University of Nottingham for their friendship and encouragement and support for the work.

Thank you to Sinikka Neuhaus, Katarina Blennow, Haya Fakoush, Henry Kulaya, Sally Coulton, Lars-Olof Välemark, Ingrid Sturén, Brigitta Jönsson for all our early conversations about the theoretical underpinnings for Section 1.

This book would not have been written without the generosity, expertise and insights of the practitioners in the case study schools. Whilst the schools, school leaders and teachers have all been anonymized in the text, I would like to record my gratitude to Asta Baranauskiene, Ed Cornwall, Jane Daffe, Beth Hilditch, Maliki Konteh, Ginette Osborne, Cherry Pearce and Melanie Tuck for all of our debates and dialogues as we shaped and theorised pedagogical practice for refugee children. Thank you also to Marianne Blake, Sara Fletcher, Sian Hampton, Rachel Spencer, and Dave Tungate, Adrian Sharpe and Susannah Bates for giving their time and demonstrating their inclusive stance and leadership.

Thanks also to Elizabeth Walton, Susan Jones, Simon McGrath, Volker Wedekind and Clare Brooks for guidance at key points of the writing and especially to Christine Hall for her continued guidance and support and for her comments on every stage of the manuscript. Thank you also to my family, to Colin, Joel and Anya, who always believed in this work and that the book would be written.

Finally, thank you to all the young people who willingly shared their experiences and wanted to contribute to an endeavour that might make it better for those who come after them. I have been overwhelmed by their kindness, humour, tenacity and optimism. They chose their own pseudonyms so are anonymous in the text but this book is for them and those who work so tirelessly to support them.

Jo McIntyre

I would like to thank the many staff, volunteers and associates of the Refugee Support Network, who provided many of the contacts and interviewees for the place and policy sections of the book. Also Adrian Matthews and Marie-France Faulkner at Cambridge Refugee Resettlement Campaign; Adeela Bainbridge and other staff at the British Red Cross, particularly those on the Surviving to Thriving project; staff and pupils at the Iqra Academy in Peterborough; John Jordan-Hills at Cambridgeshire County Council; Jo Schofield, UASC Regional Co-ordinator for the East of England; Louise Gooch at the Strategic Migration Partnership for the East of England; Charlotta Nuboer-Cope at the Oxford orientation programme; Elizabeth Adlington and Chris Jackson for comments on draft chapters; the East of England UASC Leads group; and to Hamid Khan of the RSN Youth Advisory Board. The biggest thanks, of course, must go to the many young people who talked so openly about such deeply personal and often traumatic experiences. Most of them must remain anonymous, but they will know who they are.

Fran Abrams

FOREWORD

For those refugee children fortunate enough to reach safety, their journeys do not stop there. Indeed, it could be said that their journeys are just beginning, even if simply finding safety has, for many, taken years and involved hundreds or even thousands of miles.

Safety is, of course, the overwhelming motivation for the vast majority of children who flee their homes and communities. But finding safety is just the start. Children also need hope. Once safe, refugee children, like all children, need opportunity and a sense of belonging if they are to be able to thrive.

Education is undoubtedly the answer. Education not only provides refugee children with the hope and means to succeed, but also anchors a child, whose life experience is often defined by chaos, fear and isolation, within a society, a school, a classroom, where he or she can belong.

When I arrived as an unaccompanied refugee child in the UK aged six, I spoke two languages – Czech and German, but not a word of English. It's lonely – arriving in a foreign country, not speaking the language and knowing no one. It was my school that changed that for me and began my journey from lonely refugee child to university graduate and finally to becoming an MP and a peer – something I never would have dared to dream of as a frightened 6-year-old child. And what I didn't learn in class I learnt in the playground – making friends and learning about my new home, alongside other refugee children, was in some ways as important as the academic opportunities that my school gave me. I'm still in touch with some of those friends today, 80 years on.

Our continent is witnessing the biggest refugee crisis since the Second World War. Children in their hundreds of thousands are the innocent victims. Losing your home and family is tragedy enough for anyone, especially a child, but we must do all we can to make sure these tragedies do not also mean losing the opportunity to learn to read and write and build a successful life. It is only through education that the scars can begin to heal. That's why I brought an amendment to ensure that when young Syrian refugees came to the UK they could move into higher education immediately, rather than being locked out of the education system for three years while their claim was processed.

Being a refugee doesn't have to cost a child its future. Teach them, and my experience tells me that they can and do go on to achieve great and extraordinary things.

Alf Dubs

1　Introduction

Joanna McIntyre and Fran Abrams

Of the 25 million refugees across the world, more than half are children. This book is about how to provide an inclusive education environment for refugee children, a topic of global significance which also has huge implications for classrooms in localities many miles away from zones of conflict, persecution, political instability and increasingly inhospitable climate environments. These children, many of whom have, in recent years, made their way to Europe on forced migration routes, are trying to establish new lives in countries vast distances from their homelands. Since 2015, Europe has been home to more child refugees than at any point since the Second World War (Save the Children 2016).

Once refugee children have reached a point of safety and begin the process of resuming their lives in their new contexts, access to education becomes a real priority. Refugee education operates at global, national and local levels. Although there are international agreements about the ways in which nation-states should operationalise their commitment to provision of high-quality inclusive education and opportunities for lifelong learning, education systems are experienced very differently at the local level by refugee children who have resettled in different countries (Dryden-Peterson 2016). Those working in the field of refugee education in high-income countries often have to negotiate between the competing demands of highly meritocratic and performative national education systems and their own vocational commitment to compassionate inclusive education for all.

The local context for the research evidence discussed in this book is England, but the evidence and arguments are also intended to speak to other similar international resettlement contexts. The main contribution the book seeks to make is to provide a theoretical model for the inclusion of refugees in national education systems. This theoretical model has been shaped by practitioners; it is responsive to the voices of young refugees for whom education represents the first steps in rebuilding lives with possibility and meaningful futures. We see the model not as an abstraction but as a practical tool to be used in planning and operationalising the ethics of inclusive education.

This introductory chapter sets out why and how we've come to write this book, which we hope will be both thought-provoking for policymakers and supportive of day to day practice in schools and colleges.

The rationale for the book and our approach

The focus of the book is on the challenges faced by young refugees and by those working to include them in secondary education in schools and colleges. Refugee education is an extremely significant, ethically charged, emotive and complex subject. By its nature it is multi-dimensional and interdisciplinary, drawing on different kinds of voices and approaches and knowledge from different disciplinary areas. As authors, we bring some of that interdisciplinarity to this project: Jo's work is as an education academic and Fran is a journalist. The book therefore brings together two different professional perspectives; we come from different traditions and work with different professional codes of ethics[1] and different styles of writing. Resolving some of these differences and deciding on how best to present our findings and thoughts has been, at times, a challenging process. But, since our first collaboration, when Fran joined Jo on a field trip to compare the experiences of education practitioners working with refugee children in Sweden and England, it has seemed to us that the benefits of bringing our perspectives together have outweighed the challenges. The debates we have engaged with together and separately have shaped the development of this book, which reflects our differing perspectives and the traditions of our fields. Drawing from different disciplines and expertise is integral to furthering understanding of the challenges that young refugees face. What unites us is a commitment to refugee education, to improving the experiences of the young people and those who work with them.

The process of developing our ideas and evidence for this book involved researching different elements of the book separately, then coming together to discuss our findings and plan how best to communicate them. We have sought to retain the distinctiveness of our voices and approaches to understanding the issues rather than trying to produce one authorial voice that blends different perspectives and starting points. Accordingly, we have attributed individual authorship to the sections of the book each of us wrote and readers should expect a change of voice and approach at each transition point. To set the context for the reader, we take this opportunity to explain a little more about the different approaches we took to preparing the different chapters within the book.

Jo's work in and with schools

Jo is an academic working in a School of Education in an English university. She was a teacher for a number of years before starting work at the university. She is committed to working with teachers and to portraying the work they do and the communities and children they work with through an asset-based perspective. As well as the comparative work with Sweden, Jo has adopted a place-based approach to understanding the challenges and opportunities for those working to support older refugee children in education in England. This work, and the findings underpinning the theorisation of this book, have been informed by her research with practitioners in the field, experienced teachers in schools that have been identified as sites of good practice for refugee education.

Jo is an experienced teacher educator and works with practitioners at different stages in their careers, including those just entering the profession. In her work, Jo often notices that teachers feel pulled in different directions as they try and enact the role of the 'good teacher' (Connell 2009), fulfilling obligations to ensure strong pupil outcomes, as measured by mandated assessments and audited in performance management regimes and school league tables. At the same time, she knows that there is a fundamental vocational dimension to teachers' work, often unrecognised in performance terms but manifest from the outset in a pre-service teacher's desire to become a teacher. This is the sense of wanting to make a difference, a commitment to social justice and to contributing to making their students' lives better. This is especially the case for school leaders who seek to maintain a commitment to strong inclusive values predicated on social justice agendas within an education landscape where league tables and the marketisation of school choice create 'moral dilemmas' (Stevenson 2007). This moral tension is often particularly marked for head teachers seeking to foster an inclusive school environment for refugee pupils (McIntyre and Hall 2018).

The school leaders and teachers in the case studies reported by Jo in Section 1 of this book were selected because they adopt and have maintained an inclusive stance towards refugee pupils. We sought out examples of teachers who are demonstrating an ethos of compassionate professionalism towards students who are often marginalised in mainstream education. These teachers' attitudes echo those described in the findings of a seminal study by Pinson, Arnot and Candappa (2010). Pinson et al.'s study was of teachers' responses, within a hostile immigration policy environment, to the needs of the 'non-citizen' child in English schools. Both authors of the current book were aware that many practitioners feel overwhelmed by the nature of the refugee 'crisis' as mediated in public discourse and popular media, and by their sense of powerlessness and inadequacy in responding to the needs of young people who arrive in schools and colleges with lived experiences so dramatically different to any they can imagine. Teachers propelled by a sense of vocational purpose often desire to do *something*, but are not always sure what it is they can do. For this reason Jo's sections of the book set out to describe and discuss ways of working observed in the case study schools, in the hope that practical theorising will enable more schools and individual practitioners to feel empowered to work with refugee children.

This book goes beyond simply sharing what has been observed in these schools. Throughout Section 1, readers will hear the teachers' voices as they explore and clarify what they do, in interviews and structured discussions in which they interrogate theoretical concepts they are introduced to through their engagement with the research study. The teachers move beyond simply applying the terms to their practice; they refine the concepts and ultimately shape the theoretical perspectives that underpin this book. They use the concepts and theories to name, interrogate and develop their pedagogy. Hall and Thomson quote the adage that there is 'nothing as practical as a good theory', emphasising that pedagogy incorporates 'ideas, theories, ways of seeing the world, relationships and values' as well as more visible markers such as teaching methods and assessment practices (2017, 4). It is this notion of pedagogy and practical theorising that defines the ambition of this book: namely, to offer an accessible practical theorising that draws directly on teachers' voices, ideas and experiences to help define an inclusive approach to the education of refugee children in our schools and colleges. We follow this journey of practical theorising throughout Section 1 and revisit it in the conclusion, where we share the participants' collective recommendations about pedagogical principles for policymakers and fellow practitioners, before issuing a call to action to legislators of national education systems.

Fran's investigative work on the ground

Debates about refugees are constantly played out in the public media. In an era in which 'post-truth' became the *Oxford Dictionaries'* international word of the year (2016), we believe that it is vital to support honest and open public discussion of the people involved, of current policy and of how the public discourses about refugee education today have been influenced by the past histories of refugee children in England. As right wing populism increases its influence on the international political landscape of Europe, the USA and Australia, the importance of ethical journalism in reporting and contributing to the public debate is paramount.

We are writing this book at a significant time in English history, following the result of the Brexit referendum which led to the country leaving the European Union. This has followed the development of the intentionally hostile environment for immigrants (Kirkup 2012). As immigration policies proliferated and bureaucratic practices intensified, children seeking asylum and refuge in England felt the brunt of changes that equated their status as asylum seeker/refugee with becoming a potential security threat. For example, in 2016, the Education Minister felt obliged to raise concerns about schools being asked to carry out immigration checks on pupils, a direct result of a proposed Immigration Bill requiring Schools Admissions Panels to deprioritise finding school places for 'illegal migrants' (Kuenssberg 2016). It is within this context that we sought to investigate the refugee children's experience of accessing education in the country many had travelled to at such personal cost.

Fran is a journalist with 30 years' experience of reporting on education and other domestic social and political issues. She is the author of five previous books, all of which have in some way focused on marginalised or under-represented groups. Their subjects have included those living on the minimum wage, young people at risk of dropping out of education and a group of teenagers in a comprehensive school striving to work out who they were and how they fitted in the world. She has also written two history books, one on the Suffragettes and one on the history of modern childhood, charting how the relationship between family and state has changed over a 120-year period.

For Fran, the joy of being a journalist is to be licensed to give a voice to those who might otherwise remain voiceless, and to shed light where it might not otherwise shine. While journalism is not a direct route to effecting social and political change, it is one of the tools which can be used by those who hope to do so. So when the opportunity to help with the writing of this book arose, it seemed one not to be missed. There can hardly be a group within our society today who are so regularly discussed without their voices ever being directly heard.

When we wrote the proposal for this book we included the following quotation from American Vice-President Hubert Humphrey: 'The moral test of government is how that government treats those who are in the dawn of life, the children … those who are in the shadows of life; the sick, the needy, the handicapped.' For young refugees arriving on English shores, the test of England's government must be the test of more than one key agency – social services, for instance, have a major role to play. The health services often have a great deal of work to do in restoring physical and mental fitness. But the education service has a special role to play: it is through education – if it is done well – that these young people can find their sense of belonging, and can begin to see a clearer path to becoming fulfilled and useful members of society.

The word 'useful' is a key one here, for young refugees are often seen as a problem to be solved, whereas in fact what they are is a resource. In times of historically low unemployment and with an ageing population, the economy is crying out for ambitious young people who are receptive to the idea of becoming skilled workers, valued members of their local communities and, potentially, the voices of the voiceless for the future.

Fran's aim in co-authoring this book has been to try to put a human face on the issues, tracing the stories of these young people and examining the barriers and opportunities they face on their journey towards fulfilment and citizenship. It is to provide some practical pointers for policymakers, based on the experiences and aspirations both of young people themselves and of those who work with them. She hopes her contributions to this book will be of interest to all those whose lives may bring them into contact with young refugees, and that a sharing of their experiences may enable both those young people and the adults in their lives to overcome barriers more effectively.

Who is this book about?

We need to begin by talking about terminology. According to the legal definition set out in the 1951 United Nations Convention on the Status of Refugees, a *refugee* is someone who has been forced to leave their home country because of a 'well-founded fear or persecution, war or violence'. Increasingly, we are also seeing the use of the term 'climate refugee'. The legal status of refugee brings rights and entitlements for the individual in their new host country. The term *asylum seeker* is applied to someone awaiting confirmation of refugee status. The term *forced migrant*, and more recently in the popular press 'suspect migrant', are also used.

In England, schools do not record or track the numbers of refugee children in their population. Most schools refer to refugee or asylum-seeking children as 'new arrivals' or use the descriptor 'EAL' (meaning having English as an Additional Language) or, in college settings, 'ESOL' (part of an English for Speakers of Other Languages group). Throughout this book, practitioners variously use these terms. We use the term *refugee* to distinguish children who are forced migrants from other new arrivals, such as economic migrants. We are aware that there might be some children awaiting confirmation of their status who are still classed as asylum seekers; when we know this to be the case we use the appropriate legal term.

Our focus is on older refugee children aged 15 and above in the later stages of secondary education and post-16 provision in England.

The structure of the book

The book draws on observations, conversations, interviews and focus groups with refugee children and those working with them. Throughout the book we intersperse the text with extracts or descriptions of our conversations with children we have met. The book is divided into three sections. It begins with a practical theory of meaningful inclusion, which is intended to offer a message of hope and encouragement to practitioners and policymakers seeking to 'get this right' in schools and colleges. It moves on to describe how we got to where we are. It concludes with ways forward for practitioners and a call to action for policy makers and academics in the field of refugee education.

Section 1, **Theorising practice in schools,** is based on Jo's work with the case study schools. In chapter 1, the field of refugee education and the conceptualisation of the refugee education 'crisis' are outlined and then the theoretical framing for the book is introduced in chapters 2 and 3. This framing is predicated on a commitment to inclusive education under-pinned by a strong motivation for social justice. Ravi Kohli's (2011, 2014) concepts of *safety, belonging* and *success* provide an operational frame whilst Nancy Fraser's (2003) concepts of *redistribution, recognition* and *representation* provide a lens through which to explore moral norms for operationalising Kohli's concepts when working with refugee children. Chapters 4, 5 and 6 explore each of the concepts of safety, belonging and success, looked at through the lens of the case study schools and the dialogues and debates of the practitioners as they refine the concepts that underpin their work with refugee children. Throughout these discussions and debates, the practitioners raise questions about barriers and enabling fac-tors in their work drawing on Fraser's moral framing to explain and explore these barriers and enablers further. Section 1 draws these ideas together to close with Chapter 7, a rich descrip-tion of Fern College, a bespoke post-16 provision for refugee and asylum seekers developed according to the theoretical perspectives discussed in this book.

Throughout Section 1, there is deliberate stylistic use of the 'we' pronoun which acknowl-edges, for Jo, that research is a collective endeavour, that sometimes the 'we' refers to other academics, sometimes to the practitioners in the study, depending on who Jo has been work-ing with as the thinking for the ideas in this section has developed. So the second interlocutor varies but the implied 'I' is always Jo.

Section 2, **Contexts,** explores some of the background factors which impact on the educa-tion of refugee pupils. This part of the book, which draws on Fran's work, includes the experi-ences, feelings and aspirations of a range of young people as well as interviews with and reflections from those whose professional lives bring them into contact with young refugees. In an extended chapter on the context in the east of England, we explore how arrival and set-tling in England works in one area of the country, and we hear from those who have a per-spective on how factors outside the classroom could be made to work more smoothly to improve school experience.

A historical chapter charts the factors that have aided and impeded the journeys of earlier groups of arrivals and draws conclusions about the contextual factors that are still relevant today. A chapter on policy concludes this section: it examines the ways in which the actions of the state impact on the educational lives of these young people, and points to possible policy initiatives or changes which could help the young refugees to succeed.

In Section 3: **Ways forward,** Jo and Fran become the 'we' as we reflect together on the lessons from history and on our observations of current practice. We consider what we have learned about the lived experiences of policy for those working to support children from refugee backgrounds through education. We then return to the practitioners in our case studies to report on a collaboration in which we designed a set of pedagogical principles for policymaking and future practice in the field of refugee education. The book concludes with a call to action and a set of recommendations for school leaders, teachers, policymakers and future research.

Throughout the book, our focus is on teenage refugee and asylum seekers who arrive in the upper years of secondary education, they are legally classed as children and we refer to them as such throughout the book. They are part of the millions of children who have spent years on forced migration journeys until reaching places of refuge many miles away from where they began their journeys. Beneath the statistics are individual and extraordinary stories of individual children trying to resume ordinary lives and who view education as a means through which they can begin to participate and contribute to their new society. Their stories, and the experiences of those who work with them, offer hope for the future as we reimagine educational policymaking which prioritises wellbeing. This book offers a theorised model of high-quality inclusive education for all to inform policy and practice to ensure that refugee children can experience education which enables them to lead lives they and others value in their new place.

Note

1   British Educational Research Association [BERA] (2018) *Ethical Guidelines for Educational Research*, Fourth edition, London. https://www.bera.ac.uk/researchers-resources/publications/ethicalguidelines-for-educational-research-2018.
    British Broadcasting Corporation (BBC) 2019 Editorial Guidelines https://www.bbc.com/editorial guidelines/guidelines

References

Connell, R. 2009. Good teachers on dangerous ground: towards a new view of teacher quality and professionalism. *Critical Studies in Education*, 50(3), 213–229. doi: 10.1080/17508480902998421.

Dryden-Peterson, S. 2016. Refugee education: The crossroads of globalization. *Educational Researcher*, 45(9), 473–482.

Fraser, N. 2003. Social justice in the age of identity politics. In Fraser, N. and Honneth, A. (Eds), *Redistribution or Recognition? A Political-Philosophical Exchange*. London: Verso.

Hall, C. and Thomson, P. 2017. *Inspiring School Change: Transforming Education through the Creative Arts*. Abingdon: Routledge.

Kirkup, J. 2012. Teresa May interview: 'We're going to give illegal migrants a really hostile reception'. Accessed 25 May 2012. https://www.telegraph.co.uk/news/uknews/immigration/9291483/Theresa-May-interview-Were-going-to-give-illegal-migrants-a-really-hostile-reception.html.

Kohli, R. 2011. Working to ensure safety, belonging and success for unaccompanied asylum-seeking children. *Child Abuse Review*, 20, 311–323. doi: 10.1002/car.v20.5.

Kohli, R. 2014. Protecting asylum seeking children on the move. *Revue Europeene Des Migrations Internationales*, 30(1), 83–104. doi:10.4000/remi.6768.

Kuenssberg, L. 2016. Theresa May had plan to 'deprioritise' illegal migrant pupils, December 1, 2016. Accessed 17 January 2020. https://www.bbc.co.uk/news/uk-politics-38165395.

McIntyre, J. and Hall, C. 2018. Barriers to the inclusion of refugee and asylum-seeking children in schools in England, *Educational Review*, DOI: 10.1080/00131911.2018.1544115

Pinson, H., Arnot, M., and Candappa, M. 2010. *Education, Asylum and the 'Non-citizen' Child: The Politics of Compassion and Belonging*. Basingstoke: Palgrave Macmillan.

Save the Children. 2016. Children on the move in Europe. Accessed 12 January 2018. https://savethechildreninternational.exposure.co/children-on-the-move-in-europe.

Stevenson, H. 2007. A case study in leading schools for social justice: When morals and markets collide. *Journal of Educational Administration*, 45(6), 769–781.

SECTION 1

Theorising practice in schools

Joanna McIntyre

In Section 1, our focus is on working with practitioners in schools and colleges to develop a practical theory for meaningful inclusion within education. This is based on Jo's previous research in the field of refugee education, where some of the early ideas of theorisation were shaped with colleagues in Swedish and English research projects. Chapters 2 and 3 outline the academic starting points for the book and introduce the concepts of *safety, belonging* and *success* (Kohli 2011, 2014) and the concepts of *redistribution, recognition* and *representation* (Fraser 2003). Taken together, these theories provide a lens through which to explore moral norms for operationalising schools' work with refugee children. In Chapters 4-7 the reader is introduced to the case study schools. Chapter 4 focuses on the concept of safety, Chapter 5 on that of belonging and Chapter 6 reconceptualises what success means in work with refugee and asylum-seeking children. Each of these chapters begins with a pen portrait to illustrate the good practice exemplified in each case study and also includes dialogues and debates with the practitioners to illustrate how they made sense of and refined the concepts that underpin their work with refugee children. They draw on Fraser's moral framing to explain and explore the barriers and enablers to operationalise these concepts. Section 1 draws these ideas together to close with Chapter 7, a rich description of Fern College, a bespoke post-16 provision for refugee and asylum seekers developed according to the theoretical perspectives discussed in this book.

References

Fraser, N. 2003. Social justice in the age of identity politics. In N. Fraser and A. Honneth (eds) *Redistribution or Recognition? A Political-Philosophical Exchange*, London: Verso.
Kohli, R. 2011. Working to Ensure Safety, Belonging and Success for Unaccompanied Asylum-Seeking Children, *Child Abuse Review* 20, 311-323.
Kohli, R. 2014. Protecting Asylum Seeking Children on the Move, *Revue Europeene Des Migrations Internationales*, 30 (1): 83-104.

2 Safety, belonging and success

Joanna McIntyre

Three important principles underpin the work of this book. First, a humanitarian issue: the scale of the global refugee 'crisis' demands socially just responses from resettlement destinations. Second, a philosophical issue: education is a fundamental means of supporting young refugees to experience inclusion in their new context. Third, a social issue: inclusive high-quality education provision for all benefits both newly arrived students and also their peers in the resettlement context. This is especially important in societies where anti-immigration rhetoric and isolationist policies feature significantly in public discourse.

The opening section of this chapter begins by outlining the context of refugee movements and the perceived refugee 'crisis' in Europe, and then discusses the field of refugee education. The second half of the chapter introduces the first of the two theoretical framings for the book, Ravi Kohli's notion of the resumption of an ordinary life. Kohli's three concepts of 'safety', 'belonging' and 'success' are adapted to develop an inclusive model of education which meets the needs of all students, including those who have been forced to leave their homes in order to try and build new lives in a new resettlement context.

Before proceeding, it is important to explain some of the terms in this chapter. There is specific terminology which is utilised to group and identify people, and when talking about (im)migration these are often deliberately loaded terms:

> because we deploy labels not only to describe the world but also to construct it in convenient images, ... labelling was not just a highly instrumental process, but also a powerful explanatory tool to explore the complex and often disjunctive impacts of humanitarian intervention on the lives of refugees.
>
> (Zetter 2007, 173)

I use the term 'resettlement context' to describe the United Kingdom. Resettlement is an official term for the processes by which a nation-state will agree that people who are granted refugee status (or another form of humanitarian protection) by the UK while they are abroad are then brought to live in the United Kingdom. However, many who make the journeys to distant countries which they enter legally, through official schemes or through dangerous illegal routes, are unlikely to return to their original homes. With respect to this group, the term seems to be increasingly used in academic literature to refer to contexts like the United Kingdom where refugees aim to live lives of permanence, seeking citizenship and building their future there. I also use the term 'host country' recognising that the term is problematic because of its connotations with short-term benevolence, with the refugee positioned as temporary visitor.

The refugee 'crisis'

This section begins by outlining the situation in Europe following the rise in numbers of people, including many unaccompanied children, making perilous journeys into and across Europe in recent years. These are people forced to leave their homes because of increasingly precarious conditions in some African and Middle Eastern countries, exacerbated by the continuing conflict in Syria. The label 'migrant crisis' was first used in media depictions of the situation in 2015, when it is estimated that around one million migrants arrived into Europe, nearly a fourfold increase on the previous year (BBC 2016). This period also saw an increase in the numbers of people trying to enter Europe through the eastern and central Mediterranean routes making dangerous journeys across the sea. It is estimated that half of these displaced people were leaving conflict zones in Syria, Afghanistan and Iraq (Pew 2016). By the time of writing, in 2020, the numbers arriving into Europe have lessened but the drivers for displacement – conflict, human rights violations, political unrest and increasingly climate change – continue to force people to leave their homes, and numbers could quickly escalate again. At the same time, across Europe anti-immigration policies are foregrounded in populist views of international and domestic issues.

The movements of people across borders are not modern phenomena; Castells comments that 'as a result of war, conquest and political struggle they are as old as human history' (2003, 17). However, the current political salience of issues associated with migration has risen, along with the rise in right-wing political parties and governments in Europe and elsewhere. Headlines and images in the popular press perpetuating notions of a migration crisis stoke public discourses of fear that the migrant stranger poses a threat. Governments utilise this fear in election campaigns to prove they have the prowess to protect the public through hostile immigration policies and increased securitisation measures (Bauman 2000). Media portrayals of the 'crisis' also contribute to political manifestos about the causes of economic austerity across much of the Global North. In Europe, increasingly populist governments have been elected on mandates which lay the blame for challenges in the domestic sphere on the increased movement of people into Europe. Thus, the social contract between peoples that existed following the Second World War has been eroded from a position of mutuality towards fear of the other as depictions of a refugee 'crisis' effectively move public attention to focus on blame and away from what is actually a 'political, cultural and socioeconomic crisis' (Lucassen 2018, 406).

When a term like crisis is used so pejoratively, it is important to ask: who is this a crisis for? As outlined above, popular discourse positioned the mass movement of people fleeing into Europe as a crisis for the hosting nations, with the incomers as a perceived threat to security and a demand on the state's welfare provision. However, a more compassionate reading might reposition this as a crisis for those needing to flee from their homes and to consider how hosting countries should frame a welcome and response which is both sympathetic and acknowledges responsibility for the ways in which decisions taken in high-income countries in Europe have had an impact on political insecurity, unrest and climatic change in Africa and the Middle Eastern regions. Such a reading would mean that the nation-state's international commitments and responsibilities to enact humanitarian rights for refugees were foregrounded, rather than the implied threat that they pose. However, whilst a minority of countries in Europe responded to the 'crisis' by offering a public national welcome, for example Germany's open border policy, most states introduced restrictive legislation and border control policies (Skleparis 2017). The response from Britain aligned to the latter. Analysis commissioned by United Nations High Commissioner for Refugees (UNHCR) of the press coverage of the refugee situation across Europe found that the coverage in the UK media in 2015 was the most negative and divisive (Berry, Garcia-Blanco and Moore 2015b).

It is within this context that the UK response to the refugee 'crisis' was framed. The response was very much bound up in discourses of securitisation, with an official government preference for providing humanitarian aid for refugees in camps on the borders of the conflict zones rather than supporting those who had made it into Europe. On 2 September 2015, the publication of photograph of the body of Aylan Kurdi (family name Shenu), a three-year-old Syrian boy of Kurdish background who drowned whilst his family were crossing the Mediterranean Sea to Europe, led to significant change in the public discourse. This tragedy brought the human face of those making the journey into public awareness and, in particular, highlighted that many refugees were children. There followed a shift in government policy, which included a commitment by the prime minister later that year to resettling 20,000 refugees from the conflict in Syria under the Vulnerable Persons Resettlement Scheme. Reports of the inhumane conditions in the refugee camps around Calais led to the Dubs Amendment (named after its sponsor in the House of Lords) in 2016, an official agreement that up to 3000 unaccompanied children living in the refugee camps near Calais could be brought to live in the United Kingdom. In April 2016, the Vulnerable Children's Resettlement Scheme was introduced. This was targeted at supporting refugee children and their families from the Middle East and North African regions.

There has been subsequent criticism of the limited extent to which these policies have been implemented. Nearly four years later, for example, fewer than 400 children have benefitted from the Dubs Amendment. At the same time, families with children and unaccompanied asylum seekers who have made perilous journeys into Europe continue to put their lives at risk by trying to cross into the United Kingdom. Once they have arrived from mainland Europe into England, the label of asylum seeker or refugee dictates their early experiences as they have to successfully navigate bureaucracies associated with the stringent immigration policy, alluded to in earlier, before they can begin to encounter aspects of everyday life in this new context (McIntyre and Hall 2018). For young refugees, the most important marker of everyday life is accessing education.

Gatrell uses the term 'refugeedom' to refer to 'the principles, rules and practices adopted by government officials and others in order to manage refugees ... whilst enabling us to relate refugees' experiences, conduct and responses to these prevailing systems and norms' (2016, 178/9). Refugeedom is a useful concept as it allows consideration of the ways in which refugee children are managed in the systems of bureaucracy which foreground the nation-state's commitment to securitisation and protection in the face of perceived threats to social cohesion that it is feared new arrivals bring. This is most evident in the ways in which politicians feed the notion of a refugee 'crisis' (Watters 2008). However, as has been argued elsewhere, education is perceived as having a key role in promoting social cohesion (Cantle 2008, Shuayb 2016). This is enhanced by an ethos of inclusive education where diversity is recognised and celebrated.

I now turn to explore some of the themes relating to refugee children in education – the focus of this book.

The 'pull' of education

Whilst evidence suggests that many asylum seekers and refugees have limited options available to them and that they are reliant on the destination choices made by agents or people smugglers (Spinks 2013), there are some 'pull' factors for those who can exercise some agency over the direction of their forced migration route. According to a recent report by the UNHCR, 'among those who eventually did undertake the journey to Europe, education was a key factor shaping their decision. Education is also a key element for refugee and migrant children's social inclusion into host communities' (UNHCR 2019a).

Ammar's story

Ammar arrived in England when he was 16. Until the conflict took hold in Syria, he and his family had lived a relatively privileged and peaceful life. Ammar came from a family of lawyers, but his ambition was to be a doctor. He attended school in Syria until the bombs began hitting his neighbourhood and disrupting his everyday life. School often had to shut because of bombings, and he lost friends as their families moved away or, more tragically, were hit in the attacks. When he was 12, and in Year 8 at school, his family decided it was no longer safe for them to stay. They moved to Egypt, where Ammar tried to attend school; with over 100 other students in the classroom, however, he felt that he was unable to learn and study effectively. The family decided to move to Europe, Ammar recalls feeling hopeful that he would be able to resume his studies and pursue his ambitions of becoming a doctor.

However, when his family were waiting to get on a boat to Greece, the captain of the boat said he could only take Ammar, '*you couldn't argue with the men in the charge of the boats*'. His father thrust into his hand an envelope which contained Ammar's papers and promised to find him on the other side. When Ammar arrived in Greece, he found out that his family had not made it onto any of the boats. He was initially held in what he describes as a prison until an organisation called PRAKSIS managed to get him out and then took care of him for the next nine months. Again, Ammar tried to attend school, but having learnt French and English at school he struggled with the Greek language. He focused on trying to plan to get to England to join an aunt and spent his time listening to, and learning English through YouTube videos, so on arrival into England, '*I could blend into the system straight away*'.

Ammar eventually made it to England, four years after leaving his home in Syria. He managed to conduct the interview with the immigration officials in English and was moved to live with his aunt in the Midlands. He and his aunt tried to get him into a school, he went to the local council to fill in the necessary forms. Six months later, he had heard nothing and was becoming increasingly depressed: *'They destroyed the whole idea that I had in my mind, while I waited in Greece, while I waited to go legally to England, that this would be perfect, that they would take care of me. I felt nobody cared. I wouldn't achieve what I wanted and therefore my life would be bad.'* Eventually, he was moved from his aunt to the care of a foster family and they and a local refugee charity helped get him a place in a college where he began studying for five subjects at GCSE. He realised that he would also need science GCSEs to become a doctor and he and his foster carer, a teacher, bought the relevant books and accessed the science syllabus online. A few months later, he achieved all seven of his GCSEs and his foster carer managed to find him a place at an academic Sixth Form college. When we spoke to him, he was enjoying his A levels, saying that,

> *every day is better than the year before, every day I am learning something ... education is the only way.*

Four years from the date of his arrival in England, and eight years after fleeing from his home in Syria, Ammar is studying medicine at a university in the United Kingdom.

For Ammar, the primary goal on arriving in England was to attend a school in his new city. As Matthews observes, 'schools are a stabilising feature in the unsettled lives of refugee young people' (2008, 32). It is generally accepted that including refugee and asylum-seeking children in education is a 'good' thing for both the individual child and also the 'host' society. Education is a key marker of integration, but also a process of integration (Ager and Strang 2008). In schools, the refugee child sees models from peers and teachers of how to learn the rules and ways of being in their new society.

The ways in which refugee children are included within education systems varies according to how nation-states interpret their duties to enact international agreements about the education of young people on forced migration journeys. The various interpretations and implications of these global rights and agreements are discussed in Chapter 3, where it is argued that ensuring a refugee children's right to education is an act of social justice. For now, I explore the ways in which education for refugees has been conceptualised in the academic literature.

Refugee education arguably began at scale during and after the Second World War. During the war, education for refugees was conceptualised as a temporary measure preparing the child for their return; after the war, by contrast, the education of refugee children became about preparing for a future in a different home context. Dryden-Peterson et al. outline how nation-states' refugee education provision varies according to their perceptions of the role and purpose of education for refugees in terms of possible futures for the child (2019).

High-income contexts in Europe in this framing could offer a possible future of long-term inclusion through models of education which include the newly arrived child in national education systems, provide access to high-quality education and, crucially, engender a sense of social belonging (2019, 349).

In the English context, key voices within the field of refugee education (for example, Arnot and Pinson 2005) observe that refugee and asylum-seeking children are marked by their invisibility in education policy and practice. Excluded from educational policies, they are subject to exclusionary policies and practices which are determined by immigration and welfare policies. In this way the refugee child is positioned through policy as both a potential threat to security and a potential drain on welfare resources (Watters 2008). This latter positioning is critiqued for assuming a victim narrative and lack of agency whereas the lived experiences of the young people's journeys often demonstrate resilience and independence (Rutter 2006). In these somewhat contradictory depictions of threat, supplicant and victim, the identity marker 'refugee/asylum seeker' is foregrounded and important elements of intersectionality are diminished.

This largely deficit portrayal is not confined to studies of refugee education in England. The challenges faced by refugee children, along with the challenges they present to fixed education systems and pedagogies, are well documented. These include, for example, studies of their experiences of racism (Baak 2019), bullying and prior trauma and a focus on their psychological needs (McBrien 2005, Rutter 2006). An overriding challenge is that despite coming from various global contexts, refugee children are often treated as a homogenous group (Rutter 2006, Matthews 2008). Policy for schools in highly regulated accountability systems tends towards standardisation and assuming a stable cohort of similar students. Providing for children who arrive from a diverse and often-fragmented set of educational backgrounds is a challenge for schools in such systems. As such, priority is given to ensuring that the child can quickly access the mainstream curriculum by focusing on addressing linguistic needs through intensive attention to learning the language of the host country. This means that what the young person can bring to schools and classrooms in their new context is often overlooked because of a tendency to focus on what they cannot do and therefore what they need. In this book, we meet teachers who are working with children who come from a range of contexts with a range of different experiences and expectations of education. As an illustrative example, in the case study schools featured in this book, the teachers' perceptions were that Eritrean and Syrian children seem to adapt quite quickly to the 'norms' of English curricula, possibly because their own experiences are from education systems informed by European influences from their countries' colonial histories. In contrast, some students in the case study schools arrive with no experience of formal schooling or formal literacy practices.

There is a growing strand of work in the field which explores various good practice for educational provision for refugee children in education systems in high-income countries. For example, Hamilton and Moore's work is on best-practice school interventions for refugee children in New Zealand (2004), and Stewart's work is an influential exploration of the experiences of refugee children in Canada and the most appropriate ways to support them (2011). There have also been extensive reviews of literature and research which explore the barriers and opportunities for best practice for refugee children in the United States (McBrien 2005) and Australia (Baak et al. 2019). What emerges from this work is confirmation of Dryden Peterson et al.'s observation of the role of government's attitude towards responsibilities for the possible futures of refugee children in their state and how this impacts on education provision for the refugee child (2019).

The two most influential texts in the English context explore the experiences of forced migrants through an analysis of policies which frame these experiences. Firstly, there is Rutter's 2006 study of the effects of educational policy on different groups of children who arrive as forced migrants. She argues for a deeper ecological consideration of the child's pre- and post-migration experiences. Through case studies of the experiences in London schools of children originating from the Sudan, Somalia and the Democratic Republic of Congo, Rutter demonstrates how a preoccupation with their experiences of trauma and their linguistic needs negates important aspects of their prior educational experiences and their potential. Secondly, Pinson, Arnot and Candappa provide a sociological reading of the effects of the UK government's asylum policies and how these affect the experiences of children in the school system and those teachers who try to adopt a compassionate stance in order to provide a humanitarian response whilst navigating competing demands for them to reach performative targets (2010). This text builds on an earlier study by two of the authors which explored the work of local authorities in England and identified best practice for those working with young refugees to be a holistic model of targeted (multi-agency) support that provides for their social, emotional and learning needs within an 'ethos of inclusion' and 'celebration of diversity' which draws on parental and community involvement (Arnot and Pinson 2005).

The work of Arnot and Pinson has been influential to thinking about how to provide an inclusive education for refugee children in schools. Taylor and Sidhu extend Arnot and Pinson's holistic best-practice model in their study of the contribution of schooling to refugee experiences of resettlement in Australia, adding the importance of strong leadership support and a whole school approach to the characteristics of inclusive education that Arnot and Pinson identified (2012, 53). These holistic models are predicated on a commitment to social justice which draws on discourses of refugee children's right to education and their entitlement to an equitable model of inclusive education. Most resettlement contexts have ratified the UN Conventions on the Rights of the Child (UNHCR 1989) which incorporates the right to 'an education to fulfil their potential'. At the same time, there is international recognition that global commitments to, and definitions of, inclusive education, should extend beyond the needs of children with disabilities to include **all** learners, including refugee and asylum-seeking children, and challenge exclusionary policies that make some groups vulnerable and marginalised through structural inequalities (UNESCO Concept note 4 2018).

The young people who are the focus of this book are the intended beneficiaries of the global promise of universal human rights. In the everyday practices of schools, Dryden-Peterson challenges us to explore 'how to realize the right to education for all and ensure opportunities to use that education for future participation in society?' (2016, 473). It is at the discretion of the nation-state as to how these are interpreted in practice. Questions about how these principles are enacted in the lived experiences of young refugees and those seeking to support them are tied up with questions of social justice when it comes to ascertaining whether policy enactment serves to include or exclude marginalised young people because of their refugee status.

Education for all: moving beyond 'right to rights' towards a socially just frame

> The world has another decade to meet the 17 Sustainable Development Goals, including SDG 4 – the commitment to an inclusive and equitable quality education and lifelong learning opportunities for all. But if we do not ensure that all refugee children have access to school, that goal will never be reached.
>
> (UNHCR 2019b, Stepping Up: Refugee Education in Crisis)

There are more people under the age of 18 on the move across the world than at any other time in history. In Europe there are more child refugees than at any time since the Second World War saw the vast movement of displaced people fleeing persecution. The experiences of the Second World War led to many nations coming together to share a commitment to ensuring that conflict and persecution at this scale would never happen again; from this emerged the Declaration of Universal Human Rights (United Nations 1948) and then the Refugee Convention (United Nations 1951). One central tenet of these universal human rights is the right to education. Education as a basic human right benefits the individual, the national state and the international landscape as it forms the foundation on which to build peace and drive sustainable development (UNESCO 2019). In 2015, the international community reaffirmed a continuation of a commitment to the right to education for all through the Incheon Declaration and the 2030 Sustainable Development Agenda. The ambitions of the Sustainable Agenda for education are encapsulated in Sustainable Development Goal 4 (SDG4), which seeks to *'ensure inclusive and equitable quality education and promote lifelong learning opportunities for all'* by 2030. This agreement about the right to education also applies to refugees and asylum-seeking children settling in those resettlement countries which have ratified SDG4.

However, despite international agreements, the experiences of refugees and other marginalised groups tell us that the lived reality is different from that which is endorsed by imperatives enshrined in international agreements. Hannah Arendt famously rejected the notion of universal human rights, claiming that they only applied to those who had some form of national citizenship rather than those who were 'stateless', as many displaced people find themselves to be. Arendt's contention that the 'right to have rights' (1951) only applied to those who were members of a sovereign state seemed to challenge the fundamental premise that human rights are universal entitlements regardless of citizenship status. However, others, such as Benhabib (1996, 2004), have argued that Arendt's apparent contradiction allows for attention to be paid to the ways in which different nation-states fulfil their obligations. It is important at this point to recognise that concept of rights-based education is not uncontentious. There are different levels of obligation inherent in the different global commitments such that the International Covenant on Economic, Social and Cultural Rights (ICESCR 1966) and the Covenant on the Rights of the Child (UNHCR 1989) are the only legally binding agreements (McGrath 2018). International agreements such as the Incheon Declaration (WEF 2015) and the 2030 Sustainable Development Goals (United Nations 2015) are commitments of intent towards delivering education for all and different nation-states interpret their responsibilities towards enacting these in varying ways. In this context we move towards a more nuanced exploration of the right to education, which looks to realisations of the commitment being moral and socially just.

In so doing, we need to consider how to talk about SDG4 in the context of resettlement countries, especially in Europe, where there has been a growing public discourse about immigration and associated threats to cultural and societal norms. Until young refugees have equitable access to education provision with their peers in that context then they are excluded from their 'right to have rights' and become what Arendt described as modern 'pariahs' living lives of exclusion in comparison with other young people in their new neighbourhoods (Arendt 1951). However, it is not enough to draw attention to whether the commitment to SDG4 is being realised or not. If, as I argue here, there is a need for a socially just response to bring about maximum benefits for the individual newcomer and to the resettlement society, then we need to find a language to speak to policymakers and a narrative that illustrates what is possible and what those working in the field of refugee education stand for.

There is a moral imperative for host societies to provide an inclusive high-quality education to the newcomer because of the benefits this brings to the young refugee but also for developing reciprocal understandings and knowledge in order to promote a cohesive society, within the resettlement context and beyond.

Ravi Kohli's resumption of ordinary lives – a practical frame

There are four important aspects to SDG4: *access* to an *equitable quality* and *inclusive* education and *lifelong learning* on par with peers in the context. How realistic is this when applied to refugee children in resettlement contexts where other children have been in the education system for 10-11 continuous years from a young age? What does this mean for young people who have had to endure disruptions to all aspects of their lives, not least education? In order to know how schools can work with SDG4 better, we first need to find a way of understanding the experiences of the young people who have been forced to leave their homes in search of security and a better future.

Refugee children experience different transitions in (and out of) school as they seek to resume some sense of normality and to find a sense of 'home' after periods of disruption. Ravi Kohli's conceptual map helps to put the young people back in the frame after our focus in earlier sections of this chapter on questions of the scale, of (inter)national policies, structures, practices and discourses. Kohli reminds us that the day that the decision is made to leave the place of origin the young person on a forced migration journey has 'given up their past in order to have a future' (2014, 85). They experience the 'death of everyday life' (ibid., 86) as they try and recreate a sense of home:

> Home is a place that is stable, safe and splendid in its ordinariness, allowing movements to and fro without further threats of rupture.
>
> (Kohli 2011, 312)

This pursuit for home is framed by Kohli as a quest for ordinariness. He tracks the journeys of young asylum seekers from their places of origin on their search for a new place to call home where they can resume ordinary lives. Kohli articulates how these journeys continue along three 'tracks' after the young people have reached a resettlement destination: 'the search for safety, the growth of belonging and the will to succeed within new environments' (2011, 313). These three tracks work across three related dimensions of movements or transitions across geographical spaces (where young asylum seekers need to create new, often temporary, social worlds and relationships), across time (chronological time, which can be experienced as periods of short bursts of frantic activity and long periods of waiting), and maturational and psychological transitions (where as they grow towards adulthood 'out of place' they have to contend with their memories and thoughts about their present, future and their past). Once they have reached a resettlement destination, these transitions continue as they move through patterns of acclimatisation, adaption, early participation and absorption of their new context before they can fully contribute to, and benefit from, a reciprocal relationship with their new 'home'.

In an earlier project comparing the experiences of young refugees and their educational opportunities in Sweden and England we were attracted to Kohli's concepts of safety, belonging and success and utilised these in our conversations with headteachers, who were trying to model an inclusive approach to new arrivals in their context (McIntyre et al. 2018). We were particularly attracted to the apparent simplicity of the notion of 'resumption of ordinariness' and were interested in how far the concepts of safety, belonging and success could help us understand the role education can and does play in this journey. Kohli himself talks about the place of school in the process of becoming ordinary:

> asylum-seeking children begin to feel safe in the day to day by finding predictable patterns, shapes and rhythms of living, by being in a good school...
>
> (2011, 317)

Kohli's conceptual approach had resonance with the headteachers in our study and with our observations of the experiences of the young people we talked to during the process. We[1] believe Kohli's ideas can be utilised as a theoretical frame for understanding the role schools can play in facilitating young refugees' journeys towards resettlement. The next sections proceed to describe how we see each dimension working from an educational perspective.

The 'search for safety' - access and inclusion

Kohli describes how young asylum seekers, after arrival in a resettlement context, 'stand at the borders of legal, practical and psychological safety'. Schools have an important role to play in this process. Legally (if we can assume that SDG4 ratification equates to legal obligation), the child has a right to access education provision, as has been discussed earlier. However, how this works in practice can have important implications for the child's psychological safety. In McIntyre and Hall, we wrote about the barriers firstly the individual child has to overcome to access a school place and then the obstacles that head teachers seeking to include new arrivals need to navigate (2018), especially in contexts where individual children's examination results are deemed to be a measure of the success or not of the school. Once in school, the child is likely to be free from previous fears of threat to life but there will be other factors that can continue to make them feel unsafe. These can be associated with a range of different factors: bullying, racism (Stewart 2011), or sudden memories of trauma or loss.

Kohli explains how young asylum seekers need to practice 'thin' stories of themselves whilst on the move, as a protective device. Some of these fabricated stories may well have had to be continued in the resettlement context and may become part of their everydayness at school. Finding spaces to become authentic are of especial importance in school settings. This can be partly achieved by: looking at what the young person brings rather than what they lack (e.g. the language of resettlement context) through asset-based holistic initial assessments; providing empathetic peer buddies to help them navigate the new environment, the explicit and hidden curriculum, and a broad network of pastoral and academic support. There is insufficient space to explicate here the dimension of safety in education; the journey to our understanding of this concept is articulated in Chapter 4. However, it is important to recognise that we need to reconceptualise the search for safety as a collective shared endeavour rather than an individual one. Schools are places where healing can happen and there are strategies that schools can and, in many cases, do put in place to ensure that this process can begin. Refugee children have worked hard to get to the point where they can access education; after long periods of waiting on the journeys they are ambitious for their futures. It is therefore key to explain how their current context in schools – whether this be in a temporary withdrawal unit (and we need to consider the effects of this exclusionary practice), or in a mainstream class with support, or studying a reduced functional skills type curriculum – will fulfil their present needs and prepare them for the next step in their educational journey.

Once the search for safety has been achieved and acclimatisation has begun, as they make sense of their new context, then they are able to transition into 'belonging'.

The growth of belonging – an inclusive and equitable quality of education

'Belonging and belongings mark the progress of resettlement' (Kohli 2006, xii). For Kohli, the experience of belonging is linked to wellbeing and is an ongoing active process both for the individual new arrival and for the actors in their new social spaces, in this case – education settings. However this is not a simple process. Pinson, Arnot and Candappa take the themes of compassion and belonging as central concepts in their sociological analysis of the position of asylum seekers and refugee children in British schools (2010). They explore the ways in which, despite hostile immigration policies, individual teachers and schools operate a compassionate stance which at times is at odds with official policy. At the same time young people find it difficult to achieve a sense of belonging due to exclusionary practices within ostensibly inclusive schools and a growing sense of othering from practices associated with assimilating, or not, to a British identity. A further complication is associated with age, as studies illustrate that achieving a sense of belonging is easier for children who arrive at a young age; '[m]igration during adolescence … when social and cultural identities are critical, may be problematic' (Anderson 2004, 79). It is also easier for refugees with permanent residency rather than temporary leave to remain to feel a sense of belonging. Despite this, there *are* ways in which schools can work with their student community to help with the process which are discussed below and more fully in Chapter 5.

Kohli emphasises that young people can 'use their own talents and capacities to grow webs of belonging' (2011, 318). As mentioned in the previous section, it is important that education providers recognise that the new arrival comes with their own strengths and experiences and that access to a high-quality education begins with a holistic assessment of what the child can do. Considerations of a broad curriculum offer where they can be in classes with their new peers learning alongside them for at least part of their time is an important aspect of this process. Helping the child to maintain connections to past cultures and traditions, including faith and language, are also integral. This allows children to work with what they know well and demonstrate what they have, rather than what they (are perceived to) lack. In the Swedish-English project mentioned earlier, we saw examples of new arrivals from Afghanistan who had worked as tailors in their hometown working alongside their new classmates to prepare costumes for a school fashion show. Similarly, we saw an example of a mathematics lesson where the teacher used flip learning so that the children worked at home with materials in their strongest language to learn the concepts and then in the lesson sat in mainstream classes alongside their peers working to apply this knowledge through exercises which encouraged pair and group work, but were not totally reliant on language.

So, schools can become places of healing, where students can work together to belong, and societal norms can shift. This is achieved through an avoidance of 'othering' alongside an awareness of the individual child beneath the label of 'refugee', working with heterogeneity rather than assumed homogeneity (Rutter 2006), in culturally responsive ways which allow the new arrival to work with their peers to co-create a sense of place and home in the school setting. Anderson advocates for strategies that avoid assimilation and focus on integration and multiculturalism, which she emphasises need to work in a symbiotic relationship (2004). Thus, schools can develop a school culture evidencing tolerance and respect for cultural diversity and awareness of the global world beyond the school gates. There is also a need for schools to adopt an ecological approach that considers the full range of pre and post-migration factors that make up the young person's past and present experiences. In this way refugee pupils can begin to experience elements of success in their new environment.

The will to succeed – high-quality education and lifelong learning

Kohli draws on various research studies which illustrate the ways in which asylum-seeking and refugee children can demonstrate considerable resilience and motivation to achieve within their new context because of their 'want to succeed educationally and materially' (2011, 319). However, we need to recognise that schools and schooling are not neutral spaces and that they are shaped by powerful dominant discourses which the young person needs to navigate. For a young refugee, as they move through belonging to success this means that they move from adaption, participation and absorption of social and cultural practices before they eventually can enjoy a reciprocal relationship with their new home. This means that they have progressed from the early stages of arrival and safety, where they were dependent upon others and had restricted movements (in terms of choice of schooling, school subjects, friendship groups), towards a point where they are able to enact agency and choice. But this may have involved compromise: '[t]o be successful in school means immigrants must surrender great parts of their language and their culture' (Gunderson 2000, 693). They have to work within a system and curriculum that is dominated by, in resettlement contexts in the Global North, a western mainstream view of values and beliefs. Rutter's case studies of refugee children in schools in England offer a powerful illustration of the ways in which new arrivals from different parts of the globe are more likely to achieve success if their past educational experiences have been in systems similar to the one in their resettlement context and/or in environments where they had been able to experience confidence in their national cultural identity and where teachers had high expectations for them (2006). Rutter concludes that more needs to be done to understand how refugee children build on the progress they may or may not have made in school; 'definitions of successful settlement must encompass the long-term experiences of refugees' (ibid., 204).

The term 'success' is not a neutral concept and needs to be considered from the perspectives of both the individual and the resettlement society. A starting point might be to think of success as a process, rather than an outcome at the end of a period of schooling. The capabilities approach (Sen 2009, discussed more fully in Chapter 3) helps here as we consider how experiences of education and schooling have prepared the young person to go on to live a life they value and which is valued by others. In this way we can consider the place of lifelong learning which takes on particular importance if the refugee has arrived as an older teenager with only limited time within compulsory education in the resettlement context. In such cases, success could perhaps be reconceptualised in terms of agency and informed autonomy. Rather than leaving school with few or no recognisable qualifications, a successful outcome would be for the young person to be informed about what the possibilities are for next steps and to know that, whether this be in work or continued education, there are and will continue to be opportunities to engage with education or training. In this way they can strategically make choices and have agency in the next set of movements and transitions that lie ahead. For schools to help young people to achieve this leads to a bigger set of questions for those national education systems in resettlement contexts which are subject to rigid accountability regimes and performance measures. Such systems are predicated on an economic model of schooling where the focus is on individual outcome at the end of a period of schooling. There is a need now to reconfigure the moral compass if schooling and education are going to contribute fully towards creating new societies where individuals are empowered to live the lives they choose. All contexts will need to think beyond borders and the nation state towards developing responsible global citizens.

In Chapter 6, we propose a conceptualisation of success as a continuous process made up of meaningful points of departure. Learning does not start and stop with school, but schools can be the foundations of lifelong learning where individual success is marked by being equipped to make meaningful choices at different stages. We suggest, therefore, when considering Kohli's conceptual map through an educational lens, that we shift the focus for the individual from the resumption of ordinariness and anonymity to the search for participatory lives of *meaning and value*. We also emphasise that success can happen at different transition points, but that safety and belonging can also mutate at different points of experience. We therefore reconceptualise Kohli's diagram as a series of interlocking cogs rather than overlapping circles (Figure 2.1). If one circle shifts slightly then the alignment is broken and the young person might need to work through aspects of safety and/or belonging again in order to be able to experience a sense of success. Movements in the resettlement context can shift from a sense of restriction bounded by bureaucratic and structural barriers towards a sense of autonomy and flexibility of choice. Education can help young people with extraordinary experiences of past displacement and uncertainty progress towards meaningful lives in new contexts that can become home.

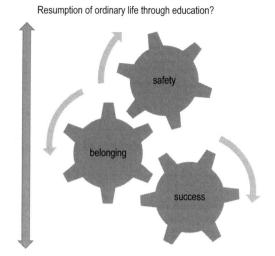

Figure 2.1 Education and Kohli's concepts

Conclusion

Kohli's ideas about the resumption of an ordinary life address the reality that, post-resettlement, many refugee children feel 'stuck' despite reaching places of sanctuary after long journeys. Kohli theorises these journeys as movements that children on forced migration tracks make across the three dimensions of geography, time, and maturational and psychological alterations – transitions through the concepts of safety, belonging and success (Kohli 2011, 2014). Kohli was working in the field of social work; we bring his theory of resumption of ordinary life to our empirical work to establish a *normative operational basis* for judging educational policies and practices. The greatest marker of success as outlined above might be reframed through questioning how far education can lead to an outcome where individual young people, arriving as refugees, go on to participate on a par with others in their social lives. This is the basis of Nancy Fraser's framing of social justice as 'participatory parity' (2003) and is why we offer the two theoretical approaches in this book, which argues that it is by working with these ideas in tandem that we can better understand why some young people are in-/excluded and find ways of thinking about schooling that can help young people find opportunities to go on to lead lives they and society value. Kohli's *resumption of an ordinary life* offers us practical concepts for working with refugees in school contexts. It helps us to develop pedagogical principles for supporting their individual moves towards success and lives they and others can value in their resettlement context. Nancy Fraser's *participatory parity* provides a moral normative basis for thinking about the various ways in which local, national and global policies, practices and structures allow for education for refugees in resettlement contexts.

We conclude that the realisation of Kohli's model in education is contingent on Fraser's socially just framing with a concomitant relationship between redistribution and recognition and representation. If we are to achieve participatory parity and a resumption of ordinariness and meaningful success for the young people who arrive searching for a new home in a reset-tlement context then there is a co-dependent relationship between the theoretical lenses we are working with. I therefore now move, in the next chapter, to explore how Fraser's theory of 'participatory parity' offers a socially just framing for education for refugee children.

Note

1   Throughout Section 1, there is deliberate stylistic use of the 'we' pronoun which acknowledges that research is a collective endeavour, that sometimes the 'we' refers to other academics and sometimes to the practitioners in the study, depending on who I have been working with as the thinking for the ideas in this section have developed. At times, the 'we' includes the reader.

References

Ager, A. and Strang, A. 2008. Understanding integration: A conceptual framework, *Journal of Refugee Studies*, 21(2), 166-191.

Anderson, A. 2004. Resilience, in Hamilton, R. and Moore (Eds), *Educational Interventions of Refugee Children*. London: RoutledgeFarmer, pp. 53-63.

Arendt, H. 1951 (2017 edition). *The Origins of Totalitarianism*. Harmondsworth: Penguin.

Arnot, M. and Pinson, H. 2005. *The Education of Asylum-Seeker and Refugee Children: A study of LEA and School Values, Policies and Practices*. Cambridge: Research Consortium on the Education of Asylum-Seekers and Refugee Children.

Baak, M. 2019. Racism and Othering for South Sudanese heritage students in Australian schools: Is inclusion possible?, *International Journal of Inclusive Education*, 23(2), 125-141, doi: 10.1080/13603116.2018.1426052.

Baak, M., Johnson, B., Sullivan, A., Slee, R., Brown, J. L. and Miller, E. 2019. School practices to support students from refugee backgrounds. Refugee Student Resilience Study Key Issues Paper No. 4. University of South Australia.

Bauman, Z. 2000. *Liquid Modernity*. Cambridge: Polity Press.

BBC. 2016 Europe migrant crisis, *BBC News*, 4 November 2016. https://www.bbc.co.uk/news/world-europe-34131911. Accessed 18 January 2020.

Benhabib, S. 1996. The democratic moment and the problem of difference, in Benhabib, S. (Ed), *Democracy and Difference: Contesting the Boundaries of the Political*. Princeton, NJ: Princeton University Press, pp. 3-18.

Benhabib, S. 2004. *The Rights of Others: Aliens, Residents, and Citizens*. Cambridge: Cambridge University Press.

Berry, M., Garcia-Blanco, I. and Moore K. 2015b. Press coverage of the refugee and migrant crisis in the EU: A content analysis of five European countries report prepared for the United Nations High Commission for Refugees. https://www.unhcr.org/protection/operations/56bb369c9/press-coverage-refugee-migrant-crisis-eu-content-analysis-five-european.html. Accessed 19 January 2020.

Cantle, T. 2008. *Community Cohesion: A New Framework for Race and Diversity*. Basingstoke: Palgrave Macmillan.

Castells, S. 2003. Towards a sociology of forced migration and social transformation, *Sociology*, 37(1), 13-34.

Dryden-Peterson, S. 2016. Refugee education: The crossroads of globalization, *Educational Researcher*, 45(9), 473-482.

Dryden-Peterson, S., Adelman, E., Bellino, M.J. and Chopra, V. 2019. The purposes of Refugee education: Policy and practice of including refugees in National Education Systems, *Sociology of Education*, 92(4), 346-366.

Fraser, N. 2003. Social justice in the age of identity politics, in Fraser, N. and Honneth, A. (Eds), *Redistribution or Recognition? A Political-Philosophical Exchange*. London: Verso.

Gatrell, P. 2016. Refugees – What's wrong with history?, *Journal of Refugee Studies*, 30(2), 170-189.

Gunderson, L. 2000. Voices of the teenage diasporas, *Journal of Adolescent and Adult Literacy*, 43(8), 692-706.

Hamilton, R. and Moore, D. (Eds) 2004. *Educational Interventions for Refugee Children: Theoretical Perspectives and Implementing Best Practice*. Abingdon: Routledge.

International Covenant on Economic, Social and Cultural Rights (ICESCR). 1966. https://www.ohchr.org/Documents/ProfessionalInterest/cescr.pdf. Accessed 4 January 2020.

Kohli, R. 2006. *Social work with unaccompanied asylum-seeking children*. London: Palgrave Macmillan

Kohli, R. 2011. Working to ensure safety, belonging and success for unaccompanied asylum-seeking children, *Child Abuse Review*, 20, 311-323.

Kohli, R. 2014. Protecting asylum seeking children on the move, *Revue Europeene Des Migrations Internationales*, 30(1), 83-104.

Lucassen, L. 2018. Peeling an onion: The 'refugee crisis' from a historical perspective, *Ethnic and Racial Studies*, 41(3), 383-410, doi: 10.1080/01419870.2017.1355975.

Matthews, J. 2008. Schooling and settlement: Refugee education in Australia, *International Studies in Sociology of Education*, 18(1), 31-45, doi: 10.1080/09620210802195947.

McBrien, J.L. 2005. Educational needs and barriers for refugee students in the United States: A review of the literature, *Review of Educational Research*, 75(3), 329-364.

McGrath, S. 2018. *Education and Development*. Abingdon: Routledge.

McIntyre, J. and Hall, C. 2018. Barriers to the inclusion of refugee and asylum-seeking children in schools in England, *Educational Review*, doi: 10.1080/00131911.2018.1544115.

McIntyre, J., Neuhaus, S. & Blennow, K. 2018 Participatory parity in schooling and moves towards ordinariness: a comparison of refugee education policy and practice in England and Sweden, *Compare: A Journal of Comparative and International Education*, DOI: 10.1080/03057925.2018.1515007.

Pew. 2016. Number of refugees to Europe surges to record 1.3 million in 2015. 2 August 2016. https://www.pewresearch.org/global/2016/08/02/number-of-refugees-to-europe-surges-to-record-1-3-million-in-2015/. Accessed 18 January 2020.

Pinson, H., Arnot, M. and Candappa, M. 2010. *Education, Aslyum and the 'Non-Citizen' Child: The Politics of Compassion and Belonging*. Basingstoke: Palgrave MacMillan.

Rutter, J. 2006. *Refugee Children in the UK*. Maidenhead: Open University Press.

Sen, A. 2009. *The Idea of Justice*, Cambridge MA: Belknap Harvard University Press.

Shuayb, M. 2016. Introduction, in Shuayb, M. (Ed) *Rethinking Education for Social Cohesion: International Case Studies*, pp. 1-7. Basingstoke: Palgrave Macmillan.

Skleparis, D. 2017. European Government's responses to the 'Refugee crisis': The interdependence of EU internal and external controls, *Southeastern Europe* [L'Europe du Sud-Est], 41(3), 276-301.

Spinks, H. 2013. Destination anywhere? Factors affecting asylum seekers' choice of destination country. Research Paper no. 1, 2012-13, 3 February 2013. Parliamentary Library: Canberra. Available at https://www.aph.gov.au/About_Parliament/Parliamentary_Departments/Parliamentary_Library/pubs/rp/rp1213/13rp01. Accessed 24 January 2020.

Stewart, J. 2011. *Supporting Refugee Children: Strategies for Educators*. Ontario: University of Toronto Press.

Taylor, S. and Sidhu, R. 2012. Supporting refugee students in schools: What constitutes inclusive education?, *International Journal of Inclusive Education*, 16(1), 39-56.

Watters, C. 2008. *Refugee Children*. Abingdon: Oxford University Press.

UNESCO. 2018. Concept note for the 2020 Global education monitoring report on inclusion. https://unesdoc.unesco.org/ark:/48223/pf0000265329. Accessed 4 January 2020.

UNESCO. 2019. Global Education Monitoring Report 2019 Migration, displacement and education: Building bridges not walls. https://en.unesco.org/gem-report/report/2019/migration. Accessed 4 January 2020.

United Nations. 1948. The Universal Declaration of Human Rights. https://www.un.org/en/universal-declaration-human-rights/. Accessed 4 January 2020.

United Nations. 1951. Convention related to the status of Refugees. https://www.unhcr.org/5d9ed32b4. Accessed 4 January 2020.

United Nations. 2015. 2030 agenda for sustainable development. https://www.un.org/sustainabledevelopment/education/. Accessed 4 January 2020.

UNHCR. 1989. United Nations conventions on the Rights of the Child. https://www.unicef.org.uk/rights-respecting-schools/wp-content/uploads/sites/4/2017/01/UNCRC-in-full.pdf. Accessed 4 January 2020.

UNHCR. 2019a. Access to education for refugee and migrant children in Europe. https://www.unhcr.org/neu/wp-content/uploads/sites/15/2019/09/Access-to-education-europe-19.pdf. Accessed 4 January 2020.

UNHCR. 2019b. Stepping up: Refugee education in crisis. https://www.unhcr.org/steppingup/. Accessed 4 January 2020

World Education Forum (WEF). 2015. Education 2030: Incheon declaration and framework for action. https://unesdoc.unesco.org/ark:/48223/pf0000245656. Accessed 4 January 2020.

Zetter, R. 2007. More labels, fewer refugees: Remaking the refugee label in an era of globalization, *Journal of Refugee Studies*, 20(2), 172–192.

3 Redistribution, recognition and representation

Joanna McIntyre

A commitment to equity, justice and fairness underpins the theoretical framing for the book. In this chapter, I introduce the second of the two theories – 'participatory parity' (Fraser 2003). This theory is drawn from feminist political philosophy and means that justice requires social conditions such that all can participate and interact with one another as peers. This is a theory of social justice which works with the three components of recognition, redistribution and representation to promote equitable access and inclusion. Fraser establishes a *normative moral basis* against which policies and practices can be measured.

Moving from education as a right to education as a socially just imperative/frame for inclusion

What is meant by social (in)justice in this context? This is too vast a concept to explore fully here so what follows is only a partial introduction. This is offered in order to provide a rationale for the focus on a normative moral and operational frame for working with refugee children in resettlement settings. Most models of social justice have been framed in terms of redistribution of goods and symbolic recognition. Petersen et al. offer the following definition of social justice:

> being concerned with notions of equity and fairness in the distribution of resources within given spaces (local, national and transnational, for example); the recognition of particular, and often multiple, identities; and access to democratic decision-making processes.

> (Peterson et al. 2016, xi)

The first aspect of this draws on the tradition of distributive justice. One of the most influential thinkers in this area was John Rawls, who proposed that we reconceptualise models of socially just societies through imagining a new social contract (1971). In order to do this fairly Rawls asked that we consider this by operating within a 'veil of ignorance' with no knowledge of what our own roles and identities might be within this new social order. This thought experiment was intended to ensure that the new social contract was not created by people who could work it to their own advantage with their own vested interests. Rawls' 'justice as fairness' approach was predicated on the idea that this new social contract should be based on an idea of 'society as a system of fair social cooperation between free and equal persons' (Rawls 1985, 229)'.

Rawls developed this idea over time, guided by his underlying principle that the worst off in society be advantaged through a form of distributive justice, where any individual, regardless of their background or individual characteristics, should have a 'basic moral equality with everyone else' (Ryan 2012, 513) and that inequalities (such as redistribution of goods) are permitted if they work to the advantage of the worst off; this is the 'difference principle' which seeks to ensure fairness. So Rawls advocated for equal rights, equality of opportunity and a commitment to promoting the interests of the worst off in society.

But can an abstract theory of distributive justice apply to our focus here on education and marginalised groups? Amartya Sen offered a detailed response to and critique of Rawls' approach, arguing that it is dependent upon a social contract drawn up within an idealised nation-state, comprising just institutions, ideal social arrangements and conceptualisations of citizenship that were dependent upon the existence of a sovereign state (2009). Sen argues that we now need to consider ideas of justice within the realities of today's globalised world. Sen does not offer any answers and does not formulate a 'fully worked-out theory'; as Robeyns explains, however, the approach is relevant because 'we need theorising to help us with making comparisons of injustice, and to guide us towards a less unjust society' (Robeyns 2017, 57). In his Capabilities Approach, Sen helps us to question whether a fair distribution of resources, as advocated by Rawls, is enough to ensure that individuals can fulfil their aspirations.

Sen, and later Nussbaum (2006), challenge Rawls by calling for theories of justice which relate to lived experiences and practices. Sen is interested in questions of human wellbeing and his approach is broadly based on the idea that individuals have capabilities and attend to what opportunities they have to achieve their potential in terms of being and doing that which they value – their functioning (cf. Sen 2009). Robeyns simplifies this by articulating the main question that Capabilities Approach seeks to answer: 'What are people really able to do and what kind of person are they able to be?' (2017, 9). In this book, our[1] focus is on Kohli's and Fraser's theoretical concepts, but it is important to acknowledge that the Capabilities Approach allows us to judge how far society provides real opportunities for people to be able to 'lead lives they have reason to value' (Robeyns 2003, 545). This is important to our conceptualisation of 'success' in Chapter 6.

For us to consider this in relation to refugees' experiences of schooling, there is a need to think about SDG4 in its entirety and move beyond simply focusing on access. A wider conceptualisation of educational social justice calls for recognition of the ways in which educational spaces, the planned, enacted and lived spaces of schools and schooling need to become more fluid if they are to be able to accommodate the needs of new arrivals and to recognise how the resettlement education system may need to shift a little to accommodate changing societal demands at the local and global level. In this way, young new arrivals might find they can experience education provision which prepares them for lifelong learning and to go to lead lives they and others value.

The second dimension of Petersen et al.'s definition above refers to this concept of recognition. Recognition (and misrecognition) is particularly important to theories of social justice, especially when considering how political and societal contexts allow for groups that are usually marginalised from mainstream society. Debates about recognition in this context are linked to normative values of how things should or should not be. However whilst the notion of recognition is integral to social justice this must at all costs avoid 'essentialising difference' (Kiwan 2016). Honneth, drawing on the Hegelian tradition of human flourishing, argues for the need for mutual recognition and the importance of social relationships in avoiding mis-recognition and in supporting the development of self-realisation and the maintenance of an individual's identity (1995). In order for Honneth's concept of recognition to be achieved, an individual must experience feelings of self-confidence, self-respect and self-esteem, and this is only possible within social arrangements which allow for recognition for and from others. This is particularly important when we consider recognition in relation to universal human rights. It is not enough to be able to have written commitments to, or an official ratification of, the entitlement to education if young refugees are living within socio-political contexts which do not allow for this right to be fully realised. Honneth's position is that without the necessary social arrangements for this to happen then individuals are disrespected, being denied the capacity to exercise rights that others in the resettlement context can exercise in order to legitimately take part in social life. Integral to recognition theories is a consideration of power dynamics when marginalised groups struggle for recognition (Young 2011). In the case of SDG4 in resettlement contexts, access to education is not enough if others from more powerful groups are provided with education of a higher quality which newcomers are excluded from by nature of their status as refugee or asylum seeker. It is also an issue when refugees are treated as one homogenous group. So recognition needs to account for multi-faceted intersecting identities – bound up with identification by gender, by sexuality, by ethnicity, by age, by religion, by country of birth, as well as their newer identity classification of refugee.

Access to education without considering whether it is high-quality inclusive provision is not therefore always a societal 'good' in itself, especially for individuals who have not been able to have consistent education provision through forced upheaval or who have been locked out of mainstream provision for a range of reasons. It is unlikely that a newly arrived 16-year-old who has been given access to part-time college provision for just 7 hours a week, consisting of basic skills (language, numeracy and perhaps information and communications technology [ICT]), will be able to realise their potential capabilities. However, it is also not enough to simply draw attention to the paucity of some provision without offering a means of understanding what transformative provision might look like.

Kiwan suggests that social justice can be reframed within educational debates as 'justice as inclusion' where the focus is on inclusion as 'process' as well as 'outcome', arguing that this has implications for 'the societal' and 'the pedagogical processes of involvement' (2016, 4–5). This would necessitate a consideration of how the newcomer is represented and how they are valued and given opportunities to contribute to the evolution of a new society as the resettlement context shifts beyond assimilation to practices which ask: 'How can society include?' and 'How is society excluding?' This calls for a relational approach to social justice which acknowledges power dynamics and the role of education to be a process for and out-come of more socially just societies within and across borders. It moves beyond meritocratic individual responsibility for social mobility and associated assumptions about the neutrality of structural barriers towards a more critical understanding of the ways in which in/visible barriers replace national borders. Access and recognition are not enough; they can mask ongoing inequalities. However, there are some school spaces which recognise that refugees can represent 'social hope' (Dillabough 2016, 63), especially where all members are given opportunities to interact on an equal basis.

Nancy Fraser's participatory parity - a normative moral frame

Nancy Fraser poses what looks on the surface like a straightforward question: she asks whether individuals and different groups can participate on a par with others in their social life (2003). For Fraser, this is an important indicator of social (in)justice. If the answer is no, then we are required to consider what are the barriers to the achievement of *participatory parity* for those individuals or groups who are currently marginalised or excluded. The concept of participatory parity is the normative core of Fraser's theory of social justice; in order for it to be achieved, then there must be a fair (re)distribution of socio-economic resources alongside a reciprocal recognition of cultural identities. This latter focus on cultural recognition moves beyond a naming of difference, which could be described in terms of deficit and othering, towards a mutual recognition of the positive values and cultures heterogeneity brings to a society. Whilst there has to be a symbiotic relationship between these concepts of *redistribution* and *recognition*, Fraser adds a third concept, that of *representation*, which requires a consideration of how different voices within society are reflected and contribute to dominant political discourses. These three dimensions are necessary prerequisites for participatory parity and provide a useful lens through which to view how sections of society can operate and interact on an equal basis with others, encompassing economic, cultural and political factors. Fraser later developed this to consider how (in)justice operates within a plurality of scales, thus allowing a consideration of global, national and localised framing of policies and issues (2010).

But what has this to do with our focus here? How does a moral normative frame such as participatory parity allow us to understand better what the experiences of young refugees are in secondary education in England? Fraser's 'participatory parity' lens allows us to consider how far systemic factors affect the ways in which schools and those within them respond to the needs of young new arrivals. Fraser is concerned with the relationship between de jure inclusion and de facto exclusion (Knight 2015, 100). Young new arrivals who are provided with access to some form of educational provision in a withdrawal unit within a mainstream setting, a reduced hours timetable outside usual curriculum hours in a post-16 setting because of over-demand for places, or transported to settings away from their local school because of a lack of capacity, are experiencing exclusion under the auspices of inclusive practices.

Through the course of this book, we will consider the ways in which young refugees and the people working with them are able to access meaningful education provision, which will equip them to make choices about their future, as peers in their new context are able to do. This means we focus on the distribution of socio-economic resources in terms of policy and practice. We also will be examining the extent to which there is a recognition of the needs of different groups of refugees, and importantly of different individuals within these groups.

We will consider the ways in which policies and practices are culturally responsive without stigmatising or othering the young person. Further, we will also look to how political obstacles are negotiated or avoided, such as policies and decision-making processes that marginalise and exclude newly arrived children from their right to an education. In this we will look to how national policies in the English resettlement context are influenced by global and international policies and discourses. Throughout, we need to ask how the voices of the young people themselves and their advocates are (mis)represented in decisions about their educational experiences and opportunities. Considering these concepts together can help to develop a socially just response.

Schools and the young people in them (or out of them) work within a set of social, institutional and environmental contexts. These can be policies, practices and discourses which constitute the normative domains/parameters within which people go about their lives. An important aspect of Fraser's approach is that it shifts the focus from individuals (and what they are perceived to lack) to social conditions. It also allows us to consider what we experience/observe in localised spaces and their relationships to national and global perspectives. So, we can see that educational policy and practice within an English city or town are affected by national and global responses to narratives of a refugee 'crisis' (McIntyre and Hall 2018). We can also extrapolate the English experience to other resettlement contexts.

Two extracts from the recent Global Education Monitoring (GEM) report (UNESCO 2019) provide illustrations of the ways in which young refugee children are potentially disadvantaged by decisions about distribution of resource within England:

> Immigrant students tend to concentrate in suburban areas and schools with lower academic standards and performance levels ... Non-native speakers in the United Kingdom were more likely to attend school with disadvantaged native speakers.
>
> (UNESCO 2019, 22)

> The new National Funding Formula in England (United Kingdom) abolishes specific funding for migrants but allocates funds to compensate for such disadvantages as 'deprivation', 'low prior attainment' and 'English as an additional language'.
>
> (UNESCO 2019, 23)

The first point refers to the policy of dispersal, which I write about more fully elsewhere with my colleague Chris Hall (McIntyre and Hall 2018). Families with school-age children and unaccompanied new arrivals seeking asylum and refugee status within England are first and foremost subject to immigration policies which, we argued, were steered by international discourses (ibid.). If they successfully navigate these institutional procedures, they then have to work through a series of welfare policies and bureaucracies. The first of these is housing. In order to 'relieve the burden' on London and the south-east of the country (Home Office 1998, 8.22), the government introduced a dispersal policy to create a greater geographical distribution of new arrivals. In practice, however, this accommodation tends to be in areas of cheap housing in localities which frequently populate the bottom of tables of socio-economic deprivation indices (McIntyre and Hall 2018, 6). It is no coincidence that schools in these identified areas are also likely to be at the lower end of performance tables (this is not to suggest deficit models of schools in these areas, but rather to highlight the multifaceted systemic factors of injustice that are prevalent, such as poverty, ill-health and unemployment).

The second quotation from the GEM Report, which appears to be linked to the redistribution of financial resources, is also linked to the concept of recognition. It echoes a point made in an article in which Swedish colleagues and I reported our analysis of comparisons of English and Swedish educational policy for refugee children (McIntyre, Neuhaus and Blennow 2018). We found that in England, ostensibly refugee children are rendered invisible in policy discourse and in data reporting (ibid.). Of course, some new arrivals will also meet the criteria of 'deprivation', 'low prior attainment' and 'English as an additional language', but this won't necessarily accommodate all their needs. There has been no guidance for schools and practitioners on supporting refugee children in schools since 2007, and there is no mechanism for collating data about new arrivals in schools; accordingly, in policy terms, there is a lack of recognition and representation as they are effectively excluded from the discourse. In McIntyre et al. we conclude that there is a 'useful invisibility' of refugee children in educational policy, allowing public discourse to focus on refugees as an immigration policy matter, leaving schools and individual teachers wishing to offer a socially just response to work through and underneath policy (2018). A number of schools do this, and it is important to understand the ways in which they do in order to support others wishing to learn from them. In Chapters 4–7, we explore the ways in which schools can work within a normative operational frame to try and achieve this.

Bringing in the moral frame

Fraser's framework offers a tripartite approach to 'participatory parity' – a moral basis for shaping equity for new arrivals in schools. For Fraser, the imperative is to examine the 'social arrangements that permit all to participate as peers in social life … overcoming injustice means dismantling institutionalised barriers that prevent some people from participating on a par with others, as full partners in social interaction' (Fraser 2007, 27). When considering refugee education policy and practice, interrogation of the barriers to parity can be examined on three levels using Fraser's heuristic (Figure 3.1).

If the barrier is:	*the solution could be:*
viewed as economic	**redistribution** of material or human resources
caused by cultural barriers	**recognition** of cultural values and measures that promote recognitive justice
thought of as a political issue	**representative** measures, increased ways of according equitable representation/ political voice

Figure 3.1 Applying Fraser's heuristic

Through dialogues with the practitioners in our case study schools, reported in the following chapters, we can see that Fraser offers a means by which they make sense of how national 'big' policy is enacted by 'small' policies and practices in their own contexts. Policy is not static and 'out there' – we all 'do' policy and can shape policy enactment. The participants reflected that the participatory parity lenses gave them a language to understand their context, and they felt this was empowering.

Redistribution

In considering how far refugee and asylum-seeking children can participate in a socially just society within England, Fraser's distributive lens is particularly interesting. Fraser's 'objective condition' for social justice and parity is predicated upon a fairer distribution of material resources (2003). Historically, the United Kingdom has been characterised by economic and social inequality, and this continues to the present day; although this study is located in one of the world's ten richest economies, there is uneven distribution of wealth. Within the United Kingdom, just 10% of households account for 44% of all wealth, whilst the poorest 50% account for just 9% (ONS 2018). This unequal distribution of wealth is echoed in the structure of the education system, where 6% of the school population attend fee-paying private schools. These are predominantly children of more affluent families, who are significantly more likely than poorer students to go on to study at a prestigious university (Sutton Trust 2010). The majority attend state schools where the social inequalities are even more magnified, with differential government funding for free schools, academies and local authority schools. Since 2010, successive cuts to school budgets have had the most negative impact on schools in economically deprived areas (Reay 2017). As I have articulated earlier in this chapter, because of the UK's dispersal policy, refugee children are likely to attend schools serving communities of higher economic deprivation. All of these factors play a part in how schools can choose to distribute their human and material resources.

Distributive features of justice have been a feature of equity and educational policy in England for some time. Historically, there has been an acknowledgement that not all students are equitably positioned. This is the case for a range of reasons relating to pupils' family background, including level of education, occupation, residential status, financial security and class allegiance. In particular, the latter two have created systemic structural barriers to equality. Of course, this assumes a particularly stable notion of family context, which is not usually reflected in refugee pupils' experiences. Family education and income could have been high in their home context but count for very little once they have been forced to migrate.

The policy focus within England has been on distribution of funding to allow for schools to deploy staffing, organise timetabling and resourcing to ensure that pupils make progress against national academic benchmarks. Between 1998 and 2010, refugee children were included under national strategies programmes targeted at 'narrowing the gap' for identified under-achieving groups, and there were specific programmes within this, including the New Arrivals Excellence Programme (DCSF 2007). A change of government in 2010 led to a cessation of the national strategies programme, and all documentation and guidance were subsequently removed from government websites. At the time of writing (the spring of 2020), there has been no subsequent government policy documentation about the education of refugee children. Department for Education and Home Office policies relating to 'migrant children' have been largely confined to the welfare needs of unaccompanied children in local authority care.

Historically, schools working with refugee and asylum-seeking children would have received specific funding through the Ethnic Minority Achievement Grant (EMAG), which was introduced in 1999. This funding was targeted to support pupils for whom English was an additional language and to raise the achievement of underperforming pupils from ethnic minority backgrounds. EMAG funding was devolved to local authorities who usually retained some of the funding to finance training and support at the wider local authority level whilst also devolving money to schools with particularly high intakes of pupils meeting the EMAG criteria. In 2011, this EMAG funding was stopped. Schools then received Direct Grant Funding, with no stipulation as to how this money should be allocated. This meant that there was no longer specific funding targeted for supporting those refugee children who would have fallen under the auspices of EMAG funding. In 2016, the government announced that all schools would receive their allocated budget based on a National Funding Formula (NFF) administered centrally. The level of funding is based on the number of students on roll, the numbers of children with specified additional needs (including EAL, so most refugee children are included) and the number of 'looked-after' children (which includes unaccompanied children). However, there are no measures to ensure that the funding is allocated to specific groups, and decisions about how to spend the overall budget are left to individual schools. Recent austerity measures, coupled with a national shortage of teachers, have resulted in a great proportion of this budget being allocated to cover staffing costs and operational needs rather than targeted at pupils with additional needs such as refugee and asylum-seeking children (Hutchinson 2018).

In theory, students with EAL arriving in school should attract three years of additional funding. If a refugee child qualifies for this and arrives after the age of 15, in years 10 or 11, the school will receive proportionally less than the three years' allocation. The case study chapters will illustrate how the needs of refugee and asylum-seeking children extend beyond acquisition of a new language. The label EAL can mask other aspects of educational need. However, these needs are not addressed in the decision-making process about fiscal resources for schools. There is funding to support raising achievement for pupils with low attainment in year 6, but if refugee children arrive after the testing period, they will not bring that funding with them upon arrival at secondary school. Many refugee and asylum-seeking children should qualify for Pupil Premium funding targeted at disadvantaged pupils in local authority care and/or in receipt of free school meals. However, the school leaders in the study explained that this was difficult to access because of linguistic and cultural barriers which often militated against refugee parents registering their children for free school meals. For older new arrivals, aged 16–19, there is a Vulnerable Student Bursary intended to facilitate access to education for those in financial need. This bursary is only available to asylum seekers or refugees in local authority care and is not available to asylum seekers with families. If students have arrived in England as part of the Vulnerable Persons Resettlement Scheme (VPRS), there is also specific funding for their education.

This very complex distribution of resources was not clear to those working in our case study schools. Most of the practitioners had no knowledge of how much of each year's school budget was specifically targeted at supporting new arrivals, with one claiming that *'funding is mysterious'*.

Prior to 2010, resources and the provision of expertise to support new arrivals were devolved to local authorities to work with targeted schools and settings. This led to the development of specialist teams in local authorities whom schools could draw on for support. Some local authority teams had refugee education teams as part of this work. However, since 2010, policy in England has been predicated on the requirement that schools should be held accountable for each child making progress against identified academic benchmarks. The national strategies programmes of the previous administration, which included the New Arrivals Excellence programme, were discontinued, with the justification that it was time for central government to step back to foster the 'school system improvement journey'. This led to the abolition of dedicated resourcing and specialist support. So in recent years, refugee children have not been recognised as a specific group in need of additional funding, provision or time. This has led to the current situation in which we have inadequate systems even to measure how many refugee children are in English schools, and only partial data on access to education for unaccompanied children in care (Ott and O'Higgins 2019).

The most evident aspect of injustice in resourcing for refugee children is the maldistribution of school places, which means that some have to wait months before they can resume their education. The schools in this study work to ensure that they can accommodate new arrivals: firstly by promptly offering them a place in school and then by working to ensure that they have an inclusive, high-quality experience of education. They do this because there is a commitment from the senior leadership team to make *'brave'* decisions although, as one leader in a case study school commented sardonically, in the current educational climate, this isn't necessarily seen as *'the wisest'* thing to do. Headteachers are under extreme pressure to ensure that they meet performance targets in terms of league tables of examination results, to ensure positive Ofsted inspection reports and to compete to attract parents in the school choice marketplace. Children with additional needs who arrive midway through the school year are perceived as a strain on limited resources and it is especially difficult for refugees to find a place in a school if they arrive at the age when most children in the system are preparing for high-stakes examinations. Patently, it is the case that refugee and asylum-seeking children cannot begin to live lives of parity if they cannot at least find a place in a school.

Our previous research confirmed both the existence of these barriers to inclusion of refugee children in schools in England and the relative invisibility of refugee children in policy and data (McIntyre and Hall 2018; McIntyre et al. 2018). Until the visibility of refugee children in educational policy and discourse improves and targeted funding is provided for supporting them, the largest barrier to their resumption of an ordinary life will be in the inequitable distribution of funding for schools. The current distribution mechanisms penalise schools in areas of high economic deprivation such as those nearest to cheaper rental accommodation in dispersal areas.

An investment in high-quality inclusive education in school is crucial in ensuring that the young refugees can go on to have access to equal participation in the jobs market and in society in the future. The case study schools have demonstrated ways of utilising resources to this effect. However, not all schools operate in this way and until there is a change in the pattern of distribution of targeted resources for refugee children, many refugee and asylum-seeking children will find themselves excluded from a futures-oriented model of inclusive education. As discussed above, the move to the national funding formula, coupled with the lack of visible data on refugee children in schools, has repositioned resource for refugee children under the labels EAL and Pupil Premium. This masks the educational and welfare needs of newly arrived individual children, something that I now move to discuss in considering Fraser's second lens: recognition.

Recognition

Fraser's second condition of participatory parity is the 'intersubjective condition' (2003) which relates to the concept of recognition. According to Fraser, social injustice occurs through misrecognition of cultural values which differ from the dominant patterns, and this leads to status inequality for those whose cultural values do not fit neatly with those that are privileged in the hierarchy. School systems predicated upon social and cultural capital that reflects the most privileged in society reproduce inequalities and social exclusion (Bourdieu and Passeron 1977). Having access to the preferred sorts of social and cultural capital means that a child is more likely to thrive and prosper through education. It is therefore easier to succeed in an education system if the child enters school with the sets of knowledges, skills and experiences that are reflected in dominant models of pedagogy, curriculum and assessment. Refugee and asylum-seeking children arrive bringing different experiences of prior education. They are likely to need support to fit in and assimilate to the prevailing model of education in their new context. If their needs are to be recognised then schools and teachers need to be able to accommodate and support this transition.

In a similar way to the different centralised and local approaches to redistribution of fiscal resource discussed above, it is clear that historically, there have been deliberate moves to redress the effects of marginalising pupils from dominant modes of curriculum in school settings. These were most manifest in increased recognition of the importance of multiculturalist educational policies and practices from the late 1970s to the mid-1990s (Kymlicka 2010, 97). In the English context, these were linked to national initiatives and championed at the local authority level, especially in areas of the country, such as the inner cities, where there were diverse communities. In the 1970s there was a shift from a focus on (mainly Commonwealth) immigrants needing to assimilate through education, towards a recognition of the importance of multicultural approaches to facilitate integration. The Bullock Report (DES 1975), for example, celebrated the importance of valuing each pupil's 'mother-tongue'. This set the groundwork for the Swann Report in 1985 which championed multicultural approaches and contained a statement on racial equality (DES 1985). This highly influential report recognised that the education system did not adequately reflect or serve Britain's multiracial and multicultural society; it shifted attention from how to educate children of ethnic minority backgrounds to fit a dominant model towards educating all children about how to live in a diverse society, in order to 'bring about a true sense of belonging to Britain' (Joseph, Foreword to the Swann Report, 1985).

However, there followed a significant shift in policy signalled in a speech by the then Prime Minister Margaret Thatcher where she raised concerns that 'children who need to count and multiply are being taught antiracist mathematics, whatever that may be' (1987). The 1988 Education Reform Act signalled the introduction of the National Curriculum, the content of which was heavily steered by the Conservative government to minimise multicultural and antiracist perspectives (Tomlinson 2009). However, whilst references to multiculturalism did not feature in the National Curriculum documentation, multicultural approaches which favoured educating all pupils about diverse cultures and beliefs were still prevalent in the 1990s because of the prominent role of local authorities in steering localised policy and practice, especially in ethnically diverse communities (Bleich 1998). A plethora of materials generated by local authorities and phase and subject associations supported teachers in adopting approaches that supported pupils in their diverse classrooms. During the New Labour era (1998–2010), the EMAG grant ensured that local authorities had specialist teams supporting the education of children from ethnic minority heritages. Alongside this, the introduction of citizenship education aimed to support the development of a more tolerant diverse society, as did the policy focus on community cohesion following the Cantle Report on a series of disturbances in northern cities in England in 2001 (Cantle 2001). Although there was some criticism that these multicultural approaches did not fully include antiracist perspectives, it is clear that there was an attempt at the local level during this period to develop culturally responsive pedagogies in order to create more inclusive and supportive classroom environments. Marginalised groups, including refugee children arriving at this time, would be more likely to feel a sense of welcome and inclusion in school.

In more recent years, and especially post-2010, changes at the national level to create a more centralised education system, combined with pressures on schools to compete in the school choice marketplace, have had a widespread impact on what schools and individual teachers feel they have the space to do. In many schools, this has moved the focus away from celebration and recognition of diversity in classrooms towards a focus on examination performance and on individualised social mobility, especially for those pupils from 'disadvantaged backgrounds' where disadvantaged is marked by poverty or by virtue of being raised by the state and 'looked-after' by the local authority. When this is coupled with an increasingly hostile immigration policy landscape, any celebration and recognition of diversity in education polices have been silenced. As has already been stated, at the time of writing, there has been no significant mention of refugee and asylum-seeking children in educational policy documentation in England for a number of years. This, along with the disappearance of funding aimed at supporting children from diverse ethnic backgrounds, has meant that schools working with refugee children are drawing on inclusive pedagogies from memories of previous policies and practices.

English education policy has been particularly influenced by global measures of accountability which foreground an economic model of comparing educational outcomes, as demonstrated in the PISA tables (OECD 2019). These economic models are reproduced within national education policy. Since 2010, there has been a renewed emphasis on a defined set of knowledges that schools need to teach in order for pupils to perform well in external high-stakes examinations. We have already articulated how this has an impact on decisions about where to focus resources, but there are also implications for refugee new arrivals whose prior experiences, knowledge and skills are not necessarily recognised by this exam-focused curriculum. They need to assimilate to this set of privileged knowledges, pedagogies and assessments if they are to individually perform well in examinations and on a par with peers in the English context. This does not allow for recognition of their individual skills and aptitudes. At the same time, refugee children and other new arrivals are subsumed under the homogenous label of EAL, whereby what they lack (English) is foregrounded rather than what they bring (multilingualism). The label EAL does not recognise and value their assets. Others have written about how language policies in England and the USA are usually targeted at prioritising a monolingual approach, aiming to replace the first language with English rather than celebrating the cognitive skills associated with multilingual expertise of the children (Wiley 2017). Furthermore, whilst policy dictates that schools have to explicitly teach (and display markers signifying allegiance to) British values, official educational discourse does not foreground diversity in cultures and values.

All of this has led to a public silencing of the formerly key role of holistic culturally responsive curricula and pedagogies. So, if the refugee or asylum-seeking pupil's assets and potential contributions are not recognised by the dominant models of education they encounter in schools, then this is a misrecognition in Fraser's terms. Many schools do attempt to recognise and value the contributions of refugees to society through activities such as Black History Month and Refugee Week, but if these are confined to these special occasions, then this leads to what Fraser describes as the reification and displacement of children from refugee backgrounds, positioning them as 'other' and implying that they have to do something extraordinary in order to be valued by their new society.

Fraser's lens of recognition helps us to understand what some schools face in terms of barriers to establishing safety, belonging and success for their newly arrived pupils. The descriptions in Chapters 4-7 indicate that the case study schools have relied on 'brave' decisions by those advocating for inclusion for refugee children in such a highly pressurised school system.

Within educational policy and enactment in England, there is clearly a symbiotic relationship between the concepts of redistribution and recognition. Fraser describes this as 'their practical entwinement'. Here this entwinement serves to disadvantage children from refugee and asylum-seeking backgrounds who cannot immediately compete in the high-stakes performance framework of schooling (2003, 48). This preoccupation with examination performance as the only measure of success creates a hierarchy of cultural values based on a set of privileged knowledges and skills required by the prescribed test-focused curricula and pedagogies. The stratification of schools by results in the school marketplace sets up an economistic hierarchy of schooling. Both contribute to the inequalities in the experience of refugee and asylum-seeking children. Recognition of their cultural values is diminished and, in some ways, displaced by the emphasis on dominant models of school accountability and the focus on distribution of fiscal resources which accompany this.

In an increasingly globalised world with 'a growing tide' of neo-liberalism (and, I would add, populism), Fraser argues that there needs to be a third dimension which directly explores how political injustice occurs when people are represented in ways which exclude them (2004, 382). Refugees/asylum seekers/new arrivals are collective terms for people who are grouped together because of a range of individual circumstances that have forced them to leave their homes and seek sanctuary elsewhere. When they arrive in their new context, they lose intersectional aspects of their identity as their status as asylum seeker/refugee becomes prominent. This labelling serves to both depersonalise (through homogenisation) and marginalise them; their lives become controlled by immigration and welfare processes. I now explore how the misrepresentation of refugee and asylum-seeking children in English educational policy and discourse is a further obstacle to achieving lives of parity in their new context.

Representation

I have already described how, since 2010, the needs of newly arrived children are invisible and silenced in educational policy in England. This is an obvious form of misrepresentation in Fraser's terms. If schools are not required to work with and fully support these children, then it is likely, given the pressures of accountability, that some will choose not to. Policy invisibility is a political act of injustice that affects both those schools that want to be inclusive and those that do not. Most importantly, it affects the children who are marginalised as a consequence of this invisibility.

Usually, groups seek to improve parity of representation through ensuring their voice is heard. Notwithstanding earlier comments about the issues with the homogeneity implied by grouping diverse individuals from a range of contexts and situations under the label 'refugees', it is notable that there has been little engagement by refugee groups in the development of policy around education; they are excluded from membership of those groups making decisions about educational provision in national policy and in formal schooling contexts. By contrast, individuals from refugee backgrounds are actively involved in non-formal educational provision, for example youth projects in Non-Governmental Organisations (NGOs)which support children waiting for a place in a formalised education setting.

In the model of schooling and associated policies that are dominant in England at this time, there is a deliberate move to, ostensibly, leave decisions about curriculum and pedagogy to individual schools in order to support conceptualisations of a school-led system of school improvement. This has led to the removal of guidance and good practice examples from government websites. Children from refugee backgrounds are not unique in finding themselves misrepresented and disenfranchised as a consequence of this approach. Despite this, some schools are able to become 'hopeful, lived spaces … educating refugee and migrant-background students' (Wrench et al. 2018, 1209). They do this despite the political injustices in the education system, often by stealth and bravery, navigating spaces and working underneath official bureaucracies to be compassionate and inclusive and taking risks about enrolling students because they believe that what they are doing is more important. Ciara's comments illustrate this when describing the ethos of the Senior Leadership team in Lilac Lane School (which is featured in Chapter 6): *'They said, "Well, we can take the hit, we* accept that that's the right thing for those individuals" whereas there are some schools would have said 'No, it's about results.'

A significant marker of inclusion is if the child can see people like themselves represented in adults that shape their experiences of life in their new society. Across western contexts there have been moves to try and increase the representation of minority groups within the teaching workforce (Keddie and Niesch 2012). However, most schools in England do not reflect the diversity of their intake, a point raised by Sally in our conversations again at Lilac Lane: *'Our staffing, it's not as diverse as I'd. You know for me, it's quite ironic schools talking about being inclusive but having an all-white middle class staff.'* Representation of refugee children is inevitably complex. Although this can partially be met by considering representation of ethnic minority groups in the workforce, representations of social class are harder to address. Assumptions about the class of families and children who have had to forcibly migrate to England and thus become dependent on welfare systems do not necessarily reflect their lived experiences of social class in their home contexts.

The importance of increasing the diversity of the teaching workforce has been recognised by the government in England, especially in relation to gender and ethnic minority representation (DFE 2018). However, moves to address this are hindered by successive years of problems with teacher shortages and also by bureaucratic and technical barriers to recognising previous teaching experience and qualifications gained outside the UK. This means that teachers with refugee backgrounds find it costly and difficult to utilise their professional expertise and join the teaching workforce. Funding for programmes to support refugees into teaching is difficult to source, though some charities have projects that aim to do this. A PGCE training programme at University College London Institute of Education specifically aimed at refugees and asylum seekers wishing to teach in post-16 contexts had its funding withdrawn in 2013.

As well as a lack of representation of the refugee community within the teaching workforce, there are also questions to be asked about how newly arrived students are made visible and represented in student populations. Younger refugee and asylum-seeking children are more likely to be placed in mainstream schooling; the picture is more complex with older children. Children arriving at the age of 15 or older find it difficult to access a school place because of the considerable pressures on schools during those years, despite the fact that an individual child's performance outcomes will only affect the school data if they have been in education in England for the past two years. So some refugee children might be on school rolls but educated in separate provision to relieve pressure on mainstream teachers focused on preparing classes for the high-stakes examinations. Children who arrive aged 16+ find it particularly difficult to access mainstream education, which in England at post-16 level is usually stratified into academic or vocational provision with specific entry criteria. Most attend, if there are spaces, college ESOL classes (English for Speakers of Other Languages, a form of adult English language instruction) and, where there is capacity, basic numeracy and ICT classes. These courses rarely make up full-time provision for these students.

Studies of unaccompanied children show that if they are able to access education it can be categorised under the following three headings: mainstream, English language provision and other transitional bespoke provision (Ott and O'Higgins 2019). In practice, even when the student is on roll in mainstream provision there are many examples of internal exclusion where the students' day-to-day experiences diverge sharply from the daily experiences of their native peers.

In England, there has been a concern to make schools more democratic through strategies to give pupils voice in their education. In reality, mechanisms for engaging student voice raise questions of power and legitimacy (see, for example, Noyes 2005) as fundamentally schools are hierarchical structures where adults have more power and ownership of the debate than children. Such mechanisms rarely aim to redress issues of inequality through attending to the voices of the disenfranchised, such as refugee pupils. Where they do, there is a concern that language and cultural barriers will prevent schools from being able to engage meaningfully with pupils' representatives from refugee backgrounds.

I have already articulated the ways in which refugee children are unlikely to find themselves and their experiences represented in curriculum. My previous comments have been about the ways in which, because of the dominant models of curriculum and assessment in English schools, such students are unlikely to find their own cultural values and perspectives reflected in what they are studying in class. There are also debates about how far children from refugee backgrounds can be represented in such contexts as there is a danger of reification (through tokenistic mechanisms such as assemblies during refugee week) and of the emergence of a simplified homogenised group identity marker (EAL or the label 'refugee' itself) that does not represent all experiences. Fraser negotiates this, arguing that such tokenistic representation is a form of status subordination and proposing that the solution lies in seeking to understand how subordinated individuals can have a more equitable experience. As the curriculum shifts to focus on global issues relating to climate change and conflicts across the world, spaces are opened to discuss the causes of forced migration. This needs to be handled sensitively to avoid othering children in the classroom who might not want to make their histories public – but there is potential for educating all children about their roles and responsibilities from a global perspective. In time, this might lead to greater understanding which could serve to reduce marginalisation and foster parity.

The political dimension of Fraser's framework allows us to examine how far misrepresentation can impede refugee and asylum-seeking children from experiencing the concepts of safety, belonging and success.

Conclusion

Fraser's tripartite model provides a moral frame for schools' work with newly arrived children. The moral framing allows practitioners and those working in the field of refugee education to explore what the barriers are to operationalising the kind of education all children in our society deserve. An education system which aims for parity of participation and the opportunity for new arrivals to resume an ordinary life moves inclusive refugee education towards a rights-based education system which is fundamental for the future of all in our society. In this book, the two frames of 'resumption of ordinary life' and 'participatory parity' become interdependent (Figure 3.2).

Figure 3.2 The interdependence of the operational and moral frames

For adolescent refugees in resettlement contexts the playing field is not level; they are always going to have to work harder and to do more to achieve anything resembling participatory parity. The next stage of this book is to consider how the theoretical approaches outlined in these two chapters have been developed with practitioners to create a set of pedagogical principles (outlined in Chapter 11). These principles are intended to inform work in schools seeking to help new arrivals, those working with new teachers as teacher educators and those involved in different local and national policymaking roles. In this way we hope to move beyond identification of barriers and blocks to the realisation of SDG4, towards new ways of working and a new language for those working in resettlement contexts. This offers a more hopeful and transformational educational response to those who have had to make the choice to move and to seek a new space to become home.

In the following chapters, I present the work with four case study schools and work with the practitioners within those schools to develop a practical theory of meaningful inclusion for refugee and asylum-seeking pupils.

Note

1 Throughout Section 1, there is deliberate stylistic use of the 'we' pronoun which acknowledges, that research is a collective endeavour, that sometimes the 'we' refers to other academics sometimes to the practitioners in the study depending on who I have been working with as the thinking for the ideas in this section have developed. At times the 'we' includes the reader.

References

Bleich, E. 1998. From international ideas to domestic policies: Educational multiculturalism in England and France, *Comparative Politics*, 31 (1), 81–100.

Bourdieu, P. and Passeron, J.C. 1977. *Reproduction in Education, Society and Culture*. (2nd Edition). New York: Sage.

Cantle, T. 2001. *Community Cohesion: Report of the Independent Review Team – The 'Cantle Report'*. London: Home Office.

Department for Children, Schools and Families (DCSF). 2007. *New Arrivals Excellence Programme*. London: Crown. Available at https://ealresources.bell-foundation.org.uk/sites/default/files/document-files/New%20Arrivals%20Guidance.pdf.

Department for Education (DFE). 2018. Statement of intent on the diversity of the teaching workforce – Setting the case for a diverse teaching workforce. Available at https://www.gov.uk/government/publications/diversity-of-the-teaching-workforce-statement-of-intent. Accessed 18 January 2020.

Department of Education and Science (DES). 1975. The Bullough Report: A Language for Life. London: Her Majesty's Stationery Office.

Department of Education and Science (DES). 1985. The Swann Report: Education for All. London: Her Majesty's Stationery Office.

Dillabough, J. 2016. Gender, social, justice and citizenship in education: Engaging space, the narrative imagination, and relationality, in Peterson, A., Hattam, R., Zembylas, M. & Arthur, J. (Eds.), *The Palgrave International Handbook of Education for Citizenship and Social Justice*. London: Palgrave Macmillan, pp. 49–71.

Fraser, N. 2003. Social justice in the age of identity politics, in Fraser, N. & Honneth, A. (Eds.), *Redistribution or Recognition? A Political-Philosophical Exchange*. London: Verso.

Fraser, N. 2004. Recognition, redistribution and representation in capitalist global society, *Acta Sociologica*, 47 (4), 374–382.

Fraser, N. 2007. Re-framing justice in a globalizing world, *Anales de la Cátedra Francisco Suárez*, 39 (2005), 89–105. Available at https://www.semanticscholar.org/paper/Re-framing-justice-in-a-globalizing-world-Fraser/d2170289b4fcbd284dec04b93fb50e5a49145102.

Fraser, N. 2010. Injustice at intersecting scales: On 'social Exclusion' and the 'global poor', *European Journal of Social Theory*, 13 (3), 363–371.

Home Office. 1998. Fairer, faster and firmer: A modern approach to immigration and asylum. Available at https://www.gov.uk/government/publications/fairer-faster-and-firmer-a-modern-approach-to-immigration-and-asylum.

Honneth, A. 1995. *The Struggle for Recognition: The Moral Grammar of Social Conflicts*. Bristol: Polity Press.

Hutchinson, J. 2018. Educational outcomes of children with English as an additional language. Available at https://d1eeqy5w9fvriv.cloudfront.net/app/uploads/2018/02/16105734/Educational-Outcomes-of-Children-with-EAL.pdf. Accessed 18 January 2020.

Keddie, A. & Niesch, R. 2012. Productive engagements with student difference: Supporting equity through cultural recognition, *British Educational Research Journal*, 38 (2), 333–348.

Kiwan, D. 2016. 'Race', 'ethnicity' and citizenship in education: Locating intersectionality and migration for social justice, in Peterson, A., Hattam, R., Zembylas, M. & Arthur, J. (Eds.), *The Palgrave International Handbook of Education for Citizenship and Social Justice*. London: Palgrave Macmillan, pp. 3–25.

Knight, A. 2015. Democratizing disability: Achieving inclusion (without assimilation) through 'Participatory Parity', *Hypatia*, 30 (1), 97–114.

Kymlicka, W. 2010. The rise and fall of multiculturalism? New debates on inclusion and accommodation in diverse societies *International Social Science Journal*, 61 (199), 97–112.

McIntyre, J. & Hall, C. 2018. Barriers to the inclusion of refugee and asylum-seeking children in schools in England, *Educational Review*, doi: 10.1080/00131911.2018.1544115

McIntyre, J., Neuhaus, S. & Blennow, K. 2018. Participatory parity in schooling and moves towards ordinariness: A comparison of refugee education policy and practice in England and Sweden, *Compare: A Journal of Comparative and International Education*, doi: 10.1080/03057925.2018.1515007

Noyes, A. 2005. Pupil voice: Purpose, power and the possibilities for democratic schooling, *British Educational Research Journal*, 31 (4), 533–540.

Nussbaum, M. 2006. *Frontiers of Justice*. Cambridge, MA: Belknap Harvard University Press.

OECD. 2019. Pisa 2018 Results. https://www.oecd.org/pisa/publications/pisa-2018-results.htm. Accessed 20 January 2020.

Office of National Statistics (ONS). 2018. Wealth in Great Britain Wave 5. https://www.ons.gov.uk/peoplepopulationandcommunity/personalandhouseholdfinances/incomeandwealth/bulletins/wealthingreatbritainwave5/2014to2016 (accessed 18 November 2019).

Ott, E. & O'Higgins, A. 2019. Conceptualising educational provision for unaccompanied asylum-seeking children in England, *Oxford Review of Education*, 45 (4), 572-576.

Peterson, A., Hattam, R., Zembylas, M. & Arthur, J. (Eds.) 2016. Editors' introduction, in *The Palgrave International Handbook of Education for Citizenship and Social Justice*. London: Palgrave Macmillan, pp. xi-xx.

Rawls, J. 1971. *A Theory of Justice*. Oxford: Oxford University Press.

Rawls, J. 1985. Justice as Fairness: Political not Metaphysical. *Philosophy & Public Affairs*, 14(3), 223-251. www.jstor.org/stable/2265349. Accessed 4 August 2020.

Reay, D. 2017. *Miseducation: Inequality, Education and the Working Classes*. Bristol: Polity Press.

Robeyns, I. 2003. Is Nancy Fraser's critique of theories of distributive justice justified? *Constellations*, 10 (4), 538-553.

Robeyns, I. 2017. *Wellbeing, Freedom and Social Justice*. Cambridge: Open Book Publishers.

Ryan, A. 2012. *The Making of Modern Liberalism*. Princeton, NJ: Princeton University Press.

Sen, A. 2009. *The Idea of Justice*. Cambridge, MA: Belknap.

Sutton Trust. 2010. Private school pupils 55 times more likely to go to Oxbridge than poor students. https://www.suttontrust.com/newsarchive/private-school-pupils-55-times-likely-go-oxbridge-poor-students/. Accessed 11 December 2019.

Thatcher, M. 1987. Speech to Conservative Party Conference. Available at https://www.margaretthatcher.org/document/106941. Accessed 25 November 2019.

Tomlinson, S. 2009. Multicultural education in the United Kingdom, in Banks, J.A. (Ed.), *The Routledge International Companion to Multicultural Education*. Abingdon: Routledge, pp. 121-134.

UNESCO. 2019. Global Education Monitoring Report 2019 Migration, displacement and education: Building bridges not walls. Available at https://en.unesco.org/gem-report/report/2019/migration. Accessed 18 January 2020.

Wiley, T. 2017. Diversity, super-diversity, and monolingual language ideology in the United States: Tolerance or intolerance? *Review of Research in Education*, 38 (1), 1-32.

Wrench, A., Soong, H., Paige, K. & Garrett, R. 2018. Building spaces of hope with refugee and migrant-background students, *International Journal of Inclusive Education*, 22 (11), 1197-1212, doi: 10.1080/13603116.2017.1420251

Young, I.M. 2011. *Justice and the Politics of Difference*. Princeton, NJ: Princeton University Press.

Brief note about methodology

Joanna McIntyre

The next four chapters draw on empirical work conducted with teachers and explore the ways this work helped to form, shape and re-shape the theoretical perspectives outlined in the previous chapter. Chapters 4, 5 and 6 focus in turn on the concepts of safety, belonging and success as we[1] work with operationalising models of inclusive education for refugee children in schools. In each chapter we turn to Fraser's tripartite model to help us to understand different factors which support or challenge practitioners working in these inclusive ways in schools. In Chapter 7 we present a case study of a unique bespoke provision for post-16 new arrivals which has been designed to put into practice the theoretical concepts of safety, belonging and success.

The data are drawn from a sustained set of conversations, observations, email exchanges and visits to schools that were selected because they were identified as sites of 'good practice' with refugee and asylum-seeking children. We acknowledge that the term 'good practice' is contentious. The schools were recommended to us by professionals in the different locations who had strong vernacular knowledge of schools' reputation for doing good work. As such, these are sites with strong theoretical yield. The schools are situated in three English cities.

Each school has been given a pseudonym. Jasmine Gardens Academy was recommended by a local NGO refugee charity which had an active youth project supporting over 100 14–19-year-old new arrivals in the city. This meant that the NGO had a good 'on the ground' knowledge of schools which actively aimed to include students from refugee backgrounds. Lilac Lane Academy was recommended by a local university's initial teacher education department within the city. The Larkspur Secondary Academy became known to us because it had been awarded a gold standard inclusive schools marker and when we contacted the CEO of the academy chain it sat within we learnt that the school had a high number of new arrivals on roll. These schools became the case studies for the book. Chapter 7 consists of the portrait of bespoke provision for unaccompanied asylum seekers aged 16–18 which we call Fern College. There was a fifth school, Heather Academy, recommended by the same NGO that led us to Jasmine Gardens Academy. For logistical reasons, Heather Academy did not become one of the case studies but in the chapters to come we draw upon an extended group interview with its senior leadership team as they reflect on the ways in which they work to ensure an inclusive ethos for new arrivals.

Each of the following three chapters includes a case study exemplifying the concept of safety, belonging or success. The beginning of each chapter is influenced by the portraiture approach taken by Christine Hall and Pat Thomson in their descriptions of schools which prioritise creative arts as expositions of their theory of vernacular change (2017). Whilst each of the case studies schools in this book presented rich illustrations of all of Kohli's concepts in their practice, each chapter offers an interpretation of a single concept in one specific site. The descriptions loosely follow Sarah Lawrence-Lightfoot's method of portraiture in that they aim to capture the '"essence"; qualities of character and history' of each school's work with new arrivals and to offer a description which is 'probing, layered, and interpretive' (Lawrence-Lightfoot 2005, 5). We wanted to illuminate the good practice that was happening in the schools so that the teachers 'felt seen' (ibid., 6). Drafts of each chapter have been shared with the practitioners and their comments have helped shape the final versions of the case study chapters presented here. This intentionally reflects the questioning stance of the researcher and the practitioners in each site as the discussions and exchanges re-shaped theory and practice over time. The portraits are based on field notes, emails, conversations and interviews with senior leaders, practitioners and students in the schools.

In addition to the visits to the schools there were a series of focus group meetings bringing the practitioners together. These focus groups and the one to one discussions are drawn upon in the second half of each chapter where the concept is discussed more fully. Illustrative quotations from interviews and focus groups are utilised alongside examples from academic literature to tease out a clearer understanding of theory and practice. Each chapter ends with a definition of the concept in educational practice.

Note

1   Throughout Section 1, there is deliberate stylistic use of the 'we' pronoun which acknowledges, that research is a collective endeavour, that sometimes the 'we' refers to other academics and sometimes to the practitioners in the study, depending on who I have been working with as the thinking for the ideas in this section have developed. At times, the 'we' includes the reader.

References

Hall, C. and Thomson, P. 2017. *Inspiring School Change: Transforming Education through the Creative Arts*. Abingdon: Routledge.
Lawrence-Lightfoot, S. (2005). Reflections on Portraiture: A Dialogue between Art and Science. *Qualitative Inquiry*, 11(1), 3–15. https://doi.org/10.1177/1077800404270955

4 Education and the search for safety

Joanna McIntyre

Gare's experience

I got an interpreter when I came here [to England]. And they said to me 'You are here, you will be here for life.' And then because I'm here, I have to understand what people say, I have to understand when I go somewhere like the supermarket. Like having something to eat, I need to speak English. That's why I really like it here [at the education provision]. So because I like it I can speak English. … so I came here for just for English. But now I know what your culture is like. I know what English people are doing. I know what English people like. So it's not just learning English, it is learning about culture as well.

… When I first came to England, I didn't feel safe because I was thinking about the police like in my country. They are like very bad to us. I just thought … and I was crying when I was with them: 'Please don't do anything to me. I'm not here to do anything. I've just run because of my country and the bad things they do there.' But when I came here [to the education provision] and I know who the English people are, how they care about us. It was wonderful.

JMc: *How did they show they cared about you? What kinds of things did they do that make you feel that?*

I haven't been to a doctor for my whole life. But here every single week, I have to go to an appointment with my dentist, my ears, my eyes, if I have a little problem they want to talk to me. They want to, like, switch over the problem. Yeah, sometimes I have a problem here; J just takes me to somewhere and talks about it with me. 'What can I do? How can I help you? What's wrong with you?' Yeah, so that's why I know they care. And the first time they made an appointment for me with the doctor. Well next time I do it because I know how to do it then. So I am there when they do something so I know how to do it for next time.

JMc: *So they include you and show you how to do that. So here, you've learned about how to book appointments, about how to get to different places in [the city]. You've learned English obviously and maybe maths as well and things like that. Have you learned other things?*

I am learning how to live without parents.

This chapter reflects on the search for safety, which is graphically illustrated in Gare's words. The chapter is divided into four parts that follow from the introduction. Parts one and two draw on data derived from our empirical research. In part one, I present a descriptive case study of Larkspur School, focusing on the practices and organisational structures the staff have put in place in one institution to help new arrivals experience a sense of safety. Part two draws on data from focus group discussions and interviews with practitioners. Its purpose is to enrich the discussion of education and the search for safety by its focus on how teachers from a range of institutions define and refine their understandings of what it means to build a secure environment for their students. In part three, the concept of safety is analysed through the tripartite lenses of redistribution, recognition and representation. The fourth, concluding, part of the chapter draws on the case study and focus group points to pull the discussion together and clarify the concept of safety in the specific context of new arrivals.

Case study: Larkspur Secondary Academy

> *'As a new student, school is something mysterious. First you have to adapt to the school system, then you start getting used to the rest.'*
>
> *(Emir)*

Larkspur Secondary Academy opened in 2013 and is currently a small 11–16 school which has seen growth each year, with the ultimate aim of accommodating 900 pupils. Larkspur is located in a city in the east of England, which has seen a steady rise in migration since the Second World War because of its traditionally low levels of unemployment. The majority of the city's workers are on lower-than-average wages and, since the decline of the manufacturing industries, are now employed in retail or in one of the large distribution centres. There is a high demand for short-term contract workers. Larkspur is located on the north-east side, near to one of the busy orbital roads that surround the city.

First impressions: communicating safety

The welcome on the Larkspur Secondary Academy's website is framed by the branding of the multi-academy trust to which it belongs. Whilst this conveys a sense of the school being part of something bigger there is also a sense of the specificity of the place. This is conveyed by the ways in which the academy celebrates its diverse school population, with an emphasis on how different languages are catered for and celebrated. There is an image on the landing page of two pupils enjoying sharing a book – it is a student atlas and is perhaps a not-so-implicit message that the school values being connected to a global community, through its commitment to celebrating its multilingual identity. This message is explicitly echoed in the commitment on the website to recognising and valuing children's home languages. The inspection report on the website praises the Academy's work with a wide range of community activities and singles out the work the school does with new arrivals, especially with their approach to languages, and the confidence this approach instils in those students for whom English is an additional language. The school was recently awarded the highly regarded Inclusion Quality Mark.

Larkspur sits in an urban estate comprising neat streets of mainly semi-detached houses, which are a mixture of private ownership and social housing. One side of the estate is bounded by a busy orbital link road, on the other side of which lies a business site housing two large engine manufacturing companies. Driving into the estate from the busy link road, it is initially hard to find the school amongst the grid of residential houses and occasional convenience stores and takeaways. However, as with most schools, the key to finding it is to find the bus route and trace this through the estate. The school is located off a quiet road at the end of a cul-de-sac. Like most modern-build schools in England, the visitor first needs to negotiate the locked gates and the security double porch entrance before 'signing in' through the photograph computer system. All of this communicates that safeguarding and security are paramount.

The reception is a spacious area echoing the website branding of the multi-academy trust's logo and colour scheme. Whilst this is an official space with an air of business about it, it is also a welcoming space for the students and for their parents and carers. On my first visit I position myself on the sofa in the reception area whilst waiting for my meeting and observe interactions with a parent who is trying to enrol her child – this is now the summer term and her child would need to go into Year 7, the youngest and largest year in the school. The parent is told that there are already 64 children on the waiting list for that year group. The year manager takes time to ensure that the parent has understood this, as English is not her first language, and the parent leaves armed with information about what to do next and with reassurances that the school will keep in touch. As I wait, I observe a member of staff come in through the reception with a child she has collected from home. The child has overslept and is due to be sitting a GCSE paper that morning. Another parent arrives to collect a child who has been unwell and is being looked after by a member of the pastoral team.

So this is a place of comings and goings, of the handover of children, of welcoming visitors. It communicates calm and order. It feels reassuring.

A multilingual school

On the other side of the reception area are doors leading into the main school. Each Tuesday, a tour takes new arrivals through these doors to visit the different areas of the school. On the walls, the new arrivals see various notices detailing the life of the school: rules and expectations, clubs and events, the curriculum area they are passing. On the upper floor, the tour takes them past the Language of the Month display and the Young Interpreters Board. They will finish their tour in the 'Base'.

Donna, a member of the Senior Leadership Team, explains that because the school has only been open for a few years, the upper years had capacity to accommodate in-year admissions. Because of this, Larkspur has become a school for new arrivals to come to when they arrive in the city. This means that the school has a higher-than-average proportion of pupils who speak languages other than English as their home language. Donna started work at the school shortly after it opened; because the school had started small, with just one year group (who now form the basis of Year 11), she was able initially to assess every pupil's English as an Additional (EAL) proficiency level. Whilst this is no longer possible now that the school has grown, the lessons learnt about the multilingual backgrounds of a large majority of students (nearly half of the pupils in the upper years) have influenced the ways in which the school inducts new arrivals today. The weekly tour is part of this induction.

> *'The first hurdle to overcome is the language barrier with the parents and that is where the Young Interpreters come in.'*

According to Donna, the idea behind the Young Interpreters Scheme is to promote languages and bilingualism across the school, to encourage inclusivity and to provide buddies who share a common language with new arrivals. Students volunteer for this and are provided with training. They wear badges, making them easily identifiable. They support parent and community events and translate documentation and letters. Donna explains that although the school can receive additional funding for most new arrivals because they fit the criteria of economic disadvantage, many of the families do not complete the necessary paperwork. The young interpreters assist here too, explaining the documentation and translating as appropriate. However, Donna says that sometimes the barriers are more than linguistic: *'You get some that are very proud who will say "I've not come here for handouts".'* This becomes an issue for the school since without the pupil premium documentation the school cannot access the funding.

Another important initiative is the decision that all Pupil Panels should have a representative from pupils with an EAL background. The Pupil Panels are involved in: interviewing new members of staff; student voice consultations about behaviour and safety; curriculum and teaching and learning projects; and planning for school activity days. According to Donna, newly arrived students need to be represented on these panels because they have such a high profile within the school.

Whilst Donna is able to ascertain the range of languages spoken in the school – *'I think it is thirty six'* – she is less confident at being able to state where the new arrivals came from: *'You'll get a birth certificate from one country and a passport from another country and then they will tell you they are from somewhere else. And if you ask them what languages they speak they will tell you a different one.'* This means that, unless the school has been made aware by social services, it is not always clear how many pupils are from refugee backgrounds. What is clear, however, is that whilst new arrivals make up a large proportion of the student body, the group of new arrivals are themselves a very diverse group reflecting families and languages from all over the globe. This means that each newly arrived child comes with a particular set of experiences of schooling. The school works hard in the initial meetings to ensure that they gather enough information to be able to accommodate each pupil appropriately.

The first aspect of this is to assess their proficiency in English. If they have no English at all then they will spend some immersion time in the Base *'for a few days or even a few weeks'*. However, there is a commitment for the new arrival to be placed in lessons with their peers as early as possible through *'the immediacy of physical education, of art, of dance'* and *'number-based subjects, maths and science'*. There is a flexible approach to timetabling – *'the timetable is reviewed weekly for these students'* – and if the new arrival wants to attend a particular subject, such as history, from the beginning, then they try and accommodate this. Like many schools in England, the school sets pupils in most subjects according to their prior performance in assessments. The new arrival will be placed in the set that best matches them, *'because everyone is an individual'*. Full immersion in the Base is rare and to begin with most of the new arrivals spend around three lessons a week there to receive targeted language support. Depending on their language needs, they will be placed in one of three EAL (mixed-aged) proficiency groups. When the EAL lead practitioner, Ema, who conducts the initial assessment on the induction day, feels that they can move levels they will change groups.

The claims on the website that the school considers multilingualism to be core to its identity seem to be reflected in the positive messages that are communicated about inclusion and a language-rich environment. EAL is part of the Languages Department. Ema, the EAL lead, and Gideon, the Head of Languages, are both bilingual and their own schooling took place outside England, so there is a sense of empathy with the linguistic and cultural needs of the new arrivals.

Safety in the Base

> *'Coming to this Base was helpful, I was told I could come here every Thursday and Friday lunchtime but after I came the first time, I asked if I could come every day.'*
>
> (Victor)

Halfway down one of the long corridors from the reception area is the Base. This small teaching room is dedicated to supporting new arrivals and Ema spends most of her time here. At lesson changeover, there is a small trickle of pupils who come to the door to ask Ema if they can join her for that lesson. The answer is usually 'No', but they are welcome to come back at lunchtime.

The room is welcoming and well organised with brightly coloured displays in a range of languages. Every available space has a purpose, either to convey messages about life in school or about specifics of English usage, or to demonstrate the range of languages spoken by the children who spend time there. The Base is always open at lunchtimes when different clubs are run. In one corner there is a stack of board games for Game Club and reading books for Reading Buddies Club. Ema explains that a number of pupils come most days to the Base, even after they have been fully integrated into the curriculum and no longer need the three lessons of English language intervention per week. On one of my visits she points to a group of girls who are chatting over a game of draughts. They have been in the school for long enough to no longer need the interventions during lesson time:

> *I think they have to have a place where they can communicate with their friends. Even the Year 9s, who are fluent in English, will still come here all the time and they will chat and socialise. And I really want them to come because they can help the others so much with their language development. So now they realise they can come here although at first they were really reluctant. But last week they came and sat and they want to be seen, to feel acknowledged by adults. It was Alina's birthday on Friday and just for a joke I said 'Are you going to bring a cake so we can celebrate?' and she brought a cake and some juice and we sat at lunch time and sang a happy birthday song. It was so nice.'*

The young people in the Base talk to Ema about the issues they have with other students in their classes, with their homework, about what their plans are for the weekend. Although some do have a common language they choose to speak in English in the Base, though not on the corridor, when I see some of the same pupils together walking to lessons. As Ema explains, *'This is a safe space where they can just hide, they can come in here and somebody will listen to them and they can let their feelings out. We have a pastoral role and especially with these kids … I am not just here to teach language, I am here sometimes to teach them about life.'* She gives examples of how some new arrivals struggle initially with the expectations of the English school system and with learning about what rules to follow. She says that she approaches this by being quite explicit and by following whole-school strategies even with a tiny group of two or three pupils in the Base. Some children make mistakes and behave inappropriately and, in such cases, Ema says her role is to enforce the rules, but then start each new session with the student with a *'blank slate'*.

Ema meets all new arrivals as it is her responsibility to assess each student's language competence. If she feels they need additional support, she will assign them into one of the three groups according to their assessed proficiency in English as an Additional Language. It is during these meetings that Ema is able to find out more about the new arrival and to make suggestions to the year teams about which subjects they could be given immediate access to. Her timetable is organised so that she is free on Tuesdays to do this work. Ema shows me a folder with all of the different assessments and questions she goes through each time she does this. It also includes documentation and activities that she works through with each child to help them adapt to life in an English school. Each child is given a New Arrivals Welcome book which introduces the school day, and includes activities like 'Things you will be asked to do at school', 'Things that your teacher will ask you', 'The Library', 'Useful phrases' and so on. There is also a section with activities related to different school subjects where the child indicates, if they have studied the subject before, whether they like or dislike the subject. There is an induction book for staff to support them in their work with new arrivals in their curriculum area. The School has also invested in an Australian training package called LILAC (Language in Learning Across the Curriculum) to support teachers across the school in improving their practice in developing the academic English skills of pupils with English as an Additional Language.

Ema keeps an audit of the assessment she makes of each child. At the time of my visit in May, she has assessed 41 new arrivals since the start of the academic year, with the largest numbers arriving between October and December (23 in these months). Since the start of the year, the school has taken 18 new arrivals into Years 10 and 11, with 8 of these going into Year 11. This is usually a difficult time for new pupils to be admitted into Year 11 because of the pressure on schools of the final GCSE examinations which occur in that year. At Larkspur, however, Gideon, the Head of Languages, illustrates how the school's results have been improved by including new arrivals in these upper year groups and entering them for a GCSE in their preferred home language, *'with most students last year getting [top] grade 8s and 9s'.* He says that this meant that the school's GCSE examination performance was positively impacted by the inclusion of these students in Years 10 and 11.

During my lunchtime visit a boy comes to the Base to tell Ema he's been moved up English sets. She congratulates him, but he says he doesn't want to go – when she asks why he says it is because when he moved up sets in Maths he lost his friendship group. She asks if this is still a problem now in Maths and he replies 'No'. She explains to me that many new arrivals feel a sense of insecurity about any changes to their routine.

Becoming safe in Larkspur

'*People need help. More mental help. When people first come they feel so alone.*'

(Victor)

Sidra vividly describes how she felt when she first arrived at Larkspur two years previously, shortly after her family came to England: '*It was so difficult, I wanted to go back. I missed everyone from home. It was really hard to make friends … I was lonely. I used to cry for the first month. … I met a girl and she could speak Punjabi a little bit and she helped me and she's my friend now.*'

Sidra found Science at Larkspur easy to adapt to because science lessons in her village school had been in English. She says she struggled at first with other subjects because it was so different from her previous experiences: '*It is really hard to come from another country and we need help with our studies.*' She speaks of how things became easier over time and how she felt about coming to the Base. At the beginning it was '*a nice safe space*', but as her English improved and her EAL lessons finished, she came to join the Reading Club at lunch-times. She says she did this for around two months and then stopped: '*I had made friends by then so I went with my friends. I am really happy now. It is better here than it was when I was at home … the teachers here were so nice to me, they really helped and I can come and find [Ema] if I need any help even if I am not coming to the Base for any lessons.*' Two years after entering Larkspur, Sidra seems settled and happy. She has a close-knit friendship group, and she is happy with the GCSE subject choices that she has now made.

In contrast, Emir, who arrived from Syria six months earlier, is struggling to adapt to life at Larkspur. He had been educated in Saudi Arabia and only visited Syria during the holidays. This all changed when the war started and his family had to move. Emir is struggling with his sense of home. He says he doesn't understand the concept of '*my country, my town – what does that mean? Just because I live there it becomes mine? Because my dad was born there, and my grandparents are from there it is mine? But I am myself.*' The teachers at Larkspur are concerned about how he is settling in and the fact that he seems to be struggling to find his place in the school and to understand the ways pupils and teachers interact both within and outside classrooms. He says that he had moved schools a lot and '*so for me this school is not my school, it is a school I am studying at*'. He feels pressure to do well at school, saying his family focus too much on grades, '*If you are at school you are at school to study*'. Emir is the son of a doctor: '*You study long and work long hours but I want to enter medicine and if I don't like it I will still continue in medicine because there is nothing else but being a doctor.*' He does not choose to come to the Base at lunchtimes.

Victor had been in two schools in Spain following his family's journey to Europe, and has been at Larkspur for nine months. Like Emir and Sidra, he had initially struggled to adapt to life in an English school. However, his teachers observe that he has settled extremely well and is making excellent progress. With ambitions to become an engineer, he is very keen to work hard and do well. He has recently been invited to tea with the Principal as a reward for the progress he had made in the short time he has been at the school. He is in Year 10 and is already matching some of his peers in some of his academic subjects. However, he lacks confidence in his spoken English and actively seeks out the Base every lunchtime. He appreciates the efforts the school has made to help him to settle: *'First they put one boy with me and I stayed near him all day and then I had an idea of how the school works. … I liked having one boy look after me because if I had a question I could ask him. If you are alone you can't ask anybody.'* Initially, he spent some time in the Base having intervention English lessons, but he is now fully integrated into the timetable for his year group and he is in the top or middle sets for most subjects. He is one of the school's Young Interpreters.

Victor has a friend with whom he says he spends time in lessons and at breaktimes, but he still chooses to spend lunchtime in the Base where he can study. At times during our interview he struggles to express himself and I suggest he can speak in Spanish or Urdu. He chooses Spanish and explains that each time he moved schools it got much harder to make friends. He says that when you are young you can make friends because you play and you don't need much language and you are all working things out at the same time. Young children spend more times in big groups all doing the same things. But as you get older: *'These things get more refined. And so when you move, you cannot reveal all of yourself. Your oldest friends know all about you, even if you are now only interested in a small number of things. So it is hard to find common interests as you grow older.'*

Ema and Gideon explain that for some children, whilst they can support their language development and their understanding of how school works, they know that realistically the new arrivals will find it difficult to make friendships unless they manage to find a common interest, such as sport. This is especially the case for the students who arrive in the upper years of the school. They say that the Base seems to continue to have a key role for these students long after they have integrated into mainstream classes.

Towards safety through education: debates and dialogues

> *'Feeling that school is there for them and that it is a safe place. That is what we want to instil from the beginning.'*
>
> (Focus group)

Previous chapters have outlined the ways in which new arrivals need to negotiate tangles of bureaucracy before accessing a school or college place within the English system. Once in education provision, then the child can expect that their first steps towards feeling safe have been met. Schools in England are required by law to ensure that all the adults working in them follow the safeguarding processes outlined in a government publication, 'Keeping Children Safe in Education' (DfE 2019). This requires all staff and adults in school settings to be aware of possible threats to a child's welfare both in and out of school. So, looking back at Gare's interview, this goes beyond the English teachers being kind. They have a statutory duty to help young people to be safe. The various processes that visitors to Larkspur have to go through before moving beyond the reception area of the school illustrate some of this safeguarding duty. During the focus group discussions as the practitioners compared ways of working, two particular comments resonated with regard to safeguarding. The first was the real risks that some of these students continue to face:

> For instance, we have a student who was trafficked to the UK and so for him safety in school means quite concrete things – so is he actually safe?

This was a salutary reminder that the things some young people are trying to escape from sometimes follow them. The second was a sad indictment: that many people in this country perceive refugee children as untrustworthy – value judgements that have presumably been shaped by popular discourses in the media:

> We've had some really awkward situations with mainstream members of staff who have never met our students. The first time they've spoken to them they were asking questions about where they came from and what their journey was like. And they will also ask our staff if we think that they are 'genuine refugees'.

In the focus group discussion, the teachers moved to explore difficult experiences of needing to convince other members of the school community that the refugee children did not pose some sort of threat. They said that because the children came from areas of the world where they had witnessed or experienced extreme conflict, they had to advocate for them in ways that they would not be asked to do for a child who had experienced violence growing up in England:

> It's really interesting that they said, 'Who are you bringing in?' You always feel personally responsible for the behaviour of the young person. Yet they are part of a school and what would you do with another 'dangerous' child who has got a history of knife crime? You'd have things in place for them. We do get that sense of responsibility, don't we?

However, it is clear that for the staff at Larkspur and the other schools in the study, the commitment to keeping young people safe goes far beyond the duties laid down in the statutory documentation.

> So are they safe from others and are others safe from them; is it a safeguarding issue; do we have the information from Social Care to make sure that we as an institution are doing what we are supposed to do? For example, there might be some students who aren't allowed to leave the site at lunchtime because they are in care. ... Sometimes we have to think about whose safety is at risk: is it staff or students? Also we need to think about how secure our space is and do they feel safe and secure in our base. So it is all that.

This is an issue that the teachers have given particular attention to for young refugees who access their provision. In the interviews and focus group meetings we kept revisiting what the concept of safety might mean:

> When I think of safety, I think of all of those things but then I think of the impact of having all of these things in order to feel emotionally safe. So things like feeling physically safe can also allow them to feel emotionally safe and that will have a huge impact on their mental health. So you need physical safety in place, as well as the routines, and then comes emotional safety.

The comment above was made during one of the days the practitioners from the schools came together to discuss the concepts and the ways in which they worked to make young new arrivals feel secure and safe in their own institutions. Like Larkspur, all of the schools in the study had created a physical space for the new arrivals that was commonly referred to as the EAL Base. In each school, children did more than learn English in these rooms. The young people I spoke to described their school's base as a *'safe space'* and utilised it in the same ways as Victor and Sidra, long after they needed intensive language support. One of the teachers explained that, because the young people had experienced and were continuing to experience so many changes, the Base in school was *'the only constant because everything else is so transient'*. For most refugee children, the Base in school for new arrivals was the first space in which they could feel some sense of permanency or continuity and begin the act of place-making as a step toward building an ordinary life.

Links between place-making and young people's sense of their own identities have been well established in the literature (for example, Hopkins 2013). Also there is emerging litera-ture on what happens when an individual's links to a significant place are disrupted or destroyed, when becoming a refugee leads to becoming physically absent from that place (e.g. Brun 2001). Emir's rejection of identification with his country of birth accords with Edward Said's notion of the pathos of the exile when 'homecoming is out of the question' (2000, 178). Where would Emir's home be – England, Syria or Saudi Arabia, where he spent the greatest proportion of his life until events in his birth country led to him being uprooted to begin again in a school in England? Emir cannot (yet?) identify with this new place and so for him the school is not *'his school'*. He is out of place.

In contrast, no doubt facilitated by time, Victor and Sidra had been able to engage in activities such as the Young Interpreters or Reading Buddy groups in the EAL Base at Larkspur. This had allowed them to begin to feel a sense of connection with the space and, by extension, with the wider school. The activities they engaged in were importantly meaningful activities – they were involved because of their more expert status: as a new arrival who had been in the space for longer than newer arrivals, and as students who had managed to acquire sufficient language to translate passages from books or information from various sources for different purposes. Importantly, the Bases in the different schools were also val-ued by the young people as being places where they could study and ask questions about their work. This meant they were places that signified an investment in the future. The Bases also were important spaces for developing positive relationships with teachers and with peers facing similar challenges. The fact that the Base always had a teacher or other adult there added to the young people's sense of being in a safe space. They were places where children could learn about expectations and ways of being in their new school contexts:

> *Routines and consistency. That will provide a feeling of safety in a time in their lives which is unsure. So many things are unpredictable about their current situation and things can change from day to day. So knowing they are safe here is important to them.*

> *(Focus group)*

For new arrivals, therefore, the Base in their educational setting is a transitional space that helps relationships and connections with the place develop. In the Base and in the educational setting more broadly there is also a sense that these are spaces where time can be experienced differently. Most commonly in schools, time is represented by division of the day and curriculum into lessons and timetabling arrangements. These are structures to support the organisation of the school, to carve up time and place to support formalized teaching and learning, and to ensure that teachers and pupils are able to access classrooms and curriculum appropriately. Interestingly, the teachers in the study all spoke about ways in which they could manipulate time to support the induction of new arrivals. At one extreme, this is illustrated by children at Jasmine Gardens Academy starting the school day 'backwards'.

Two unaccompanied Kurdish minors, assumed to be brothers or cousins, arrived from Turkey in 2015. They had suffered trauma on their journey enduring life-threatening conditions. The school decided to put them back a year – into the end of Year 8 in order to give them the best opportunities for success. Before starting at Jasmine Gardens, they had been receiving some tuition in the afternoons at their foster carers' home. This was scheduled for afternoons because the children were struggling with sleep issues, which were believed to be associated with trauma. So the school decided to 'start backwards' and replicated timings to begin with them coming in for an hour in the afternoons and then for increased chunks of time to support integration, building in the increase in time as felt right for the boys. The provision was built around what was felt to be their best interests, working up to whole days. The key was to do this at the pace they could cope with and was necessary for them to meet peers and integrate with students. One of the students had never attended school before and possibly had Special Educational Needs but this was very difficult to assess. Individualised timetables were developed for both. The daily support was gradually reduced to 6 hours a week in the EAL base with our Academic Coach. One boy followed an alternative curriculum of Functional Skills and Step Up to English, the other completed Step Up to English in addition to GCSEs in 2019. They have now moved away to be with family members and are attending college.

We were very aware that only one of them had even attended school elsewhere so we needed to adjust things in school and integrate them really sensitively and carefully in order to somehow build up the school day backwards – rather than our usual assumptions and plans. I remember it being a logistical nightmare but the right thing to do. (Amy)

This example from Jasmine Gardens and the portrait of Larkspur earlier show that there needs to be a flexible approach to timetabling. Each individual child's time in the setting needs to be reviewed very frequently and adjusted as appropriate. In all of the settings, time in the EAL Bases was decided according to the assessment of need of the pupil on arrival, but the aim in all schools seems to be to move the new arrival into mainstream lessons as soon as possible:

Most of the training I've had over however many years has been about the perfect match of mainstream lessons and withdrawal. The worst thing we could ever do is trap them in the one base and not have them being out and being integrated.

(Amy)

Setting 'by ability' was common across the schools and the practitioners spoke of how they worked with this institutional structure to support the new arrival in the best ways. Whilst there was a temptation to put the new arrivals in lower sets where there was likely to be more adult support, the practitioners tried to insist that the individual was put into the set which was most likely to suit their academic potential. The barriers to this were perceived to be linguistic, both in terms of accurately assessing where the child would flourish best and also in terms of workload for the teacher in being able to ensure that the content was accessible for the student. As we have seen, Donna at Larkspur ensured that the child was in the most appropriate set, regardless of their EAL proficiency. Amy, in her role as the lead for new arrivals and EAL at Jasmine Gardens, insisted that all new arrivals were placed in higher sets where they could access *'higher and more sophisticated vocabulary'*. Ciara had a similar role and approach at Lilac Lane Academy. All acknowledged that they had to keep revisiting the rationale for this with heads of department across their schools. Whilst there is a clear academic rationale for this, there are social ones too, as one of the unintended long-term consequences for a new arrival placed in an inappropriate set is the ongoing issue that the young person has with finding friendship groups that will sustain and have similar interests.

The schools in this study illustrate how institutions can conceptualise time and space differently to support new arrivals in feeling a sense of security and safety, to help them build connections with the setting. These structures are experienced differently by different individuals. Developing a sense of safety is a process. The process is underpinned by activities and spaces which are intended to promote a sense of wellbeing for the new arrivals, to establish school as a starting point for personal contact with others in the new context. Much of the literature about the wellbeing of refugee children involves discussions of mental health following experiences of trauma (Stewart 2011; Tweedie et al. 2017). However, there is a danger in focusing on assumed vulnerabilities of new arrivals in ways that homogenise their experiences, blurring the needs of those who have often exerted a great deal of agency on their journeys and during the initial transition in the country in which they settle (Rutter 2006). It is also important to recognise that western-centric notions of trauma associated with separation from family members might not always be culturally relevant as, in many cultures, different adults, beyond the child's immediate parents, can play important child-rearing roles (Watters 2008). It is important, therefore, that educational settings recognise that if a child is in the country with their parents they may be experiencing distress as they are actually separated from their main caregivers. Again, this speaks to the heterogeneity of refugee pupils. Refugee and asylum-seeking children can simultaneously show signs of both vulnerability and resilience (Sleipen et al. 2017). The schools in this study work in different ways to support them to have some agency in responding to their individual circumstances.

> *A lot of things are things that are going to happen to them, so is there a way of communicating how they are going to be part of that?*
> *It's about them taking control because most of the time decisions are being made about them without them having a say.*
>
> *(Focus group)*

A clear strategy that was voiced in the focus group was to create '*an environment where it is safe to talk. Because they meet so many professionals and they are worried about telling their story*'. This echoes Kohli's description of young asylum seekers moving from sharing 'thin stories' of themselves to 'thick stories' as they begin to trust and experience a sense of achieving an ordinary life (2011). Amy described watching two Kurdish students who were given an opportunity to talk to an adult without having to rely on English to express themselves: '*it was the first time they opened up about their story ... you could see the sheer joy in the boys being able to speak to someone who understands their first language and just get this out*'. However, the practitioners emphasised that it was important that the young people could choose to share or choose not to share their experiences. This meant at times that ground rules about what was appropriate to ask had to be set with staff visiting the Base or working with the pupils in lessons.

The practitioners' focus was also on creating environments which supported the young person's psychological, social and emotional wellbeing through activities that helped them build trust and, through forms of experiential learning, develop a sense of their new place. For example, at Lilac Lane Academy, new arrivals worked in a neighbouring community garden each week and Ciara felt that this time in the garden was valuable because '*the social and emotional learning help to promote a sense of safety.*' Others described how drama and arts could be healing spaces. One teacher shared the example of a student saying in Drama, '*I don't know what is going to happen but today I am happy*'. However, some attempts to create what one practitioner described as activities designed to facilitate '*exploring your limits as well as pushing themselves physically and mentally a little*' were not without some risk to wellbeing. This was noted in an exchange about drama, again in one of the group discussions:

> '*With drama, they need to be able to step out of their identity in a safe manner.*'
> '*There is something constantly on their shoulders and it must be a relief to them to occasionally be able to let that go.*'
> '*I think that they enjoy being in the moment, but there is often that sense of guilt about feeling happy or having fun*'.

But there were other considerations too. The practitioners emphasised that they felt a very particular sense of responsibility relating to the safety of this group of pupils, in a way that blurred different boundaries and was unlike the sense of responsibility they felt for the safety of others in the school. Amy described feeling responsible for a young new arrival who turned up at a summer transition day for children in local primary schools who were due to start at Jasmine Gardens in the September. The child had no place in a primary school despite having been in the country for six months. Amy's frustration was that Jasmine Gardens had accommodated her older cousin but did not know about the younger girl. Although at the time of the visit, the girl's age meant that she should be in a primary school, Amy wanted to fast-track her into Jasmine Gardens so that she was at least accessing some form of educational provision. Amy navigated the school admission processes, asking, '*Why can't we just do it, to know we are putting her in a safe place?*' For Amy, '*Being brave*' here meant not allowing bureaucracy to deprive the child of school for the last few weeks of the academic year. '*I have to make sure I do the right things I am supposed to do. And I don't want this day to end without us having put in place that she is coming back here tomorrow. ... So we got permission from safeguarding and through social care to allow her to come in and be escorted by people and be educated'.* So whilst the child did not experience any of the primary schooling to which she was entitled, she did start spending time at Jasmine Gardens in preparation for her official start there as a secondary pupil after the summer vacation.

Amy had the support of the senior leadership in the school. The Executive Principal and CEO of the Academy Trust spoke passionately about the need to keep making *'brave'* decisions because of what she described as *'a brutal system'* in which the refugee children and families were caught up. During our interview she talked about the ways in which staff in the school took their responsibility for the wellbeing of their children to extraordinary lengths, giving examples of how her staff had intervened if they felt that the new arrival was at risk. *'It's making sure they are safe, so wherever they are living is a place they are going to flourish and be nurtured.'* She recalled a distraught parent coming into school to apologise for his child's first absence since starting at Jasmine Gardens. This was because the family had been unable to afford the bus fare after had their status – and their welfare support – was changed from asylum seeking to 'leave to remain'.

These changes of status from asylum seeker to refugee, and the accompanying build-up towards a decision being made, often meant that the practitioners felt that they needed to intensify their support. They wanted to compensate for the shifting senses of security outside the educational setting by offering additional support to make sure the young people felt safe within the school. Sometimes the young people knew that a decision was coming up; on occasions, however, a decision was made without them being able to prepare for this. For example, the practitioners spoke about their feelings of powerlessness if an external agency decided that the child had been wrongly age-assessed and had to leave the provision as a result.

Amy summed this up: *'What frustrates me is that I can try and do things within my institution, but the system is broken and I don't know what is going on.'* This was seemingly most acute for those working with children over 16, where access to education seemed most precarious. *'If a child is denied access to post-16 education because the Home Office hasn't issued the paperwork, they end up working for cash illegally somewhere and they get lost. Had they not been lost they would be able to get their GCSEs to help them get a career. If I phone social services I am passed around five different people. The system needs looking at and assessing.'*

As we have seen already, with the support of the Executive Principal, Amy felt empowered to make decisions about placing the child in a different year group if that was the most appropriate thing to do to support them to access education. Children who start the school mid-year or who are 'kept behind' for a year are experiencing time differently in the setting. This is evidence of strategies these practitioners and institutions follow to allow young refugees to access education. Kohli observes that young asylum seekers and refugees experience time differently (2014) – for periods, it feels like they are caught in time waiting for something significant and living their life in pause until it does. In educational terms, this would mean waiting for a place in an educational institution. Once in an educational setting, however, there is also a sense of time running away from them – and that time spent acclimatising to the education system is time wasted as they watch peers born into this new context progressing towards qualifications that will unlock the next stage for them. The practitioners were acutely aware of this and shared experiences of their students' frustrations. They resolved that the best way to combat this was for them to be explicit about the English education system and the ways in which their students could progress their learning in order to fulfil their ambitions in the future.

So, for the practitioners, safety means many different things. Schools and educational settings can put things in place to help young refugees to feel secure and begin to experience aspects of belonging through connecting to the place, achieving some early successes through the social, emotional and academic achievements they begin to accrue. Sidra, Emir and Victor's descriptions and memories of their experiences bring Kohli's concept of safety vividly to life. They exemplify how for young people, feeling safe is based on a number of combining factors: a safe space, knowing where to ask for help, the feeling that they can get on with their studies and, perhaps most importantly, ways of making friends – which, as Victor explains powerfully, is much more difficult when you join a school in the upper years of schooling.

Throughout our conversations, the practitioners were asked about the utility and relevance of each of the three concepts underpinning Kohli's model. This chapter has outlined ways in which the concept of safety is understood in relation to working with all new arrivals, but especially those from refugee backgrounds. The discussions focused on what safety might look like for new arrivals and could be summed up by this observation made during one of the group discussions:

> *Getting to know this city, skills in English, self-care and supporting others, combatting loneliness, understanding British society and different opinions, attitudes and treatment of people.*

Although before these conversations started, the practitioners might not have used the term 'safety' when thinking about their work, there was a sense that the term could be refined from Kohli's original model to have applicability to their day-to-day work. It helped them to make sense of what they were doing:

> *It's about what can you put in place for these individuals on a day-to-day basis, but also the wider perspective. So, making sure this place is a safe place, a comforting place, a language conscious space where they can grow, make mistakes, be respected.*

Safety through the lens of participatory parity

Utilising Kohli's concepts as a normative operational frame has allowed us to name and make visible the work that practitioners and schools (can) do to help young refugees to experience meaningful inclusive education. During one of the discussions, a practitioner commented that *'models are only useful if they actually solve the problem'* and went on to illustrate how the concepts could be used to frame questions at a range of levels about provision for new arrivals:

> *if one uses the concept to ask oneself or the group or the organisation what are we doing to promote safety? What am I doing on an individual level? And what are we doing as a group and as an organisation? I think one could use that way of asking: how can we promote things to happen?*

The conversation developed from this until another practitioner explained her approach a little further:

> If that is our model for asking questions, can that also help us arrive at some principles? If we are promoting safety, what does the individual have to do? What is it, in concrete terms, or is it something that the organisation has to do? If we are talking about promoting safety at an organisational level, what do we want the organisation to do to ensure that the safety of this group of people is ensured? What concrete things do they have to do? If we worked in the ideal school what would they have in place to achieve this?

How does the (**re-)distribution** of material and human resource enable or prevent schools in the study to support new arrivals to feel a sense of safety? As we have seen in this chapter, *safety* is multifaceted concept encompassing a range of physical, emotional and psychological elements depending on the specific needs and experiences of the refugee child. This has resourcing implications. Flexibility is required to allow the child to be eased into the timetable of the school; designated spaces are required to support individual needs. Investment in a transitionary safe space such as an EAL base and in appropriately trained and experienced staff are pulls on the school budget and harder to defend when the available resource is no longer ring-fenced. Senior leaders and practitioners in the study spoke about the ways in which their schools were able provide a sense of routine and consistency for young new arrivals who had experienced, and continued to experience, so much change in their lives. The schools often had to advocate for the best interests of the young person and attend meetings with a range of different agencies. Again, this has resource implications both in terms of time and paying for staff cover costs during the school day.

We have established that *safety* is predicated upon **recognising** and responding to each child's physical, emotional and psychological needs and that this initially happens in the EAL base. All of the practitioners in the case study schools demonstrated what Pinson et al. (2010) describe as a 'compassionate stance' that underpins their inclusive ethos; the newly arrived students in the schools spoke of their Bases as *'safe spaces'*. However, the biggest threat to the child's safety comes outside of the individual school. If the bureaucracies that children face in trying to access a place at school are insurmountable and the child spends months waiting for a place, such as the primary-aged cousin described in the Jasmine Gardens case study, then they are bound to experience insecurity and face possible safeguarding risks. If the same bureaucracies mean that a child's family claim for asylum is up for review or if an unaccompanied child is approaching their 18th birthday, then the insecurity around what any change of status brings has huge consequences and militates against anything that the school does to make them feel safe. Refugee and asylum-seeking children need to be recognised and visible in educational policy within a more coordinated policy landscape which recognises the barriers to safety for vulnerable children fleeing from traumatic home contexts.

In each of the case study schools, there was some form of EAL base which fostered initial feelings of *safety* as the child became accustomed to school life in the new context. They could see themselves **represented** in the school, especially in their initial encounters in the Base. The Base was a space with visible markers of newly arrived children on display, usually in the form of words in a range of representative languages but also commonly with a large map and pins indicating points of origin for the children accessing the Base. The teachers in the case study examples were keen to ensure that their new arrivals could use the EAL bases as transitory spaces to support their integration into mainstream. In these first encounters the manifestations of diversity and an inclusive welcome within the Base communicated safety for the new arrivals as they began to experience life in their new school.

Safety as an educational concept

Schools have an important role to play in rebuilding a sense of security and trust in the lives of young people who have seen their primary social worlds disintegrate at the point at which they had to leave. Finding a place in a school in their new context is an important marker for the child who can then begin to establish some order and consistency after a period of disruption. Being able to rely on the routine of going to school facilitates the process of feeling safe (Twemlow, Fonagy and Sacco 2002). For refugee children, schools are often the main point of contact with outside agencies, with the communities within and beyond the school gates. They are the entry point to possible futures. Schools function as a gateway into life into the new society and therefore some hope of resuming a sense of an ordinary life (Kohli 2011). Schools are spaces where newly arrived students can feel safety because of the compassionate inclusive ethos of the teachers they meet there (Pinson, Arnot & Candappa 2010). Teachers working with refugee and asylum-seeking students act in academic and pastoral roles, the latter often extending beyond and complicating the role of a teacher (Stewart 2011). For children who have experienced forced migration, the importance of building early positive relationships in their new setting cannot be underestimated, and these initial relationships are often with adults in the school. Feeling safe is linked to being able to cope with situations, and coping is enhanced by having positive relationships with teachers and being able to access social support within the school context (Frydenberg, Care, Freeman, Chan 2009). The case study schools illustrate how teachers are key to helping develop the social bonds that help children feel secure in schools. Feeling safe and secure is linked to wellbeing and there is evidence that where refugees are able to reduce stressful situations in the early stages of their post-migration experiences then they are more likely to have more successful outcomes and sustained wellbeing in the future (Simich et al. 2002).

The Larkspur case study and the practitioners' discussions of the concept of safety in relation to their practice shows how schools can work to create spaces where children arriving from a range of different experiences and cultural backgrounds can be made to feel secure, despite all the changes they continue to encounter in their new context. In various ways the Bases in the schools created what Sampson and Gifford called 'therapeutic landscapes'. They did this through fulfilling four conditions for 'restoration and recovery' (2010). First, the young people were able to view their Base as a place of 'opportunity' manifested through participation in activities which improved their English and where they could learn the 'rules' of school; second, it was a place of 'restoration', where they could begin to focus on their future through study; third, it provided 'sociability', where they could begin to make connections and friendships with other children; and finally, it provided 'safety', as a place of calm order with a teacher always present (ibid.).

Safety is an important concept in relation to the education of refugee and asylum-seeking children. These young people experience safety in different ways and their sense of security can be disrupted when they reach transitional points, or where they experience unexpected changes such as age assessment investigations or changes to their status. Safety is a more than a physical construct; it is relational, spatial and emotional. Teachers can help students to trust that they are accepted and will be able to resume, or begin to plan for, their possible futures. For older students, unable to compete at the same rate towards examination outcomes as their peers, safety comes with reassurance. This is enhanced by an explicit sharing with the new arrival that what they are doing now in their education provision is not an endpoint, but can be used to pave the way forward to achieve what they want in their future, to build the foundations for belonging and success within their new context.

A definition of the concept of safety when viewed through the lens of education can, therefore, be summed up in the following way:

Safety - a multifaceted concept which permeates life in and out of the educational setting

Supported by:

- a physical safe space,
- creating environments for trust building, experiential learning; talking (or choosing not to) about their experiences; social and emotional learning; risk-taking
- consistent and explicit expectations, high aspirations, with understanding that mistakes/misunderstandings will occur
- advocates (peers, teachers and SLT)

Demonstrated by understanding how this current context will fulfil present needs and prepare for future ambitions.

The teachers in the case study schools were committed to continuing to work to create conditions that allowed newly arrived children to realise safety. They wanted to share their learning with others. The definition above gives names to their day-to-day actions and also the ways of being which influenced and informed their work. It was important for the practitioners to hear each other's experiences and to consider how safety was being achieved in other settings, as well as their own. The examples of children's stories that they shared suggest that the search for safety is an ongoing process and that a sense of safety is related to notions of belonging and success, as will be outlined in the chapters which follow.

References

Brun, C. 2001. Reterritorializing the relationship between people and place in refugee studies, *Geografiska Annaler: Series B, Human Geography*, 83 (1), 15-25.

Department for Education (DfE). 2019. Keeping Children Safe in Education: Statutory guidance for schools and colleges. Available at https://assets.publishing.service.gov.uk/government/uploads/system/uploads/attachment_data/file/835733/Keeping_children_safe_in_education_2019.pdf

Frydenberg, E., Care, E., Chan, E., & Freeman, E. 2009. Interrelationships between coping, school connectedness and wellbeing Erica Frydenberg. *Australian Journal of Education*, 53 (3), 261-276.

Hopkins, P.E. 2013. *Young People, Place and Identity*. Abingdon: Routledge.

Kohli, R. 2011. Working to ensure safety, belonging and success for unaccompanied Asylum-Seeking children. *Child Abuse Review*, 20, 311-323.

Kohli, R. 2014. Protecting asylum seeking children on the move. *Revue Europeene Des Migrations Internationales*, 30(1), 83-104.

Pinson, H., Arnot, M. & Candappa, M. 2010. *Education, Aslyum and the 'Non-Citizen' Child: The Politics of Compassion and Belonging*. Basingstoke: Palgrave MacMillan.

Rutter, J. 2006. *Refugee Children in the UK*. Maidenhead: Open University Press.

Said, E.W. 2000. *Reflections on Exile and Other Essays*. London: Granta.

Sampson, R. & Gifford, S. 2010. Place-making, settlement and well-being: The therapeutic landscapes of recently arrived youth with refugee backgrounds, *Health & Place* 16, 113-116.

Simich, L., Beiser, M. & Mawani. F. 2002. Paved with good intentions: Canada's refugee destining policy and paths of secondary migration. *Canadian Public Policy / Analyse de Politiques*, 28(4), 597-607.

Stewart, J. 2011. *Supporting Refugee Children: Strategies for Educators*. Ontario: University of Toronto Press.

Tweedie, M.G., Belanger, C., Rezazadeh, K. & Vogel, K. 2017. Trauma - informed teaching practice and refugee children: A hopeful reflection on welcoming our new neighbours to Canadian schools. *BC TEAL Journal*, 2(1), 36-45.

Twemlow, S.W., Fonagy, P. & Sacco, F.C. 2002. Feeling safe in school. *Smith College Studies in Social Work*, 72(2), 303-326.

Watters, C. 2008. *Refugee Children*. Abingdon: Oxford University Press.

5 Education and the growth of belonging

Joanna McIntyre

Gare's experience

If I hadn't come (to the education provision) I would have missed out on going to lots of different places like (lists local sites in the city) ...

JMc: *And you think that's been good to be able to go to different places here?*

I love here. I am going to live here for my whole life. I'm not going to stay home like just thinking about my parents. It's really hard. That's all I care about - nothing else, just to see them once.

JMc: *Do you live on your own?*

Yes. I'm... I'm really friendly so I make friends.

JMc: *How do you make friends?*

It's like sometimes I go to the supermarket and there are Kurdish people. I went to (City football club) to play football and these English people, they just invite me to play with them and they take my number and four days a week, I'm doing football with them. And then here (at the provision) like with the Eritrean people, I know them here and they are my friends. So I know loads of Kurdish people here with my religion, my language, so I know them like that. I didn't know any of them before. ... And like, you guys here, the teachers here are really helpful to us helping us for learning everything. But someone outside has just been racist to me. I don't know why, my skin and my beard, I don't know. The bus driver he didn't believe how old I was ... but here everyone is friendly as well. Yeah, they are good to us. Very good.

So I when I first came here, there was like ten people. And I was really shy. And I said, 'Oh, I hope they're only going to be just two people there.' Because I was a stranger when I came here.

JMc: *How do you think you've learned about culture?*

I hadn't seen any different cultures in my country. We are like Asian people and Kurdish people and that is it - that is just normal. I haven't see people from other countries like Eritrea or English people. It was different. And here we talk about different food, different things that are not allowed for me or not allowed for them.

JMc: *Do you speak many languages?*

I speak Kurdish. I understand some more languages, like Persian. But I don't talk in it too much. My first language is Kurdish and I'm getting used to speaking English. So when I came here they tried to teach me to speak English. Because I haven't any dream when I came here, because I don't know what I could maybe do - like when I finished here, if there's some option to choose to go to. I didn't know. Until they taught me and they told me what I have to do after that. So I always feel better. And I said I have - maybe I'll have - a future. I'm not just learning English for myself. I'll have something else after that. So that's good. They explained to me I'm not here just for learning English. You are here. You are in this country. You can be like others in this country. And I am going to go to college.

In this chapter, data from our empirical research is drawn upon to reflect on the growth of a sense of belonging, which we see illustrated in Gare's comments about his experiences of building connections both within and outside the education provision. I begin by presenting a descriptive case study of Jasmine Gardens Academy, a school that has a tradition and reputation within its locality for providing an inclusive environment for all pupils. The next section draws on focus group discussions and interviews with practitioners. Its purpose is to understand more about how the case study schools define and refine their understandings of what they do to support their students to feel a sense of belonging. We then apply Fraser's participatory parity tripartite to analyse the concept of belonging through the lenses of redistribution, recognition and representation. The final part of the chapter pulls these sections together and develops the discussion about the concept of belonging as it applies to new arrivals in educational settings.

Case study: Jasmine Gardens Academy

According to the Academy's website, Jasmine Gardens is over 300 years old. It was the first charity school in the small Midlands city it serves. Nowadays, it is one of the largest schools within an expanding multi-academy trust located in and around the city. Jasmine Gardens is an 11-19 school and many pupils stay onto the Jasmine Sixth Form College. Whilst the manufacturing industries historically attracted a large workforce to the city, the largest employers now are the NHS (in the hospitals serving the area), the county council and the local universities. The city has a history of welcoming migrant communities from a variety of different ethnic and religious backgrounds. In the 2011 Census nearly 20% of the city's population were not born in the UK and it is estimated that this figure has risen since 2015. There are a number of organisations in the city which work to support refugee communities. Jasmine Gardens is a Church of England school, though pupils of other faiths also attend.

First impressions: belonging to a community

The landing page of Jasmine Gardens Academy's website features a quotation from the latest SIAM (Statutory Inspection of Anglican and Methodist Schools) report which celebrates the *'harmonious community'* where *'everyone is respected'*. On the same page is a welcome from the Head Boy and Head Girl who say that *'Everyone is open to express themselves and celebrate who they are.'* They go on to draw attention to the *'enriched student diversity'* and say that everyone is valued *'in our family'*. The opening sentence in the Principal's welcome foregrounds the word *'inclusivity'* and an emphasis that everyone has an *'important role within our community'*. The website contains a range of information which conveys this sense of family, community and inclusion. As with most schools, there is a celebration of the previous year's examination successes and alongside accolades for those with the highest possible academic results, care has been taken to mention those students who should be celebrated for a wide range of achievements, including pupils who have overcome significant challenges to be awarded their grades. One pupil who is celebrated in this way is a girl who was a 16-year-old new arrival in Year 11 and went on to gain 9 GCSEs.

This notion of diversity and inclusion is also conveyed through newsletters on the website, which showcase the school's links with local community groups, and through the various ways in which all students take part in enrichment activities in school. The website communicates a rich and broad variety of academic and non-academic activities in the school. There is an emphasis on developing each individual's strengths and how each can contribute to the community or family of the academy. A section on the website details how children can be involved in student leadership across seven areas of academy life.

Jasmine Gardens Academy is located next to the city's northern ring road, near to a large housing estate which comprises rented and privately owned accommodation. Whilst the school attracts children from the locality, its designation as a faith school means it attracts pupils from across all areas of the city; the school works with over 60 feeder primaries. The school has been through a series of expansions and there is currently a period of redevelopment and new building on the site.

The school reception is located within a large open area which is used for different purposes throughout the day. This open area or vestibule is a hub which staff and students pass through on their ways to and from different parts of the school. There is a doorway directly to the Executive Principal's office, which is centrally located in the heart of the school. There are corridors leading off to different areas of the school and glancing upwards one can see a glass partition showing the second floor with the staffroom and multi-faith prayer room. During my visits there, I observe people stopping for conversations with the reception staff or others as they pass through. The area is decorated with children's art work and with information about recent and upcoming activities and events. Along with the academy's ethos and its mission statement 'Believe in yourself, in others, in God', there are inspirational quotations from alumni of the school displayed around this space. During breaktimes the tables next to the reception desk fill with children chatting and eating snacks from the snack bar. During the GCSE and A level examination period, I observe teachers and students at these tables talking in groups together about the exam paper they have just sat. The reception desk, where visitors sign in, is located therefore within a busy and social communal area. This large open social space communicates welcome and community.

Creating a culture of belonging through community

> If the Fair access panel say this student is coming to you, I should be straight away informed. Therefore we get the ball rolling with how we can make sure that this student feels welcomed, inducted and starts to belong in what is essentially their family of Jasmine Gardens, which might sound cheesy but it's what we use. And for me it's about from minute one that they're welcome, that their transition from wherever they come from isn't as traumatic as the transition that they've had already.
>
> (Amy)

As with Larkspur and the other schools, new arrivals spend time in the EAL base. This is viewed by the teachers and the students as a first point of contact where *'they've instantly got that sense of belonging'*. The next step comes soon after, through feeling part of a tutor group. The school has what Amy, the EAL lead practitioner for the Trust, describes as a *'circle of friends' approach'* which they developed as part of the school's wider approach to inclusion. *'For them to belong'*, says Amy, *'it has to come from the children'*. This means that there is an identified small group of students, usually within the same tutor group, to support the new arrival to feel part of the school community. This goes beyond showing them round for the first day; the process continues for as long as there is felt to be a need for it, so that even if the new arrival is in the Base on a full-time basis initially, there will be a group coming to meet them at break- and lunchtimes.

Like many other schools, Jasmine Gardens operates a house system; through membership of a tutor group each child also becomes a member of a house. Throughout the school there are various signifiers of house membership and what this includes, mainly articulated through sporting events. There are lots of displays and markers of enrichment activities during the school day and after school too and all children, including those who have just arrived, are encouraged to take part. Sport, music, performance and the Duke of Edinburgh Award scheme are particularly well communicated as activities for the young people to take part in and the message from the website, that experiencing the community of the academy is broader than the taught curriculum, is conveyed throughout the school buildings. The importance of students taking an active part in all aspects of life within the school is later echoed in my conversations with key interviewees. This is achieved partly through the emphasis on a broad curriculum experience, as evidenced by the range of enrichment opportunities and by the emphasis on pupils accessing the breadth of school life from the earliest opportunity.

In my conversations with the CEO of the Trust, it became evident that activities and mechanisms for creating a sense of belonging were deliberate and well considered:

> It would be about the relationships that they develop: relationships with the staff that they work with but also you want them to develop peer relationships. We do break down the belonging in the school, so they belong to a tutor group and they've got a house that they belong to and to a year group. I think it is about a pride in the uniform that they wear and really getting themselves involved with some of the clubs and activities that go on

so that they are not just accessing mainstream education. So all of those I would see as evidence that they have that sense of belonging.

This has taken time. In my conversations with Amy and with Jayne, the CEO, they both mention that the school demographic has changed over the past decade from being predominantly white to a situation where *'now the majority of the students are Asian and the numbers of black and white students are reasonably even. So it has become a very diverse school'* (CEO interview). Pictures around the school reflect this diversity and Amy explains that she is working on a display in the reception area to reflect the 85+ languages that are represented by the school community, *'to say, this is who we are and be proud of that'.*

Amy has been at the school for almost 19 years. She reflects that the school had to work hard at strategies for creating a shared sense of community, of belonging, for all children. She recalls a time when *'there were pockets in the playground that we wanted to try and breakdown'* and the steps they took to *'break down the barriers'* between different groups. This involved working with community group leaders outside of school. *'All these fantastic institutions that used to come into our school all the time ... they were really crucial for the work we were doing ... they don't exist anymore because of funding.'* She explains that they took a restorative justice approach to trying to develop mutual understanding and tolerance, *'and what is really nice is that you don't see that divide anymore'.* Amy goes on to explain that there used to be a lot of communication in the form of booklets and events about different groups of students and their culture and heritage. But now this is not needed anymore, *'because the students are driving that forward, they are the ones saying <u>our</u> mental health, <u>our</u> wellbeing, <u>our</u> celebration of <u>our</u> identity ... and the school has just evolved, it is just how diverse we are as a school ... the students in the school feel like they belong. And there's a lot of work being done.'*

That this is a Church of England school is obvious to the visitor. The academy's logo represents Christian iconography and the ethos statement emphasises that the mission of the school is to develop an educational community shaped by Christian values, within a context of respect for the many faiths making up the school community. The newsletters illustrate this with activities which celebrate Christian values through promoting understanding of all faiths. It is also reflected in Amy's observation that the Academy's focus is on wellbeing for all individuals and for developing a harmonious educational community which is underpinned by, but is also wider than, the Christian ethos: *'There are many staff that obviously drive the Christian distinctiveness forward, but also the multiple ethnicity and the multiple religious nature of our school. So that, for example, the multi-faith room is just embedded – it is no longer other, it is just part of who everyone is.'*

The academy has supported the inclusion of refugee children into the school for a long period of time and the CEO feels that this is possible because of the tolerant approach to faith and diversity. She describes the school's involvement in a Radio 4 programme about multi-faith communities,

> *I sort of grabbed about four kids off the corridor really, because it was one of those last minute things, and it was amazing what they came out with. Because they come to a faith institution where faith is important and respected, they feel very open about discussing each other's faith. So there was a Sikh student, a Muslim student and a black*

Pentecostalist student and a student of no faith. And it was like they were having a conversation about faith and they were just talking about each other's faith. And the one who had no faith said that when they started at the school they hadn't understood what faith was, but now they had a much better understanding of other people's faith. I hope that is the same for our refugee children and that they come with their cultural norms which are respected and understood and they learn about other cultural norms.

The local refugee charity had spoken to me about Jasmine Gardens before my first visit, explaining that when a new family arrived at the charity, the charity workers always hoped that they would be able to help the family get the children into Jasmine Gardens because they knew they would be well supported. During my initial visits, the school was putting together an application to become a recognised School of Sanctuary. Jayne, the CEO, recalls that although they had always tried to support refugee families and their children, demand for this had increased since 2015. A number of refugee families who had a child with a disability had been accepted into the city as part of the country's commitment to the Syrian Vulnerable Person Resettlement Programme and the school had expertise in supporting children with special needs. She remembers one Syrian boy with a sight impairment who joined them in 2015 and how the 'circle of friends' approach supported him:

'So we create a group of friends around them who are very supportive – peer support and that is very important. This student … who has a sight impairment, he was always with someone else to start with but he now knows his way around … and he recognises everyone's voice and he knows who he is talking to and he is confident now.'

Amy recalls that the school's first new arrival was 16 years earlier, before there were specific support mechanisms in place for refugee children. Jovani arrived in the city with his sibling. Through working closely with Jovani, and consulting with the local authority and national experts, Amy developed ways of working to support the student who had no English. Jasmine Gardens was in the early stages of adapting whole-school approaches to oracy and literacy, and this coordinated approach across all lessons, along with a bilingual dictionary, seemed to help Jovani to feel part of lessons. Shortly after his arrival in the city, his sibling left the area and, following social care involvement, the student moved in with a staff member and remains a part of this family to this day. The arrival of Jovani and assessment of his needs led to the decision to have a designated member of staff attend appropriate training; this marked the starting point of specific EAL support for other new arrivals. Amy, who is now an 'advanced EAL practitioner' in the city, recalls that *'Successful support, induction and integration to school and the family environment enabled his supported progress and success'.* Jovani has since completed his degree and is studying for a second Master's qualification.

Amy explains that Jovani's case paved the way for the school-wide, and now Trust-wide, approach to supporting new arrivals through what she described as a *'language-conscious approach'.* This puts the onus on each member of staff to consider the language demands of their subject area and to be very explicit about these for all children. Amy feels this has obvious benefits for new arrivals who might be acquiring English as a second, third or even fourth language. Her EAL training for the Trust *'is an integrated part of our school'* and focuses on a multilingual approach celebrating the plurality of languages and the range of cultures represented by the student body who reflect *'this kind of multilingual diverse world that we live in in our city. We need to move with it.'* For Amy, finding ways for the new arrivals to feel that they belong to the community within school and in their city is a feature of the work of the school.

Valuing each individual and their potential contribution to the community of the school is part of the CEO's vision for inclusivity across the Trust. *'It emanates from our ethos and the fact that we see every child as valued and important. ... every single child that crosses our threshold, whether they have got SEN needs or whether they are an asylum seeker or whether they are an Oxbridge high flyer, they deserve absolutely the best opportunities they can have.'* With new arrivals, Amy explains that in order for them to begin to develop early feelings of belonging, it is important that the school finds out what they can do and what their interests are. *'We have to quickly find out what their strengths are and do what is the best thing for them at that point.'* She provides the example of Banna, a young student from The Gambia whose first language was Mandika (an oral language) with whom Amy and her team worked hard to establish a point of connection. Amy described how Banna's only response in early conversations in the Base was to a picture of a goat. Later, Banna was able to explain that her responsibility to her village community had been to herd and move the goats. From this early point of connection, and people's interest in her life before she joined the school, Banna was able to build friendships. She went on to take an active role in all aspects of Academy life, in the clubs and activities as well as in academic life. Amy has kept the connection with Banna as she now trains at university to be a nurse.

Just before the summer holidays, I spend time with Riana, who talks about her experiences of joining the academy two years previously. Before enrolling at Jasmine Gardens, Riana had been in the city for three months at a different education provision. She has ambitions to go to a top university to study science and was keen to make up for time she had lost when the family were in Italy and she had not gone to school. In her home country, she had gone to a village school where she learnt English and was taught science through the medium of English. Although she was already old enough to begin a post-16 course, Amy decided to place Riana in Year 11 where she could take some GCSEs. The plan was for her to spend the summer holidays catching up with what she would have studied in Year 10 for mathematics, English and science, with the hope of her joining Year 11 GCSE classes when the new academic year started. However, Amy could see that Riana had the capacity to study other subjects and so within a few weeks of the start of the new academic year, she was accessing a full Year 11 timetable with only a few hours in the Base. One of the subjects that Riana showed a particular aptitude for was art.

Riana shares with me some of the challenges she found in making friends as a consequence of joining at such a late stage in school. Her observations echo Ali's at Larkspur. She observes that *'in Year 11 they all have their own groups and know each other really well'*. She had a buddy and a circle of friends that looked out for her and even tried to persuade her to go to the prom with them: *'I didn't know what this thing prom was'*. She reflects though that she was *'afraid of talking to people in English and didn't want to stop their conversations ... I felt like I couldn't be myself.'* She found English ways of being in classrooms very challenging, especially group work. She found comfort in art, describing how she could be her own person there, developing her own technique. She enjoyed everyone working on their own pieces but at the same time as the rest of the class, so *'you feel you are part of something'*. She explains that during that period, she felt she was happy at Jasmine Gardens because she was getting on with her education and progressing towards her goal of university. But it wasn't until the end of Year 11, when she went on a National Citizen Service (NCS) project, that she felt she had the confidence to make friends and to really feel that she belonged to a group of peers. She reflects that this was because all of those on the project had come from different friendship groups and didn't know each other well beforehand. Everyone had the same starting point and was working on a shared project as part of NCS. Rania did very well in that first year at Jasmine Gardens, achieving 9 GCSEs before progressing into the Sixth Form where she now says she feels she completely belongs. She has made good friends and is fully engaging with all opportunities at Jasmine Gardens, including taking on the role of sixth form prefect.

On one of my visits, I spend time with two refugees who are in Year 10 and, like the other students in their year group, are preparing for work experience. The academic coach who supports all new arrivals in the Base is helping them to prepare a letter to send to their work placement, a local art gallery. One of them has discovered that he is very good with textiles and is making a model of a mosque in his art and design lessons. I chat to them as they work on this in the Base and they talk to me about their friendship groups in the city's Turkish community and within school. They convey a sense of how they keep their lives in school and out of school very separate. Amy explains that although there have been large steps forward in terms of cohesion within the school gates, she is very aware that *'some of the friendships in the school are not friendships within the community because that's just the way it. … But that's just accepted'*. I glean that most of the connections that the boys made initially with their peers in school have been in lessons or through fitness sessions and sports played in school during lessons and at lunchtimes. They still come to the Base for a few hours each week, but have progressed from just working on their English to bringing homework from their other lessons to work on in there with the academic coach's support. As their confidence in speaking has improved, they said it has become easier to make friends and they feel more able to join in with the ordinary activities that the rest of their peers are involved in, such as work experience.

In similar conversations with two Kurdish refugees, they compare their prior experience of school in Turkey and say that they feel that Jasmine Garden's lessons about *'belief and religions helped us to learn about other people and to feel part of a family'*. For Amy, this is an important thread of the school's work. Reflecting on changes to the communities outside school and especially to national conversations in the wake of the Brexit referendum, she comments that *'politically we're all living through that right now'*; she feels it is important that the school explicitly teaches about difference and the importance of tolerance, *'the open conversations in classrooms are incredible'*. This helps new arrivals to understand what is acceptable in their new society, which is an important aspect of their education because, as Amy acknowledges, *'there have been some issues with our new arrivals having their own views that do not always gel with those of others'*. Through activities like work experience, the new arrivals are supported to make connections with the wider communities in the city, beyond their immediate family connections.

During my visits to Jasmine Gardens it becomes very clear that the messages of family and community, and inclusion and belonging are framed by the very visible presence of Jayne, the CEO. Amy had previously said to me that the senior leaders of the Trust put *'inclusion first and are willing to take the hit'*. Jayne explains that she will always strive to prioritise the need of the individual child regardless of some of the pressures she faces as a school leader. This means that the academy will take children onto roll during Year 11, *'never a year group you would want to come in on'* because of the focus on high-stakes GCSE examinations. Jayne also supports staff working with refugee children who go above and beyond their teaching duties on behalf of a particular child. She encourages them to work with external agencies: *'these children in particular have no other advocates left and we kid ourselves if we think there is a big infrastructure out there to support them'*. She gives numerous examples of children who have come into Jasmine Gardens as refugees with very fragmented experiences of education who have gone on to *'fly and be fully contributing members of society'*. In times of increased pressures for leaders of multi-academy trusts in England to foreground league table performance and examination results, Jayne argues that *'we put our money where our mouth is and if we are an inclusive school then we should be that ... having a refugee child should be seen as a source of celebration'*. At a national meeting of CEOs of Academy Trusts, Jayne celebrated Rania's achievements by asking her to prepare a speech about her experiences and successes since coming to England. By this point, Rania was on her way to applying to university to study chemistry and Amy and Jayne were helping her with her application form.

Amy reflects that helping refugee children to belong to school and to wider society has been hugely beneficial for her personally and professionally. She ends her interview with a rallying call for all schools to welcome new arrivals:

> I think some of the biggest joys and the real buzz that you get from doing the job that we do is from helping those that are most in need - and if those students aren't an example of that, then I don't know who is. And we can learn so much culturally, from a global perspective, and also thinking from a well-rounded individual's point of view. ... I want to work in a fully comprehensive environment ... those true representatives of our entire country, why would you not take them? I get why institutions have to say no because they're full or they think they don't have provision. Well make provision! Because actually it's one of the best things.

A few weeks after I finish my visits to Jasmine Gardens, I hear from Amy that the school is the first in the city to have been successfully awarded the designation of School of Sanctuary.

Towards belonging through education: debates and dialogues

> We've got to find a way for those students - ultimately they've got to create their own belonging. Because we can't make it happen, but we can offer opportunities for that to flourish rather than just sitting back.
>
> *(focus group)*

As Jayne at Jasmine Gardens said in her interview, there are various markers of belonging that a school can develop to help new arrivals feel they are part of a community. These range from physical indicators, such as uniforms and badges and inclusion of markers of diversity in public displays and documentation, to social indicators such as membership of teams or participation in activities. All the case study schools reflected belonging in different ways.

The post-16 settings did not have uniforms and so they worked differently to ensure that the young people could be identified as part of the provision. In the interviews, discussions and the focus group meetings, there was a shared sense that becoming part of a school and its wider community meant moving beyond indicators of 'otherness'. They tended to follow the approach of the senior leadership team at Heather Academy: *'It's about drawing out things that people have in common rather than the differences that they have, to help them feel like they belong.'* This meant that the lead practitioners and senior leadership teams had moved away from what Anna referred to as the tokenistic *'samosas, saris and steel bands'* representations of different multicultural groups. This had been replaced by a sense of valuing the assets and attributes of each individual through initial work and holistic assessments at induction and finding ways for them to make connections in order to 'use their talents and capacities' to begin to 'grow webs of belonging' (Kohli 2011).

The practitioners developed explicit strategies that supported the young new arrivals to feel valued and to develop a sense of self-worth, in accord with Maslow's link between belonging and self-actualisation (1987). In part, this was facilitated by conducting a holistic initial assessment to encourage the development of existing skills and attributes, such as Rania's art and Gare's footballing. Depending on where the students' previous educational experiences had been, they might feel more confident in some subject areas than in others. A number of practitioners observed that some students were particularly strong at mathematics and were keen to be allowed to access maths lessons with their peers. During the focus groups, we observed that refugee children from countries which had been former European colonies, such as Eritrea and Syria, found it easier to adjust to the English school curriculum if they had had experienced fairly uninterrupted schooling before leaving. This is because of the similarities of curriculum and subject disciplines across these contexts. A number of Eritrean children in the course of the visits to schools commented on their desire to study History and Social Sciences – subjects they are often excluded from because they are deemed to be too language-heavy.

For those children who had no or very little formalised schooling before arriving in England, priority was still given to helping them to feel valued by finding out what skills they brought with them. The practitioners from Fern College spoke of an unaccompanied new arrival who had no formal educational experiences, but who had been responsible for running the family shop in Eritrea. It quickly became clear that he could work with numbers and mental maths, even though he could not access written mathematics exercises. The teachers explained how his self-esteem grew as he worked through maths problems far more quickly than his classmates.

As has been discussed in the previous chapter, the schools all followed a multilingual approach to languages, which focused on improving the students' English, but not at the expense of their other languages – which were a source of celebration: *'We promote the mother tongue and think it is important that they don't lose it' (Gideon).* This meant that the children could take pride in their linguistic ability as the practitioners emphasised that fluency in more than one language was a sign of cognitive ability (Cummins 2016; Gandara 2016). Another important aspect of their individuality was their faith, if they had one. This was clearly an important tenet of the ethos at Jasmine Gardens, but all the practitioners felt that it was very important that there were opportunities for the young refugee to be able to have a sense of continuity with their past through celebrating their religion, whilst also being able to connect with new communities in their new place with a shared faith:

> *'I think for a lot of our students religion kind of defines who they are. We talked at the beginning about faith because that is what keeps you grounded and gives you your identity when everything around you is changing'.*

(discussion at Fern College)

It seems especially important that the educational provision is a space for individual's faith to be respected when the new arrival has come from a place where their religious affiliation was a source of persecution. The practitioners spoke of Kurdish refugees and young Pentecostal children for whom this was extremely relevant.

In the previous chapter we discussed individual wellbeing as a component of safety. There are also links between wellbeing and belonging: the importance of self-care was raised by the practitioners as an important aspect of a positive relationship with one's own self. For some children, this was the first time in a long while that they were encouraged to consider ways in which they could develop strategies for supporting their mental, as well as their physical, health, *'Things like taking care of yourself, so learning to look after themselves'* (focus group). Whilst this was part of schools' pastoral support for all students, it also was strategically included in curriculum activities that revolved around subjects related to what was commonly called PHSE in English schools.

The practitioners also spoke about the importance of finding ways of allowing the students to value their own personal histories and connections without intruding too much on any traumatic memories of past events leading to them arriving in England. They talked about how important it was for the young refugee to be able to be *'proud of your family and proud of who you are'* and most importantly to do so *'whilst not losing yourself or your culture'* (discussion at Fern College). During my time in the case study schools and in conversations with practitioners who had experienced different policy contexts over time, it was clear that the schools were drawing on reservoirs of experience of working with different groups of children. Policies such as the New Arrivals Excellence programme and various culturally relevant pedagogies and strategies from previous policy contexts reflecting multiculturalism and the focus on achievement for different ethnic minority groups in the New Labour era (more fully described in Chapter 6) still had resonance with the ways these schools made new arrivals feel welcome. These strategies worked with the child and tried to support them to feel connected to the curriculum, as is partly echoed by the Principal at Lilac Lane's articulation of what she felt was important question for her to pose to her teaching staff, *'What is it that we can do to help them feel part of the school within our lessons?'*

This focus on the new arrival feeling valued and being able to recognise and value their own individual strengths echoes studies which illustrate that more positive perceptions of self-esteem in young adults are directly related to an increased sense of belonging (for example, Hoersting and Jenkins 2011) whereas the risks to those who do not feel a sense of positive self-worth and value are that they do not feel that they can belong (Biggart et al. 2013). This focus on wellbeing was articulated as being one of the challenges many adolescents face as they work through identity shifts associated with growing towards adulthood. However, for this particular group of adolescents, with their extraordinary experiences of trauma and dislocation from home, the identity shifts were all the more marked. As has already been commented on in the previous chapter, time has been experienced differently by those who had recently arrived and had their normal lives disrupted. They know that there is a limited time left for them to access mainstream or 'ordinary' education and there are particular challenges, therefore, for schools and colleges, to help these students feel a sense of belonging to what is essentially a temporary or contingent space (*cf* Kohli 2014).

This was felt to be especially the case for those who had made the journey as unaccompanied migrants. The practitioners discussed how they had dealt with particular challenges and experiences which most adults in their new contexts could not begin to imagine: *'they've had to be pretty grown up to do what they've done. Because they've had to be like adults already'* (Eva). But in 'being like adults already' the new arrivals have missed out on aspects of childhood. The practitioners were therefore keen to provide opportunities for doing ordinary things that peers in their new context would be able to do as a matter of course: *'sometimes the belonging is just doing those teenage things'* (focus group).

Attending school or college each day is the kind of everyday thing that teenagers do in England. The practitioners were very aware that they were in a key position to be able to support new arrivals build social relationships with peers and the community within and outside school. The specific contribution of school in developing 'belongingness' for adolescents with refugee backgrounds is emphasised by the work of Due, Rigg and Augoustinos: 'school belonging has an impact on a range of wellbeing and developmental outcomes, including mental health, peer relationships, self-esteem and self-efficacy, and academic achievement' (2016, 33).

The case study of Jasmine Gardens illustrates many ways in which staff try to facilitate peer relationships in school: through setting up friendship buddies in tutor groups, through encouraging participation in enrichment activities and through a broad curriculum offer. Initially, as the examples of the experiences of some of the students in these chapters have illustrated, it is difficult for the new arrivals to find points of connection with their new peers, who are already in established friendship groups. But as the practitioners in one of the focus groups observe, *'you can't force them to be friends but you can put them in a context where friendships are more likely to develop.'* As Rania's experience of art illustrates, this works best when schools work to try to include the new arrivals in lessons, with their peers, which provide opportunities for experiential learning: *'There has to be a real reason for talking to each other and sometimes art and more creative things are a more natural way of talking because there is a purpose to the talk'* (focus group).

The schools also tried to create opportunities for new arrivals to build points of connection with groups out of school and in groups that crossed the boundaries between school and community. These experiences were intended to help them to feel *'able to contribute to a community which they are still finding their feet in'.* The Senior Leadership Team at Heather Academy try to expedite this by encouraging all new arrivals to take part in the Performing Arts faculty's annual school show: *'even if they can't dance or act they'll find a way of involving them and they all get to feel part of something special which is really celebrated'.* The principal of Lilac Lane said that she and the school were constantly finding ways of showing refugee children that *'you are a member of our community, you are not an add on'.* Whilst there were many examples of building links within the school, the practitioners shared experiences of ways in which they tried to introduce the young refugees to communities in their wider society. These included trips and activities in the local area, as mentioned by Gare in his interview. For example, the young people in Fern College worked with a localised version of a national project which helps them to learn about bike maintenance and to fix up an old bike, which they can then keep to give them cheap access to get around the city. Similarly, the involvement of the new arrivals at Lilac Lane in the community garden project offered opportunities to contribute and feel a *'sense of ownership and being proud'*. These activities, and various examples of work experience, helped to build the students' sense of connection with their new place. Generally, these interactions were positive; Gare's experience of racism with the bus driver was unusual within the data for this study. However, this may, of course, reflect the fact that people who choose to work with schools supporting new arrivals may not reflect the views of wider society.

The practitioners spoke at length about how they tried to help the young people to understand the ways of society in this, their new context. James emphasised that *'they want to be accepted in their new society'* and so teachers need to explicitly teach how to be, in order for that to happen. When refugees come from regimes which have allowed limited opportunities for open debate and discussion, schools work hard to help the young people manage the transition to life in England. Louise spoke about how in conversations about gender roles or sexuality some new arrivals *'have set views on certain things which I've tried to challenge but in a respectful way'*. Amy reflected that, *'there are things that a new arrival has to do which are different from their own culture in order to fit in. But also the environment should give their culture some respect.'* There was a sense that creating a sense of belonging needs to be a dialogic process; the refugee pupil and the school need to learn from the process, with both being changed – and usually enhanced – as a result.

> *If we genuinely want to create a society where we look out for each other and people respect each other and care for each other, then surely schools are a microcosm of that and have a part to play in terms of building the sort of society we want for the future. That is not elitist or exclusive and it has to be made up of every community in our society. The role of the refugee in that has a long and proud history, in many ways. Different groups have come to this country and made it better. And our responsibility is to take in those children and to be able to support them on their journey before they go on and support us in the future.* (Jayne).

Belonging through the lens of participatory parity

In this chapter we have outlined the different layers of the concept of *belonging* as it relates to refugee children in school. In considering the ways in which material and human resourcing needs to be **(re-)distributed**, the school leaders in the case study schools have already prioritised resources to underpin their commitment to inclusion. The variety of planned activities and strategies described above engendered positive relationships for newly arrived refugee and asylum-seeking children. These began with activities leading to a positive sense of their own relationships with themselves; they continued with activities designed to help develop friendships with peers and build connections with communities in and out of school. In the case study schools, many of these activities are aimed at all pupils; only a small proportion of them require additional targeted resourcing for new arrivals. Elsewhere, however, in other schools with a different whole-school ethos, it might be the case that new arrivals would benefit from the introduction of a planned series of activities such as those above; this would require dedicated funding for staffing, material resources and time.

Refugee children want to come to school to resume a sense of ordinariness in their lives, so they want to be **recognised** for the skills they bring rather than the labels that mark their differences. As we have seen, the concept of *belonging* is completely interrelated to the ways in which schools can help children to build connections and relationships on a range of levels. The practitioners in the case study schools recognised that the new arrivals needed support to build relationships with peers and the wider society and understood both how important and how difficult it is for the young people, especially if they arrive as an older child, to make connections and make friends in their new context. The practitioners help to build self-esteem and to broker relationships and build a sense of social connectedness and belonging through recognition of the assets and skills and potential that each refugee and asylum-seeking child brings.

This begins with an asset-based approach which recognises their experiences and attributes and helps to build the newly arrived child's self-esteem. Belonging is also aided by a recognition that refugee children do not all have the same sets of experiences or needs, as acknowledged by Jayne, the CEO of Jasmine Gardens: *'our refugee children come with their cultural norms which are respected and understood and they learn about other cultural norms'*. Schools like Jasmine Gardens know there needs to be an overt attempt to be explicit about both the expectations of the curriculum and assessment system in the new context and about how the child's own cultural values can be recognised through the use of a range of teaching approaches and resources that have been passed on from previous policy eras. These memories of previous policy and practice were held by the more experienced practitioners who worked hard, through feeding into whole-school approaches and training, to ensure that what they knew was shared with newer teachers. Anna, one of the more experienced practitioners, had been an EMAG lead for the local authority. She was actively involved in passing on her expertise to colleagues who lacked experience of supporting refugee children. She spoke of how important it had been in the past for multicultural and anti-racist approaches and support for new arrivals to be valued and recognised by the national education system: *'the activity was legitimized because it was coming from national government and there were regional advisors and local specialists who had something to bring ... we were having really in-depth and important national conversations. And then it just stopped.'*

The process of integration is complex and involves commitment from both the school and the individual child. Integration is underpinned by a sense of *belonging* and children from different contexts are more likely to be able to build webs of connection if they see that their cultural perspectives are **represented** in their new spaces. The case study schools attempted this in various ways by ensuring that refugee children were included where possible in student representative bodies such as councils – though the practitioners did acknowledge that this was difficult until the child had English language competence enough to be able to fully participate. The practitioners also felt that there were issues when children came from cultures and societies that had differing attitudes to collective and individual participation in such activities and where democratic participation in public life was not the norm.

Belonging as an educational concept

For the past century, socio-psychological studies have considered the nature of belonging as a fundamental component of being human (for example, Durkheim 1912 [1995]). Belonging is dependent upon and facilitated by individual, interpersonal, contextual and organisational features (Levett-Jones & Lathlean 2007). For children, schools work in specific multidimensional ways to foster belongingness (Due et al., 2016). Positive associations of belonging whilst at school can have long-lasting effects on the ability to develop peer relationships, wellbeing and future employment (Biggart et al., 2013). The importance of belonging to friendship groups is always an important aspect of life for teenagers, but is harder for new arrivals who, according to Candappa and Igbiginie, have fewer friends that non-refugee children (2003). Schools play a vital role in brokering possible new friendships. Whilst the practitioners in this study recognised that they had varying degrees of success with this, as Riana's memories of the invitation to the prom demonstrate, they still felt it was a vital part of their work, as was their brokering role to communities within and outside the school gates.

Belonging is a social process and is realised when communities and individuals come together. New arrivals are not passive in this process and working to forge new ways of connecting is a marker of agency in their new context. Considerations of how schools can imbue a sense of positive self-worth and wellbeing through valuing the individual newcomer is a powerful act of 'empowerment, acceptance and community building' (Koyama & Chang 2019, 141). This is achieved by an asset-based approach, culturally relevant pedagogies and explicit strategies for developing relationships. As the interview with Gare demonstrates, once the refugee child feels that they belong to their new society, they can begin to imagine their future there.

The case study presented in this chapter, along with the practitioners' discussions and reflections on their practice, illustrates how belongingness in schools is created by strategic actions which aim to: engender a sense of place-making and identification with their new context; broker and build relationships across a range of social networks; and build on a shared commitment from the Senior Leadership to the ongoing process of working together to create an inclusive environment.

This focus on locational and relational ties and ties of shared value creates a sense of what Tönnies described as a *gemeinschaft* model of community (2001). Tönnies contrasted the organic development of a community based on such ties, with *gesellschaft*, which he conceived of as a structural or 'mechanical construction' imposed upon a group of people (2001, 17). Metaphors of *gemeinschaft* and *gesellschaft* have been applied to school contexts and are a useful lens through which to understand the things that help school communities bond (McIntyre 2010). Schools which reflect *gemeinschaft* characteristics and prioritise social bonds and a social mission – schools such as the ones described in this chapter – evidence how belonging can be an educational endeavour for those working to support individuals whose own personal landscapes of belongingness have been so drastically altered by circumstances largely out of their control.

In conclusion, a definition of the concept of belonging when viewed through the lens of education would include the following:

Belonging – a multilayered concept based on opportunities for developing positive relationships:

- with self
- with peers (in and out of school)
- with communities (in and out of school)
- with place
- with the new society

Marked by signifiers of belonging (uniforms, badges, participation in events, activities, exhibitions, teams) along with locational and relational ties.

Belonging is a dialogic process (it has to involve others as well as the individual). Enhanced by

- making the implicit explicit – understanding of codes and rules, clear signposts and resources for navigating an education system and societal norms
- developing individual assets to promote a feeling of being valued
- teaching tolerance, promoting difference
- working with peers to create a new society where we belong together
- preparing for their future and forming hopes and goals for life.

Having outlined examples of policies and practices which help refugee and asylum-seeking children to develop a sense of belonging, in the next chapter, we turn to Kohli's final concept – the will to succeed.

References

Biggart, A. O'Hare, L. & Connolly, P. 2013. A need to belong? The prevalence of experiences of belonging and exclusion in school among minority ethnic children living in the 'White hinterlands', *Irish Educational Studies*, 32(2), 179–195.

Candappa, M. & Igbinigie, I. 2003. Everyday worlds of young refugees in London, *Feminist Review*, 73, 54065.

Cummins, J. 2016. Individualistic and social orientations to literacy research: Bringing voices together, United Kingdom Literacy Association Conference, University of Bristol, England.

Due, C. Rigg, D.W. & Augoustinos, M. 2016. Experiences of school belonging for young children with refugee backgrounds, *The Educational and Developmental Psychologist*, 33(1), 33–53.

Durkheim. 1995. *The Elementary Forms of Religious Life*. New York: Free Press (originally published 1912, trans.: Fields, K.E.)

Gandara, P. 2016. *Educating Immigrant Students and Emergent Bilinguals (in an anti-immigrant era)*. Brooklyn Museum: American Education Research Association, http://www.aera100.net/patricia-gandara.html.

Hoersting, R.C. & Jenkins, S.R. 2011. No place to call home: Cultural homelessness, self-esteem and cross-cultural identities, *International Journal of Intercultural Relations*, 35(1), 17–30.

Kohli, R. (2011) Working to ensure safety, belonging and success for unaccompanied asylum-seeking children, *Child Abuse Review*, 20, 311–323.

Kohli, R. 2014. Protecting asylum seeking children on the move, *Revue Europeene Des Migrations Internationales*, 30(1), 83–104.

Koyama, J. and Chang, E. 2019. Schools as Refuge? The Politics and Policy of Educating Refugees in Arizona, *Educational Policy*, 33(1) 136–157.

Levett-Jones, T. & Lathlean, J. 2007. Belongingness: A prerequisite for nursing students' clinical learning, *Nurse Education in Practice*, 8, 103–111.

Maslow, A.H. 1987. *Motivation and Personality* (3rd Edition). New York: Harper Row.

McIntyre, J. 2010. *Why they stayed: a study of the working lives of long-serving teachers in inner city schools*. PhD thesis, University of Nottingham. Available at http://eprints.nottingham.ac.uk/11652/1/Why_They_Stayed.pdf.

Tönnies, F. 2001. *Community and Civil Society* (originally published 1887, trans. Harris, J., & Hollis, M.). Cambridge: Cambridge University Press.

6 Education and the concept of success

Joanna McIntyre

Gare's experience

JMc: *So what would you like to do?*

In the future?

JMc: *Yes, in the future?*

So I mean I didn't have any thoughts about that because I was told if you are just an asylum seeker here in this country, you can't go to any meetings about college. And so I was like not really wanting to go to college until they are going to give me something – if I have, like, a statement, a document to say I am staying here in England. So if they give me that, then going to college will be really nice and going to university. But if I don't have anything, I can't, I'll just have to give up college.

JMc: *But if you could imagine there was no problem with that, in your dreams what would you like to do? Maybe when you're 30 years old, what would you like to be doing?*

Absolutely. I want to be a teacher to help people or I want to be a social worker. Because I know if I will be social worker and work with some people like me, I know how they are, you know, because I was like them. So maybe some social workers from here, they do not know about the journey or something. Maybe they know but they haven't seen. I have. I have seen that. I know how it feels. So maybe it would be helpful. I want to be a social worker. That's my first dream.

JMc: *I think that's really, really nice to hear. So you want to help other people? So I guess if you want to be a social worker we need to...*

Or even a support worker.

JMc: *Or a support worker. So we need to find ways to help you to achieve your dream. Don't we?*

Yes... I told them I will leave here for college. But if one day I want to come back, you have to work that for me. I want to come back to you to visit and talk to the people and say I was here.

JMc: *All right. Thank you very much for speaking to me. It's been really nice. Let me shake your hand and wish you good luck.*

Thank you.

In this chapter, I draw on data from our empirical research to reflect on how schools support their new arrivals' will to succeed. I begin by presenting a descriptive case study of Lilac Lane Academy, a school that is well known as being a centre of excellence for its work to support children from migrant backgrounds. The chapter moves on to draw on focus group discussions and interviews with practitioners. We explore how the case study settings try to help their pupils to achieve a sense of success. The chapter aims to understand how the practitioners define and reflect upon their understandings of what they do to support students who have a clear will to make successes of their educational experiences and then considers any potential obstacles to this through the application of Fraser's tripartite lenses. The final part of the chapter pulls these sections together and develops a discussion of the concept of success and succeeding as it applies to new arrivals in educational settings.

Case study – Lilac Lane Academy

Lilac Lane Academy is located in the eastern area of a university city in the south-east of England. The school sits at the end of a long street of semi-detached, mainly rented, housing off a busy arterial road which leads from the centre to the eastern edges of the city. This eastern end of the main road is characterised by takeaways and shops that reflect both the diversity and the poverty of the residents; it is a bus ride away from the tourists who come to visit the historical attractions in other affluent parts of the city. The restaurants and shops on the streets near the school reflect a history of high immigration. People from all over the globe arrive from one of the country's largest airports to seek asylum, or to look for work in the restaurants or in the factories surrounding the city; many are also employed as service workers in the two large universities or the two hospitals. Lilac Lane Academy opened in 2011 on the site of the predecessor school with around 750 pupils. By 2019, it is an oversubscribed 11-19 school with a hugely diverse student body.

First impressions: communicating success

The top half of the landing page of the website for Lilac Lane is taken up by a picture of the Principal laughing with a group of pupils in their purple uniform in the front garden of the school grounds. The picture has the strapline 'My Best Self, My Best Learning, My Best Within My Community'. This message is echoed by the welcome from the Head Boy and Head Girl underneath the picture. They emphasise that Lilac Lane *'values individuality and community'* and that all students' *'aspirations and needs'* are embraced to *'support the journey to become best versions of ourselves'*. This sense of a journey towards individual success is also empha-sised in the Principal's welcome, which focuses on how the school will provide opportunities to ensure each child can be the *'best version of ourselves'*, to *'build a passion for lifelong learning'*. This is achieved through the *'superb house system, diverse extra-curricular provi-sion, a wonderful learning environment'*, all of which is underpinned by *'pride' 'positivity and mutual respect'*.

Across the website there is a celebration of the opportunities and achievements open to the diverse multicultural school community. Whilst attention is given to academic success, with new arrivals singled out for their achievements, there is also a focus on broader conceptualisations of successes through the school's enrichment provision. The website includes an Enrichment Timetable, which illustrates the range of opportunities that are available each day, such as house drama, music, arts, tending a 'wellbeing' garden, and sports. One aspect of enrichment that stands out on the website is the provision for students to engage with poetry. Links on the website illustrate that the school has a long-standing tradition of successes in this area of expression, with a number of students winning national poetry competitions, such as the Foyle Prize and the John Betjeman competition. There are links to radio programmes showcasing this success and to an anthology of poems written by pupils, published by Picador and endorsed by the author Philip Pullman. The newsletters are on the website and the latest summer newsletter records children's successes in the following fields: public speaking, the outgoing Head Boy's published anthology of his poems, pupils' displays for the local carnival made in physics and arts, Duke of Edinburgh Awards, a German Olympiad competition, a film project involving pupils working with a professional artist, success in a national physics challenge, a Year 13 student being named City Poet of the year, four students performing poetry at a festival along with associated television and radio coverage, an art exhibition, a rugby cup and the culmination of the work of some new arrivals in the community garden. These public celebrations of such a wide range of events bring to life the vision statement on the website that Lilac Lane *'has established a success culture that we celebrate at every opportunity'*.

The school is set back from the road by a curving driveway, with trees and lawns, and the entrance is through open gates. Signs direct visitors to the reception, which is a small, welcoming room divided into two areas – on the right is the desk where visitors sign in and on the left the space opens out to a room with small armchairs for visitors. Information booklets are available in a range of languages. Around this space, on the walls and windowsill, are framed pictures and certificates celebrating events such as those listed above. On the low table, there are also newspaper and magazine clippings of similar events. The reception is a public space that communicates the various ways in which children in the school are able to participate in a range of activities. Success in a range of forms is celebrated for all to see.

Providing opportunities to celebrate success

Lilac Lane Academy is well known in the area for supporting children from a range of migrant backgrounds, including those from refugee backgrounds. There are language classes for parents who have limited English and the school's work with pupils with English as an Additional Language (EAL) is highly regarded. Ciara, the lead practitioner for the EAL department, is regularly asked to work with local teacher training providers to support new teachers in their understanding of best practice for language support for new arrivals. The progress of children with EAL is recognised in the latest Ofsted report as above the national average. Around half of the children in the main school, and some 65% of the Sixth Form, are comprised of pupils with an EAL background. The school has a high percentage of mid-year pupil admissions.

Three years ago, the school began to receive applications from bodies working with unaccompanied asylum-seeking children for them to attend the Sixth Form and responded by setting up a bespoke post-16 programme. Sally, a member of the Senior Leadership Team, explained the rationale for this decision: *'to do the right thing by a particular group of vulnerable people ... this was a really valuable addition to our school'*. The cohort of students on this programme have a base in the centre of the school for those who are unable to access the academic demands of A levels. Depending on their needs, the students follow level one or two of the school-created programme. On my first visit to Lilac Lane, I visit the Community Gardens, where a group on the first level of the programme are spending time on a range of projects working alongside members of the community. Two Syrian boys tell me that they used to grow *'oranges and plums'* in their gardens at home. Grace, the Principal, describes her visits to the gardens with the group and her words illustrate her thoughts about the importance of this kind of activity and opportunity in helping young people to experience a sense of accomplishment:

> We talked about how different, how the garden looks at different times of the year. And they put together this most amazing booklet of all the work that they've done and each of the individuals took a turn in kind of saying what their contributions were. ... They were so proud in there, that they had the plants, the seeds that they had nurtured, and that they made an impact in that garden. It had changed. They photographed it throughout each of the seasons. The pride, the pride, the sense of achievement.

The Principal is an advocate of the arts and speaks of the various ways in which the school provides opportunities for refugee pupils to take part in arts-based activities. There is a dedicated art room for them to work in and during my time in the school people speak to me about a recent initiative which involved them working with a local museum. The students were supported to analyse different artefacts and to find items that resonated with their cultural heritage; they were then involved in the making of a podcast celebrating this activity.

These are some examples of how pupils in the academy are provided with opportunities to engage with different activities in order to help them to find things in which they can excel, and to create occasions for there to be *'public celebrations'*. According to Grace, it is particularly important for new arrivals to be celebrated in these ways and to be offered a broad range of opportunities to engage with their new place and the people in it: *'that is success to me, that the students here feel comfortable being part of the community'*. The words that are repeated throughout our conversation are inclusion (*'it has to be at the heart of everything that you do'*) and pride (*'Oh my goodness the body language when you say "thank you so much you are doing a great job. I've heard good things" and they grow, they grow two inches, they grow a foot - they do - you can see the pride.'*)

Grace was not in post when the bespoke programme was established, but she sees it as an important feature of the school's inclusive work. She talks of the importance of what it symbolises for refugee pupils to have a one-to-one conversation about their successes with someone with the status of Principal and she prioritises finding opportunities to do this: *'to show the students that you are as proud of their achievements as any other achievement of any other child in school, but actually what you don't realise is that that five minute conversation can mean ten times more to that individual than it might do to any other child'*.

Sally, a member of the Senior Leadership Team, expresses similar views - that individual successes do not just happen within the classroom and are underpinned by the academy being *'inclusive of everyone and, I think, you know, the programme through the Houses, the*

House identity of the idea of caring, being the best selves we can be. You know the whole idea of having EID lunch and having Christmas lunch, not shying away from the fact we have different beliefs and different cultural backgrounds, but celebrating all of them. I think that's really important.'

Sally is responsible for teaching and learning across Lilac Lane Academy and she explains that she has to lead on accountability for the quality of provision for all pupils. With regard to the bespoke provision she explains that she has to ensure that she is continually asking of the programme, *'Are we making progress for them in order for them to be successful? And when I look at the first level and the second level, it's high quality delivery. It is making a huge difference.'* Sally emphasises that in order for the large proportion of pupils with an EAL background to experience different elements of success, it is vital that the whole school understand the work of Ciara and her team, who *'influence and share knowledge through different forums'*. The EAL department works with individual faculties, leads aspects of whole school training and advice about best practice from the EAL team has a central place within the termly teaching and learning bulletin.

Ciara, the EAL lead, has been at the academy and its predecessor school for 21 years. She recalls that when she started the school was averaging around 60 mid-term admissions a year.

> *And it does come in waves. There's no question. I mean at one stage we were saying, you know, there's a war reported in the papers and within about two months we start getting students, you know, it was really noticeable particularly with Kosovo. With Syria its very obvious, but other conflicts, you know, people would start to turn up.*

She explains that the school has *'had a reputation for working with asylum seekers and refugees since the Kosovan war'* and so social services and the refugee orientation programme in the city tend to approach them with new arrivals needing a school place. This was how the bespoke programme came about. For younger pupils who arrive during Years 7-11, Ciara and her team think carefully about how best to ensure that they will be able to achieve and flourish in the school. This means consideration of timetabling and access to the most appropriate classes. This is particularly important if the child has had a disrupted schooling experience, has limited formal education and/or is illiterate. Sometimes this means not placing them in exam classes: *'It's not an easy decision to make even then because somebody will have the counter-argument that you're depriving them of the chance to get GCSEs.'* She recalls having to make a decision like this about an Afghani boy who had no formal prior schooling and who *'was not literate in any language'*. She talks about the balancing act of providing opportunities to succeed academically and weighing this up when she feels a pupil in a high-stakes exam system is *'just doomed to fail'*. So Ciara strives to put them in the most appropriate sets and options and the heads of department are well versed in what works best in their subjects, as Ciara illustrates when she talks about a recent pupil who has joined the school and was offered a vocational pathway for one of her subjects: *'The new girl that has just arrived was down to do Sports studies and the head of PE, on her timetables she had a GCSE class, and the head of PE said "Well, actually we've already thought about that. We put her in the BTEC Sports studies class", which is actually a really good idea because she's much more likely to thrive there than in an exam-based course.'* Ciara and her team explicitly teach study skills and ways of working in groups and working independently as part of their work with new arrivals, who may have had very different prior educational experiences from the ones they encounter at Lilac Lane. Many of students that she supports in the main school stay on to study for A levels: *'there are a number of prominent sixth formers who are people who've come in from overseas, maybe three or four years ago and gone on to do really well. So the head girl in 2016-17 had been a beginner in Year 7 and became head girl and went on to a top university. And she's not the only one. There's been quite a number of people who have become quite prominent in the sixth form through sport or head boys, head girls or whatever, who have that background.'*

During our discussions, Ciara echoes what Sally and Grace say about the importance of enrichment opportunities as well as high-quality classroom experiences, especially for new arrivals who they try to point towards different activities. The school's distinctive focus on poetry is important in this respect. It has a long-standing writer in residence who runs a weekly poetry writing club for the new arrivals. As Ciara observes, *'it's great for our students to be able to participate and get recognition of their own experiences'*.

The Head Boy had been a new arrival from Nepal before starting at Lilac Lane. During his time in school, he worked closely with the writer in residence. He ends his school career as a well-known poet, winner of national competitions who is used to appearing on local and national radio and having his work published. At a summer event celebrating the successes of spoken word performances across different areas of the school, he speaks of how the range of activities he had been able to take part in at Lilac Lane had *'led him to where he is today'*. Shortly after this event, he collected his A level grades, which gained him entry to study at Oxford University.

Not all newly arrived pupils go onto achieve such high academic awards and the school helps them to find ways of achieving whatever their own goals are. Ciara and I have a series of ongoing dialogues about how the school supports pupils *'to be the best they can be'* and to feel that they can be successful. She shares a number of stories of children she has worked with over the years who have gone onto achieve their own success stories.

One of these successes was Andi, a part of the first cohort of Kosovan students that Ciara worked with over 20 years ago. Andi had arrived as a 13-year-old unaccompanied asylum seeker. Ciara recalls that he struggled to settle into school, and that his attendance was patchy. However, he did progress to college where he continued to study. He is now an established local entrepreneur, running his own business producing hand-made soaps with a shop in the city centre; he also gives talks at local schools on how to set up a business.

Ciara also spoke about Mariam, a refugee from Afghanistan who arrived in the UK with her family and started school towards the end of Year 9 with only very elementary English. Ciara remembers her as a very anxious girl who needed constant reassurance that she was making progress. Her strongest subject was art, and she liked to show teachers her *'beautifully worked sketch books'*. Her family has a background in dressmaking. *'She had a lot of support through GCSEs and took up a place in the Sixth Form, completing A Levels after three years.'* She is now in her first year of a degree in Fashion, and is particularly interested in a fusion of traditional Afghani clothes with 21st-century western design.

We also speak about Ali, who was an asylum seeker from West Africa with a *'troubled history at school: he was an angry young man who often got himself into trouble and was not easy to support'*. A couple of years ago, Ciara explains that he bumped into one of the teachers in town: he was delighted to report that he's now a trained youth worker supporting young people who are getting into trouble at school.

A current pupil, Rafal is a 16-year-old unaccompanied asylum seeker from Eritrea who *'loves to be cool and likes nothing better than to have a camera pointed at him so that he can play at being a star'.* He is currently studying elementary English and Maths at school: he enjoys it, but finds it hard to organise himself, *'preferring hanging out with friends to doing his homework'.* He recently completed a one-week course with the British Film Institute and collaborated with a group of other students to make his first short film, *'something he is very proud of'.*

Another pupil, Sara, is from Syria and came to the UK with her family on the Syrian Resettlement Programme. She joined Year 10 at school and worked incredibly hard to achieve GCSE grades good enough to qualify her for the Sixth Form. She is now studying A Levels. She is also a gifted writer who had her work published last year; she has also had her work set to music and performed by the university's orchestra. Maryam, Sara's sister, joined Year 9 and is now working hard towards her GCSEs. A year after arriving in the school with very little English, she won the Betjeman prize for her poem, an outpouring of grief for her homeland.

On one of my visits, I spend time with a group of students in the bespoke programme. They are all boys and come from Syria, Iraq, and Afghanistan. When I ask them about their future dreams they talk of being a coach driver, a mechanic, joining the army. One of the boys says, *'I just want a simple life and that's it … I will have a wife, a simple job … driving cars, maybe a taxi driver, children … I will have a small house, here in (names city). I love it here.'* I ask what he needs to do to achieve this. His response is *'Trust yourself, try and keep trying to make sure you can do it, never give up'.* Lilac Lane seems like the kind of school that will support him as he keeps trying to achieve this ambition of a *'simple life'.*

Towards success through education: debates and dialogues

> *So it's about how you get those students to have higher self-esteem and to know that what they are achieving is still a form of success.*
>
> (Focus group)

Within the field of education, success is predominantly conceived as an individual's performance in relation to academic qualifications. Indeed, during the focus group discussions, Gideon suggested that ultimately his measure of success was defined *'from the academic perspective, so doing well in your lessons and getting the learning and making progress'.* Clearly, in a system where grades count and act as currency for entry to the job market and in which schools are accountable for examination performances, then this academic conceptualisation of success has real resonance for refugee children and those who work with them in schools. However, these case study chapters have shown that new arrivals face a number of challenges and barriers to accessing the dominant knowledge in English schools' models of curricula, forms of pedagogy and modes of formal high stakes assessment. This accords with a plethora of literature critiquing the neo-liberalisation of education, the narrowing of what schools offer because of increased emphasis on standards and performance outcomes (see for example, Sahlberg 2011). Neoliberalist and more latterly neo-conservative models of education have been criticised for further marginalising vulnerable or disadvantaged groups in society (for example, Baltodano 2012). This is not just a feature of English schools: most school systems in the Global North are predicated on a model of high-stakes testing, where an individual's educational outcomes at the end of statutory schooling are an indicator of future employability and economic standing. This has particular resonance for measuring refugee children's success and their academic outcomes in terms of qualifications are usually given higher prominence by governments than are social indicators of success (Colic-Peisker 2009) such as building social relationships, although these are an early indicator of the individual's future integration into the new society. Refugee children arriving in England during the GCSE or A level stage of schooling face particular problems and school leaders face significant challenges in including new arrivals in these high-stakes year groups (McIntyre & Hall 2018).

So for the practitioners the pressures of performativity are very real. Looking back to the comments in the previous chapters about setting and streaming, the practitioners' role in ensuring that the new arrival is in the most appropriate class is closely linked to success not only in terms of integration with their peers and the establishment of future friendship groups, but also in terms of academic performance. If the students are not able to access a curriculum or setting that provides a route to GCSE or A level examination entry, then this will have consequences for their future education and employment options because, as Wilkinson points out, 'many refugee youth ... may be ineligible to participate in most post-secondary education courses due to incomplete secondary education' (2002, 173). Riana reflected on this issue and the ways in which Jasmine Gardens offered her a way forward when others seemed 'blocked':

> Coming ... with little English skills I was completely lost in my education career. This is because after doing my ESOL course in three months instead of two years my opportunities were still blocked as the further education institute hesitated to offer me a place. However Jasmine Gardens saw the potential and allowed me to take my GCSE's in year 11. I continued to work hard and pass all my GCSEs and I am currently doing my A-levels. The desire to succeed in my life has been driven by the opportunities that school has given me, coupled with my constant urge to show my gratitude to the whole of Jasmine Gardens Academy.

Riana's teacher, Amy, had worked hard to ensure that Riana could enter Year 11, which was a year below her chronological age, in order to give her an opportunity to pursue GCSEs. Each student needs a different decision according to their individual circumstances, as illustrated by Ciara's comments in the Lilac Lane case study about allowing students to experience success when otherwise they might be 'doomed to fail'. The pressures of this responsibility to make the right long-term choice are echoed by Amy:

> So there's always a dilemma for every student and I will carry an amount of guilt ... and most often, you know, you've made the right choice and the students are very happy, but then I can't help but wonder what happens beyond here when I don't see them again ... and I don't ever want to think when they are the age I am if only that teacher had made a different decision for me.

As well as streaming or setting, the new arrival's competence in the host language on their entry to the country and school is another barrier to academic success (Wilkinson 2002). The schools in this study all demonstrated exemplary practice in their EAL provision and this has meant that students identified as having EAL have performed well in high-stakes examinations in comparison with national averages. As Ciara says of Lilac Lane, '*We've been very fortunate because I think the school has really understood if they invest in EAL, they get the results.*' Despite this, students in all the schools were aware that the timing of their arrival meant that the pressures of high-stakes tests were all too real. Riana's results after a year studying GCSEs at Jasmine Gardens were incredibly impressive, yet in conversations with me she felt that they were not good enough when she compared them with her peers and with what her levels of attainment might have been in school in her home context.

During a broader discussion about what academic progress means for students who have been in the country and within the school system for a limited period, Amy summarised some of the issues:

> Sometimes teachers will say '*Ooh they're not doing very well and they are not making progress*' because they have not made the same amount of progress as UK born students. And I will say '*But they've only been in the country for a year! Have they made progress for them?*' The most recent fallout I've had is to do with careers advice because the career advisors aren't always aware of the background of the students. So it's about how you measure success and not just see it on what the data system is telling you.

As well as communicating different measures of academic success, the participants and the schools they worked in invested energy in celebrating an individual's success in a range of fields. The case study above shows that at Lilac Lane this took most prominence in public celebrations of participation and achievements in art and culture. At a time when arts are diminishing in public schools (Nussbaum 2010), these schools invest hugely in providing opportunities for their new arrivals to take part in a whole host of enrichment activities. This is because the practitioners say that it is important that schools find ways of refugee students being able to '*be authentic, to be themselves*' (Louise), as Riana does through her art work and Sara does through her poetry. As we have seen at Lilac Lane, a number of children with refugee backgrounds go on to achieve national recognition for their achievements. For new arrivals who have come from contexts with a very different ethos and for whom academic success is seen as a priority but out of reach, it is important that they have different experiences of success in their new environment. For some this might be achieved through engaging in activities that have cultural relevance to their own identities and memories of home; for others it will be through place-making activities which contribute towards successful community building, such as those outlined in Chapter 5. For the practitioners, this is about '*how you get these students to have higher self-esteem and to know that what they are achieving is still a form of success*'.

Success in a range of open-ended activities and practices challenges notions of homogenised knowledge as it is represented in high-stakes examination curricula. In so doing, it allows for equal participation in meaningful engagement (Zitcher et al. 2016) with different modes of activity, such as gardening, and with different groups of people, offering opportunities for the young new arrivals to make valued contributions to society. As Jayne from Jasmine Gardens observes, '*These children can fly and be fully contributing members of society*'. In their discussions, the practitioners shared various ways in which they had experienced their new arrivals taking part in a range of, usually enrichment, activities which helped them to begin to experience of 'being socially valued, of belonging and of being able to participate in and contribute to society' (Correa-Velez, Gifford & Barnett 2010, 19).

When education can build upon and be responsive to a new arrival's needs, interests and strengths, then it will have benefits for that individual in terms of developing agency, confidence and well-being. This draws on a 'funds of knowledge' approach where assets of individuals and the communities they represent are deliberately foregrounded by educators (Gonzalez, Moll and Amanti 2006). The teachers at Fern College talk about the strategies they used to help develop *'life skills, cooking, carpentry, problem-solving, work experience ... it's all about taking responsibility and being a responsible member of the community.'* The senior leadership team at Heather Academy describe these informal activities as going beyond formal academic provision so that the students are *'maximising their life chances'*. This broad conceptualisation of what schools can do to help students achieve successes underpins Jayne's observations: *'I think we have to be brave leaders. We have to challenge the norms and we have to keep saying to people that education is bigger than a set of league tables.'*

The practitioners in the case study schools are aware that they are providing the foundations for what they hope will be the right path for their students. Because of the students' shorter timeframe in the setting, often limited English at the start of their school experience and lack of knowledge about the English education system, the teachers know that only a limited number of refugees will end their time in the case study school with the same level of qualifications as their peers. Amy illustrates this: *'I see it as their journey begins and ends with us, but it doesn't. It obviously continues for their life path and what I want to make sure we've done is open as many possible opportunities for them as we can.'* In the discussions and during my time in the schools, this was clearly something that dominated the practitioners', and the children's, thinking. The practitioners talked about the necessity of being very explicit about this stage of the new arrival's educational journey and of the ways in which this could be built upon through further study or training. *'I think it is about being able to provide them with a route through ... so part of our responsibility is making sure that their journey doesn't end because they can't stay with us any longer'* (Jayne). Eva described a visual aid that she used to do this with the young people at Fern College. It was in the form of a ladder, which she used to demonstrate the different steps that needed to be taken to achieve academic success. In the focus group conversations, the practitioners talked about how this could be expanded to include steps towards more vocational outcomes for those refugee children who wanted to be barbers, mechanics, coach drivers. The practitioners considered that they needed to be expert in a range of options for the next step in order to help their students achieve what was described by the Lilac Lane students as a *'simple life'*.

For the practitioners, successful practice with this group of learners is about ensuring that new arrivals have experienced different aspects of success, have developed a sense of independence and self-esteem and are well enough informed to be able to make meaningful choices about what their next stages are:

> *For me, autonomy is a big part of success and if they are able to make those choices for themselves rather than having people make the decisions for them. To me, that is*

a measure of success because that is what a successful member of society would be
able to do.

(Bella)

Success through the lens of participatory parity

For new arrivals, *success* in their new context ultimately depends on their access to high-quality inclusive education because they are unlikely to arrive with ready-made economic and social networks that they can draw upon to support them to build their futures. So regardless of the pressures of performativity and the visible lack of accolades for choosing to support refugee children, school leaders need to make the decision to **(re-)distribute** resourcing in order to invest in activities which will allow refugee students to experience alternative forms of success during their time in schools. In doing so, they establish foundations for lifelong learning and develop skills for meaningful choice-making at key transition points. The case study schools in this study have an inclusive outlook that extends beyond the time the child is with them – the schools are preparing new arrivals for their possible futures. The schools see their moral duty to invest economic, material and human resources in alternative forms of success to exam results, despite knowing that these forms of success might not be used as currency in the competitive school marketplace.

Of course, this sense of positive wellbeing and belonging is enhanced by a **recognition** of the different ways in which each child can experience *success*. Again, this is linked to an asset-based approach to conceptualising different modes of valorising success. All of the strategies outlined in this chapter are underpinned by a whole-school commitment to recognition of and respect for each child. This means looking beyond the label of EAL, and re-framing what is valued in education despite the pressures of the dominant accountability metrics. It means finding ways of allowing children to experience different forms of self-expression through the arts, to join teams and participate in activities in school beyond pre-scribed test-preparation curricula and pedagogies. It means engaging in place-making activities to connect to their wider communities. These are the ways the case study schools address the barriers of misrecognition for both their refugee and asylum-seeking children; this is the model of the inclusive school they strive to create. However, there is always a sense that these practices and outcomes will not be valued by external measures of success and so the practitioners constantly have to balance how they distribute their energies between activities which will yield the all-important exam results and those which they know will be of benefit to their students now and in their futures. Finally, and perhaps most importantly, the practitioners recognise that working in a school community that is welcoming to refugee pupils means that the whole school benefits and will be positively changed as a result. Amy calls this *'a type of evolution'*. The schools in this study have worked to minimise the negative effects of privileged notions of social and cultural capital in national and dominant discourses by consciously recognising both the individual attributes of refugee children and the ways in which supporting them to live lives they and others can value will benefit wider society. Jayne summarises this when she says:

If we genuinely want to create a society where we look out for each other and people
respect each other and care for each other, then surely schools are a microcosm of that

and have a part to play in terms of building the sort of society we want for the future? That is not elitist or exclusive and it has to be made up of every community in our society. The role of the refugee in that has a long and proud history, in many ways. Different groups have come to this country and made it better and our responsibility is to take in those children and to be able to support them on their journey before they go on and support us in the future.

The strategies and approaches used to underpin success demonstrate the many ways in which *success* for children from refugee backgrounds is misrepresented in dominant discourses prioritising academic achievement in high-profile public examinations. The case study schools challenged this **representation** by offering their students a diverse set of opportunities to experience success and to consider how they could be encouraged to develop agency to shape their own successes in the future, often through taking a different route from the dominant model. These teachers' stories of working with refugee and asylum children and the stories from the young people themselves offer different representations of success. They challenge Home Office depictions of the refugee as a threat, and media depictions of the refugee as taking up our welfare resources through being needy – these children are already successes through overcoming huge adversity to make it to this point.

Succeeding as an educational concept

In English schools, the dominant discourse of success is rooted in the performativity agenda and it is indicated by achievements in external examinations; GCSEs and A levels are markers of academic achievement and are considered to be indicators of future economic and employment prospects (Benjamin 2003). However, the empirical evidence of this study counters the dominant narrative that education is all about academic attainment; instead, it offers alternative conceptualisations of educational successes which are multidimensional and indicators of future social relations and integration in the new arrivals' host society. The case study schools illustrate some ways in which children can be given experiences of succeeding in a range of forms in order to provide the foundations for self-confidence, autonomy, a positive sense of self-esteem and wellbeing. Rather than this being predicated on what Benjamin refers to as the 'consolation discourse' of success – which is 'at heart deficit' in that it is based upon an individual's measure of their own progress against themselves because they cannot compete with others in the dominant mode (ibid., 110) – the discourse of success in the practitioners' work with new arrivals in the case studies is one of empowerment and is future focused.

This notion of being future-focused is integral to conceptualising educational success for refugee students. As has been argued in previous chapters, time is experienced differently for children whose lives and education have been disrupted. So the usual markers of success, such as leaving schooling aged 16 or 18 with qualifications, are not the general experience of the new arrivals in this study. For most, the process of succeeding takes longer and the route is different. Schools working with refugee children can help them to understand this through making explicit the ways in which their pathways can be individualised and by focusing on exploring ways of helping them develop the skills to make confident and meaningful choices as they approach transitional points in their own educational journey.

Kohli describes young asylum seekers in his study as possessing the will to succeed. We have seen this too, with both the young people and the practitioners working with them striving to foster different experiences of succeeding. Kohli explains that as new arrivals grow more confident that this new home has a sense of permanency, then they can 'move more freely, more wilfully, in a planned way in circumstances they are in charge of' (Kohli 2011, 314). He goes on to say that the final stages of resuming an ordinary life involve 'reciprocation', where they can take part and contribute to society using their strengths and talents.

The schools in this study, with their future-focused ambitions, are laying the foundations for lifelong learning. This is based on a holistic understanding that throughout their lives in this new context, refugees will need to work harder to become 'ordinary' (Kohli 2011). They will need to understand the explicit rules of the dominant narratives of educational success at the same time as developing pathways into social networks and developing cultural understandings about the ways of being in their new social spaces (Morrice 2007). If they are successful in these areas then they are more likely to be able to contribute to society through 'leading lives they and others value' (Robeyns 2003).

The term success is never neutral. For refugee children, it means many different things, partly because they arrive with social and cultural capital that is different to those of their native peers, but also because success for refugee children is experienced as process. Indeed, to have safely arrived in a new country is a key indicator of success. But these children, who have often had extraordinary beginnings, are motivated by wanting more in this new context: they aim to feel settled, to belong, to contribute and to be able to achieve a sense of ordinariness with peers.

In conclusion, then, a definition of the concept of succeeding and success, viewed through the lens of education, would include the following:

> Succeeding – a dynamic concept, rather than an endpoint, illustrated when individuals feel they
>
> - can be authentic and have a positive sense of wellbeing
> - know how to make meaningful choices about next steps
> - can engage with opportunities for lifelong learning
> - are valued and able to contribute as members of society.

The schools in this study demonstrate ways of including refugee children in models of education which move beyond simply providing access to schooling. They have developed bespoke models which acknowledge the time-bounded nature of their work with newly arrived children, especially those who arrive at later stages of compulsory education. The practitioners recognise that the goal is not always to ensure swift access to mainstream because treating every child the same is not the same as ensuring an equitable education provision. They are constantly having to balance the decisions they make for each child. Even in these schools, which demonstrate an inclusive stance for their refugee pupils, there are times when pragmatic decisions have to be made. The practitioners found the lenses of redistribution, recognition and representation useful in helping them to see that their agency was at times constricted by big policies operating outside of their particular context.

This chapter concludes our focus on the operational model of resuming ordinary life through education. The concepts of safety, belonging and success have been shown to have resonance with educators in schools with a strong reputation for their work with the newly arrived refugee and asylum-seeking children. To complete Section 1, I now present a portrait of an educational provision which has been established to provide a model of holistic education for unaccompanied asylum seekers and refugees who arrive aged between 16 and 19. The design of curriculum and the ethos of the provision have been underpinned by the concepts of safety, belonging and success and by Fraser's moral framing.

References

Baltodano, M. 2012. Neoliberalism and the demise of public education: the corporatization of schools of education. *International Journal of Qualitative Studies in Education*, 25(4), 487–507.

Benjamin, S. 2003. What Counts as 'Success'? Hierarchical discourses in a girls' comprehensive school. *Discourse: Studies in the Cultural Politics of Education*,24(1), 105–118.

Colic-Peisker, V. 2009. Visibility, settlement success and life satisfaction in three refugee communities in Australia. *Ethnicities*, 92), 175–199.

Correa-Velez, I. Gifford, S. & Barnett, A.G. 2010. Longing to belong: social inclusion and wellbeing among youth with refugee backgrounds in the first three years in Melbourne, Australia. *Social Science and Medicine*, 71, 1399–1408.

Gonzalez, N., Moll, L.C. & Amanti, C. 2006. *Funds of Knowledge: Theorizing Practices in Households, Communities, and Classrooms*. New York: Routledge.

Kohli, R. 2011. Working to ensure safety, belonging and success for unaccompanied Asylum-seeking children. *Child Abuse Review* 20, 311–323.

McIntyre, J. & Hall, C. 2018. Barriers to the inclusion of refugee and asylum-seeking children in schools in England. *Educational Review*, DOI:10.1080/00131911.2018.1544115.

Morrice, L. 2007. Lifelong learning and the social integration of refugees in the UK: the significance of social capital. *International Journal of Lifelong Education*, 26(2), 155–172.

Nussbaum, M. 2010. *Not for Profit: Why Democracy Needs the Humanities*. Woodstock: Princetown University Press.

Robeyns, I. 2003. Is Nancy Fraser's critique of theories of distributive justice justified? *Constellations*, 10(4), 538–553.

Sahlberg, P. 2011. *Finnish Lessons*. New York: Teachers College Press.

Wilkinson, L. 2002. Factors influencing the academic success of refugee youth in Canada. *Journal of Youth Studies*, 5(2), 173–193.

Zitcher, A., Hawkins, J. & Vakharia, N. 2016. A capabilities approach to arts and culture? Theorizing community development in West Philadelphia. *Planning Theory & Practice*, 17(1), 35–51.

7 A bespoke model of inclusive education for new arrivals

Joanna McIntyre

Update from Gare

My interview with Gare took place during his last week at 'Fern'. It was the end of the academic year and Gare had decided to move to the larger city Further Education college rather than stay for a second year at Fern. Three months later, when the autumn term was well underway, Gare contacted one of the teachers at Fern and told her he wanted to visit them all, but was worried that he wouldn't be welcome. He said he would never forget what Fern had done for him. The teacher said their conversation ended with the following exchange:

Gare: I'm not part of the family anymore.
Louise: Yes you are. The family just keeps growing.

Louise commented that it was particularly striking to her that Gare used the term 'family'. Gare had said he would never be placed in a foster family as they could not replace his family back home.

First impressions - a mini-portrait of life at Fern

Nestled behind a large fenced tennis court enclosure in a portable building is the classroom where Gare found the group he could refer to as his 'family'. The wire fencing of the tennis court has been covered with large canvases displaying the student' graffiti-style artwork with the name of the provision and the values. There is also evidence of gardening endeavours, most marked by a freshly decorated disused rowing boat which has been re-used as a herb planter. There are a few steps leading up to the Portakabin building, which is surrounded by trees; the sounds of the nearby primary school breaktime can be heard through the branches.

It is a Thursday morning and the young people are working on their maths worksheets. They are preparing for their upcoming exams - and all are working at different levels of qualification. James is leading the lesson and there is a quiet buzz of activity which is briefly interrupted by me entering the room. I say hello to some of the children that I have got to know during my visits and note a couple of new faces. I move to the table at the back of the room next to the kitchen area where there are some freshly baked cakes on the surface. From this vantage point I reflect on how the space has been reconfigured over the nine months that the provision has been operating. It has transformed from a functional but unused teaching area to a place that represents the young people who spend their weekdays within it. Along the wall of the kitchen area is a large map of the world with markers indicating where each young person's journey started. The first two markers were placed in Iran and Iraqi Kurdistan, by December there were seven more markers placed in Afghanistan, Eritrea, Sudan, and Syria. Now there are also markers from Vietnam, Ethiopia and The Gambia. There are now 16 students in the room.

There are bookshelves with reading books and board games and comfortable seating around the edges of the teaching space. There is also a small pool table and I spot another addition to the room since my last visit, a portable piano keyboard. In the middle of the room, the young people are working at their desks and this part of the room has a more formal classroom atmosphere. From these desks the young people can see posters and photographs reflecting different activities that have taken place since the provision opened in the September of that year – wood sculpting, theatre visits, bread-making in a local windmill, bike maintenance, trips to different parts of the city and into the countryside.

James draws the maths lesson to a close as it is lunchtime. Some of the young people go with James to the school canteen whilst others stay and make their own lunch in the kitchen area. A couple of the young people have demonstrated that they are excellent cooks; today one is reheating food they prepared at home to share with the others. I ask about the cakes and they were made by the same boy who has become well known in the group for his baking skills – today's are semolina cakes. Over lunch I ask the children about their recent work experience, Silvana, who for a while was the only girl in the class, has been in the kitchens at the school for her work experience – she laughs as she tells me she had to cook English food *'pizza and pasta with tomato sauce'*. Eva, the teacher who organised the work experience, tells me that Hao, a quiet Vietnamese boy, also had a placement in the kitchen which was so successful that they encouraged him to look into an apprenticeship. She says he has since visibly grown in confidence. Four of the boys had been to a music studio for their placement, one of them is now playing on the keyboard with his friend sitting next to him listening to him play. Some of the others have been to primary schools and Aisha tells me that she now wants to be a primary teacher. After they finish their lunch they drift to the sofas and chat quietly whilst knitting or listening to music on the portable stereo. Eva tells me that following the work experience week most have returned *'much more chatty and asking lots of questions'*, explaining that this is due to their feeling more confident. She recalls that Hao said to her *'all the people on my work experience told me they understand me and I can talk to a stranger now'*.

The others drift back from the canteen and James and Eva start moving the furniture for the start of the next lesson – drama. Paul, the drama teacher, arrives and after sitting and chatting to some of the students he brings the group together for a verbal warm-up game. The young people stand in a circle and begin repeating English tongue twisters, they giggle at the silliness of their friends' faces as they contort to produce the strange sounds. As I leave the young people's laughter can be heard across the tennis courts.

Setting the context, establishing the moral frame

Fern is a bespoke education provision for 16-19-year-old new arrivals in a city in the Midlands. Its inception is interesting and worth explaining here in some detail. Since 2010, the Department for Education has had responsibility for both children's services and education, meaning that it has oversight of the work of schools, colleges and also those who work with children in social care, such as unaccompanied asylum seekers and refugee children. In 2018, local authorities were invited to bid for funding for projects to support unaccompanied asylum seekers through the Ministry of Housing, Communities and Local Government's 'Controlling Migration Fund'. This is government funding targeted at helping local authorities respond to the impact of recent migration on their communities. The Fern college bid was successful and the funding led to a pilot bespoke full-time post-16 educational provision for unaccompanied asylum-seeking young people in the city. As far as we are aware, a full-time educational provision for this group of young people is unique within the country. There was felt to be an increasingly urgent need for something like this within the city.

In the two-year period before Fern College was established, the Swedish-English research project mentioned in Chapter 1 was exploring the extent to which new arrivals accessed education provision in each country. During this process, it became clear that young people arriving aged between 16 and 19 were particularly marginalized from formal education and from elements of social life in their new contexts. In order to understand this better from the English perspective, we met with headteachers, city education experts, local charities, voluntary groups and NGOs. Through engaging with a local NGO which worked with refugees and asylum seekers in the city, we made contact with a number of teenage new arrivals struggling to build 'ordinary lives' in England after long periods of movement since leaving their homes. The NGO explained that few refugees arriving at that age would be able to find a place in a Sixth Form to study for A level qualifications so they advised new arrivals to register with the local further education college for ESOL classes. However, funding limitations meant that the 200 places available on these programmes were not enough to meet the needs such that by May 2018, there were 90 young people on the college waiting lists. According to the NGO, the college tried to compensate for this by offering additional classes outside of the usual sessions to offer students 7.5 hours of ESOL provision a week. The NGO, working with its own limited funding (a time limited grant from Comic Relief), had put together a package of programmes for small groups. The nature of the funding meant that these were short-term part-time projects rather than sustained consistent education provision.

I shared these concerns with Anna, who at the time was working for the local authority in a position with key responsibility for supporting schools and pupils with EAL needs, and with Nick, a headteacher. Both had been involved in the work with Sweden where we had seen first-hand the work of a vocational college with 16–19-year-old new arrivals. Following this visit, we met to explore possible ways forward for children arriving at that age in the city. Nick's school was part of a large trust which was sympathetic to the issues we raised and there followed a series of meetings to explore possible funding streams to open a post-16 provision for new arrivals on the site of Nick's school. However, the specific requirements of requiring students to meet external assessment outcomes meant that it was difficult to conceive of how to fund a post-16 provision where students from a diverse range of educational experiences and backgrounds, arriving at different points throughout the year would be able to meet these outcomes. In Fraser's model, the lack of recognition of the specific needs of this marginalized group in educational policy had a direct impact on distribution of funding for educational provision to meet the needs of this marginalized group.

Whilst these conversations were going on, young people continued to arrive in the city seeking support from the NGO. Sebhat, a 17-year-old Eritrean who had been waiting ten months for a school or college place said that he had nothing else to do all week and so stayed in his room in semi-independent accommodation apart from the few hours he attended an eight-week part-time arts project and a weekly youth club run by the NGO. He had trouble sleeping and suffered with recurring headaches, and was later diagnosed with post-traumatic stress disorder (PTSD) linked to experiences he had encountered on his solo journey across Libya before reaching Europe. When Sebhat felt he could leave his room, he went to church, the NGO youth group's weekly meeting, and the local library where he tried to work on his understanding of the English alphabet. He said he relied on the NGO to signpost him to opportunities to fill his time. He was finding it difficult to make connections with the others in the shared house who were much older than him. He said he was feeling lonely and spent much of his time isolated from others. He was hopeful that he would be able to access more hours at college in the next academic year.

Sebhat's experiences reflect national concerns about both social isolation and a lack of appropriately funded education provision for new arrivals, a particularly vulnerable group of young people, especially those with no family support or network.

> Unaccompanied migrant children are some of the most vulnerable children in the country, potentially at risk of modern slavery, sexual exploitation, forced criminality, organ harvesting, human trafficking, forced labour. They are unlikely to be certain of their rights and of whom they can trust. Local authorities have a duty to protect these highly vulnerable children in society … support will be most effective through a stable, continuous relationship with the child.
>
> (extracts from DfE Statutory Guidance 2017)

Conversations with the local authority in the city illustrated that our findings concurred with what was becoming its pertinent area of concern too. Anna and other educational leads in the city and the virtual school headteacher were trying to find solutions that would address safeguarding concerns and help young people in this age group begin or resume education or training to enable them to settle to lives in the city. It was within this context that the call from the Controlling Migration Fund (CMF) came for project bids to support Unaccompanied Asylum-Seeking Children (UASC) into education to help them to attain positive outcomes. The city successfully bid for CMF project funding to provide full-time bespoke provision for unaccompanied asylum seekers aged 16–19. The two-year funding allocation was to establish a pilot model of education provision and academics from the university were involved in discussions about the design and nature of the provision from its inception. Anna, who led on the bid from the city for the funding, was aware of the theoretical framings for the work with Sweden. Anna became manager of the project and was open to considering how the provision could reflect Kohli's concepts which were used to structure the interviews for prospective staff for the provision. Three staff members were appointed, Louise and Eva to work part-time with James, who was to provide full-time provision. Louise reflected during a later conversation that discussing Kohli's concepts at this early stage really appealed, *'That's what really excited me in the interview. I really want to make sure that we don't move away from that.'*

A condition of the Controlling Migration Funding was that there would be regular updates and monitoring reports to the Department of Education. Anna produced these each term and submitted them to the officials at the DfE who had national oversight of the projects. These officials were from the Safeguarding team at the DfE. There were also regular project board meetings with officials from the DfE and representatives from the different projects which were held in London. Whilst there was a requirement to report on progress in relation to original milestones outlined in the funding bids, there was a sense of autonomy over what these were as long as they met the brief 'to support UASC into Education to help them attain positive outcomes'. This meant that Anna felt empowered to make decisions about the distribution of material and human resources in considering the design of the provision. She worked closely with people within the city council to better understand how the students could access different resources such as the vulnerable student bursary. This led to her having knowledge of different funding streams in very different ways from practitioners in mainstream settings with its *'mysterious'* funding, as described in Chapter 3. Utilizing these funds allowed her to ensure that each student could buy a transport pass which meant that not only could they afford to travel (what were for some students long distances) each day to attend the provision, but also they could use public transport to attend the differing enrichment activities that were built into the curriculum design. The Trust, which had been so involved in trying to support earlier plans for a similar post-16 facility, donated the physical space for the provision and the three newly appointed teachers became staff members of the Trust. In this way the distribution of resources, a shared endeavour between Anna as project manager, the city and the Trust ensured that newly arriving young people would have access to a bespoke educational provision regardless of when they arrived in the school year.

Anna and her newly appointed team represented a combined set of experiences of teaching refugee and asylum-seeking children in different contexts. They were expert practitioners and Anna especially had unique insights and understandings of policy contexts outlined in Chapter 3, where there had been a focus on supporting children from diverse cultural backgrounds with a culturally responsive pedagogical approach and awareness of the importance of maintaining a multilingual repertoire. In this sense, Fern College was well positioned to offer a curriculum that was cognisant of the needs of the students with which it would be working. In a later conversation, Anna explained that she also felt it was important that:

> the staff working in the provision have a really good knowledge and understanding of the context that young people are coming from and how diverse that might be. So they need to know something about the countries that they are coming from and the sets of circumstances. You can almost start to predict a little bit what their experiences might have been and whether they might have had a decent amount of education or none at all and whether they are likely to be literate in their first language or not.

The team developed thorough processes to work with each new student in order to 'not only assess what they can and can't do in English and numeracy but, using an interpreter, [...] to get to know as much as possible about the young person'. In these ways, the provision was established to recognise the assets and particular needs of each member of the cohort. Mindful of the need to ensure that this reflected the cultural values of the groups who would be represented in the provision, Anna and the team also consulted expert voices in the local communities who were from refugee backgrounds or who worked closely with refugee and asylum-seeking young people. This intensive activity at the start of the project was built upon through the continued dialogue with the Advisory Group, a body set up to ensure that the provision met its objectives to offer a quality holistic education provision for older new arrivals in the city. The Advisory Group comprised a senior academic with expertise in refugee education, a consultant child and adolescent psychiatrist with expertise in young asylum seekers and mental health, an academic specializing in law for unaccompanied young asylum seekers and refugees, the city's virtual school headteacher and a representative from a social housing service specializing in working with unaccompanied new arrivals in semi-independent accommodation.

Through these measures, the provision was established to offset the 'barriers that prevent some people from participating on a par with others' (Fraser 2007, 27) in order to offer an inclusive educational experience for its young people.

Throughout the life of the provision, Anna and her team were receptive to working with academics and other 'experts' to shape the design and to evaluate the strengths and weaknesses of the approach at Fern College. The following sections of this chapter outline some of the key characteristics of the provision as observed through a sustained series of interactions with key individuals, visits to the provision and reports to the termly meetings of Fern's Advisory Group and monitoring reports for the Department for Education.

A curriculum for safety, belonging and success

Different expertise was drawn upon in the early conversations about the curriculum design for the provision. These included former and current members of the support team for new arrivals within the city, the virtual school headteacher, representatives from the refugee youth project at the NGO, and the practitioners who between them had considerable expertise in the field of EAL and mainstream teaching. UNESCO's four pillars of learning (Delors 1996) were considered alongside the concepts of safety, belonging and success. This resulted in a curriculum that combined academic subjects with a range of experiential learning opportunities. There were some key distinguishing features, namely:

- This is a full-time holistic provision
- The academic programmes are bespoke to the needs of individual learners so, for example, assessment of current English proficiency does not determine what level the student works with in other subjects
- There are two assessment points each year for external accredited programmes to allow for individualized progression
- Students can immediately access the curriculum regardless of what point in the year they join the provision
- The academic programme is enhanced by planned activities designed to foster relational, cultural and social learning
- As well as the planned curriculum there is in-built flexibility to adapt to opportunities for short- and medium-term enrichment programmes

- This is all underpinned by a commitment to place-making activities which take the group to different community groups and invite members of the community into the provision fostering a sense of familiarity with, connection to and engagement with the city
- The curriculum is evaluated in relation to safety, belonging and success and the UNESCO four pillars of learning
- Each pupil is assigned a key worker from the team of teaching staff who regularly liaises with external partners working with the child and crucially checks in with the child each day
- Attendance is monitored daily and non-attendance is followed up immediately to ensure students are supported if they face issues preventing them from coming to the provision each day
- Support for mental health is a key component, comprising group 'circle time', opportunities for one-to-one counselling sessions for students, the establishment of peer support programme for the practitioners
- Staff professional development is a feature of the project encompassing the education of new arrivals, supporting children with backgrounds of trauma, and the legalities of the UK immigration system
- There are regular meetings of the Advisory Board comprising expertise from the fields of education, children's mental health, law and social care.

We closed each of the preceding case studies in Chapters 4–6 with a summary of characteristics that define safety, belonging and success in relation to an inclusive model of education for refugee and asylum-seeking children. For ease of reference the definitions are reproduced in the text below with a few illustrative examples from the empirical data of how far the provision can be said to meet the criteria. The quotations come from one-to-one interviews with some of the students, with each of the practitioners, and from an evaluation meeting at the end of the first year where they reflected on how far the provision has met the aim of fostering safety, belonging and success.

Safety

In Chapter 4**, safety was defined as a multifaceted concept permeating life in and out of the educational setting.** In conversations with the teachers, it was clear that they have insights into their lives outside of the school day knowing who was living where and when issues outside of Fern were likely to impact the young person's experiences in the educational setting. They had regular interactions with social workers and accompanied their students to medical appointments and to meetings about their legal status. One female student was experiencing issues with her shared accommodation and Anna visited the home to try and help her to work through the problems. They explicitly told the young people that they were interested in their lives outside of the setting. According to our definition, safety is supported by having **a physical safe space.** The building described at the beginning of the chapter is located within the grounds of a mainstream school, initially the students had to sign in and out at the school reception but this process has now changed so that students wear lanyards, which means they can enter the school gates and access the Fern building. This all represents a sense of security, something that some students feel quite acutely,

> I remember one student had an issue that he didn't feel safe walking the streets, his support worker used to drop him off for a period of time. This was due to his past – child slavery. So FERN literally was a place of physical safety. I then remember at his final LAC[1] meeting where he thanked everyone who had worked with him and said he feels strong enough to deal with life without much support now. (Louise)

A further characteristic of safety outlined in Chapter 4 is, **creating environments for trust building, experiential learning; talking (or choosing not to) about their experiences; social and emotional learning; risk-taking.** During the evaluation meeting at the end of the year, the teachers reflected that this had been achieved by an emphasis on providing a range of activities that helped the students to feel that they could trust the adults in the provision and also their fellow students. Drama and dance activities, alongside projects such as visits to the climbing wall, helped the young people to build trust through a range of experiential learning which also incorporated elements of risk taking. One of the principles that was quickly established within the staff team was that it was important not to ask the individual students directly about their journeys of forced migration. As Anna reflected, '*they need the permission not to talk about their stories and their journeys. So they know there is a safe space to talk at any time but we would never ask ... on principle we don't ask our students any searching questions because they have to answer those questions so frequently in other situations.*'

A key area of the work of the provision that distinguishes it in many ways from mainstream settings is the staff's focus on mental health. The staff were acutely aware that the students were engaged in daily struggles '*combatting loneliness*'. They felt an important element of their work was to ensure that the students practiced self-care and that this included supporting others in the group. An issue that the practitioners had not necessarily anticipated, but regularly encountered was that individual students experienced recurring sensations of guilt. For many, this was encountered early on when they realized that they had reached a place of safety where they could be supported to begin building their lives in this new context. They experienced a sense of guilt as they recalled all they had left behind. At other times, they observed it when students caught themselves enjoying an activity or experience, '*I feel guilty sometimes if I'm having fun*'. This is illustrated from the following observation by James as he reflected on the emotional aspects of the work in the provision:

> I think we try to create an environment where it's okay to I guess to be yourself but to kind of to be vulnerable as well ... we kind of try to make it okay to be struggling. You know when you ask someone are you okay? It's just 'I'm fine' is the answer isn't it? But I think we try to at times try to kind of probe that it's actually okay to not be fine. And I think a few students, like one recently is very angry and he just got his [legal] status [official leave to remain]. But he just said I feel very angry and I don't understand why. And we were talking to him about it's okay to feel angry and to feel like you don't want to come to school and to feel that you are sad. You get that feeling that students feel they have to be grateful or they have to you know be happy in the provision and I think at times we

do have to kind of make them aware that it's normal to feel, you know, different feelings and we feel them the same. And, you know, I think that that's something that we just … it's something that we started to notice with various students, that idea maybe it's something Louise will explore further with them.'

Louise was an experienced teacher of EAL who was also in the final stages of a Master's qualification in Counselling. After a few months, with the support of her university supervisor, she established a programme of one-to-one counselling for students along with some group circle therapeutic sessions. Her supervisor also worked with the team of practitioners to support their understanding of working with children who had experienced trauma and conflict. Louise said that she used metaphors in the student group sessions to try and give the young people tools for dealing with their concerns. She talked about how people put on a mask to hide their feelings and present a version of themselves to the world and about how everyone in the provision came with their own emotional back packs. She reflected that one of the students said to her, '"I think our backpack is much bigger" and that kind of clarified it for me and it almost felt like he was saying to me that we don't totally get what they're going through.'

Our earlier definition of safety was also characterized by **consistent and explicit expectations, high aspirations, with understanding that mistakes/misunderstandings will occur.** The practitioners at Fern were aware that their students had varying experiences of formal education and had different starting points and so there was a need to be very explicit about expectations, I observed the practitioners using a constant meta-talk about what they were asking of the students which is a characteristic of EAL teaching. Each practitioner talked of the potential of their students and there was a clear sense of ambition for their futures, along with a recognition that part of their role was to be clear about life in British society both for future work prospects and for living in their new communities harmoniously. In the evaluation meeting the team spoke of their aim to foster an '*understanding of the diversity of British society and different opinions and attitudes and treatment of people, and things like those skills that you need to learn to be a good employee and a good citizen.*'

The behaviour within the provision was generally good, though there were occasions when the staff had to intervene because of a cultural misunderstanding or small area of conflict. Eva reflected that on one occasion when there had been an issue between some of the boys, Gare could see from the teachers' facial expressions that they were upset. This was reflected in Gare's interview, where he said that even when they had been '*bad*' the teachers were always '*good*' and '*kind*', supporting Eva's comment that '*we want them to be able to be a responsible member of the community and this is a micro community of what they have to be in society*'. Through all of this it goes without saying that the provision demonstrated that the group of young people had **advocates (peers, teachers and SLT),** not only those who worked with them daily but also the community members they met during their different activities. In the first year of the pilot, the Trust was committed to finding more public advocates and a number of high-profile visitors came to the provision, including the Mayor, leaders of the council, the local newspaper and Prince Harry.

The final characteristic in our definition of safety, **understanding how this current context will fulfil present needs and prepare for future ambitions** could be illustrated in a range of different ways. In interviews with the students, it was clear that they felt they had made real progress with their understanding of English, of life in their new city and in terms of academic qualifications. They could articulate what their next steps were and there was a sense that future ambitions were achievable without a feeling that they were running out of time. This was partly achieved by an exercise Eva carried out with the group, where she used the visual of a ladder to show how the programmes at Fern College compared with mainstream programmes, emphasizing that people make different rates of progress with the ladder and that whilst they might be a few rungs behind now there would be opportunities in the future to make up the steps.

Silvana's experiences of safety at Fern

Silvana joined Fern in December last year after arriving in England with her younger sister. She had attended school in Eritrea until grade 8. Teachers at the provision said she arrived with a good background level of education and knowledge of English, though she was stronger in reading and writing than in speaking and listening, '*I can write and read English but in Eritrea I learn English translated by my language and so I can't talk. Because all teachers are Eritrean and explain in my Tigrinya not in English.*' She enjoyed school, especially social sciences with History being her favourite subject. She had lived in a refugee settlement in Ethiopia for 14 months. Recently, she has shared the terrible conditions she experienced in the underground camp which was rife with hunger, disease and death. When she arrived at Fern she was keen to re-establish her studies and has an appetite for learning. She is always the first to arrive and has 100% attendance. For a while she was the only girl in the class. However, her academic ability meant that she quickly gained the respect of the others and she is often seen chatting with the boys in the group. Anna explained that Silvana had been reunited in the city with an uncle and an aunt but that they believed that the accommodation is overcrowded (she and her sister sleep in the living room). During her first months in the provision the staff observed that her clothing and personal hygiene were not always good. Her hair had been cut short and she was very self-conscious so wore a woolly hat all the time. These things also made her stand out as different and less '*part of things*'.

Because she lives with family members, Silvana does not have access to the allowances others in the group have as UASC. She stood out as having fewer material possessions and less money – for example, she has no bus pass. Other students soon became aware and the staff witnessed several occasions when they would find ways to help her e.g. the class winner of a £10 reward voucher gave it to Silvana. She quickly adapted to life in Fern and seems very comfortable in the classroom. When she arrives in the morning she now uses one of the laptops to listen to her favourite Eritrean musicians, since she has no internet access at home. Anna observed that since the start of the second year Silvana has become firm friends with a recent new arrival: '*this relationship has done wonders for Silvana and as the number of girls has grown to 9 in the class, they are becoming a large circle of friends with Silvana included although still*

> *more quiet than others.'* Her level of self-care improved over time, she has new clothes, and her hair has grown out so that she often wears it in plaits.
>
> At the end of her first year at Fern as with all the other students she was given the opportunity to apply for a place at the FE college. James accompanied her on the interview. Her teachers were sure she would cope academically at the further education college, but Silvana declined the offer opting to stay at Fern for another year. *'In college you are not there for a lot of time. Maybe two or three afternoons. I don't like it. Fern is friendly and it is all day. I like it.'* Silvana said she was looking forward next year to getting her own work done and then helping the teachers to help those who were new and working at lower levels. When asked about her future ambitions, Silvana said she did not know: *'maybe a teacher';* she just knew she would always want to be learning.

Belonging

At the end of Chapter 5 we defined **belonging as a multilayered concept** with the first descriptor listing a range of relational markers, **based on opportunities for developing positive relationships: with self; with peers (in and out of school); with communities (in and out of school); with place and with the new society.** Throughout visits to the provision since its inception, it has become clear that supporting the young people to build different kinds of positive relationships has been key to the ethos of belonging. These involved group activities in different part of the city and with different community members in the classroom. There were also organic activities such as small groups cooking lunch together each day or playing music together which helped engender a sense of belonging to their newly formed community within Fern. A key aspect of being able to build relationships with others in these ways is a sense of positive wellbeing. In the section on safety the examples of activities designed to promote self-care are also important contributors to individual's positive relationship with self through explicit acts designed to foster self-esteem and wellbeing. In the evaluation meeting, the practitioners reflected on how they had managed to work with students in this way,

> *With the mental health thing it is very difficult to measure because it is an individual thing and we obviously know when they are very low but what is a flourishing human? We're not going to solve all their psychological problems but if we can say that they've gone away with a positive sense of wellbeing ... and knowing how to maintain that, then we've done our job.*

For this group of young people (re)building positive self-esteem after experiences of trauma and journeys where they have experienced fear and victimization is clearly very important. Through staff taking time to build pastoral relationships with each individual it is clear that the young people feel 'known' by the teachers and by the others in the group. There are frequent references to feeling part of the *'family'* that Gare was anxious to still feel part of after he had left the provision. This was highlighted in Louise's observation that she found herself wanting to *'mother'* the students but that she needed to remind herself not to label the individuals as victims, that for many the fact they had successfully made it to here was a marker of their strength:

> *There must be a determination and if we just think about the skills that they must have had just to actually get here. All of the things that they've gone through which most sixteen year olds wouldn't have gone through and, yes, that has probably had a negative or traumatic impact but, actually, there would have been a lot of growth through that as well. I think it is important to acknowledge the two parts: yes there is trauma and suffering but also the independence and determination and some resilience. I often think I have to be mindful not to patronise them because they've managed to get here by themselves so they don't need me to mother them. So the nurturing needs to be balanced with acknowledging that they've had to be pretty grown up to do what they've done because they've had to be like adults already.*

The second of our descriptors of Belonging in Chapter 5 was **signifiers of belonging (uniforms, badges, participation in events, activities, exhibitions, teams) along with locational and relational ties.** There were obvious examples of this which have already been mentioned and James summarizes how this was achieved at Fern in the following comment:

> *I think maybe the provision you know it does provide that that place of belonging, that we are all parts of it, we are a team. We kind of try to talk about this building, this classroom being like that so we were doing pronouns today, possessive pronouns and we talked about Fern. So who's whose is Fern's classroom? And they all said ours. And I think they feel that very much. It's not, you know, the teachers' provision. It's theirs and I think you know, we've always tried to stress that with them. That it is theirs. You know, we wear our lanyard, and we're part of something. And I think, I think that that's important for them. And then I think it goes obviously beyond, you know there is that sense of belonging to a city. So I think as we've tried to take them out into the city, we're trying to develop that sense that it is theirs as well. They're not a kind of visitor. It is their city. And I think just students have said that it seems like a lot of them feel like they're very accepted.* (James)

The final of our descriptors in the definition of Belonging is **that it is a dialogic process (involving others as well as the individual). It is enhanced by making the implicit explicit - understanding of codes and rules, clear signposts and resources for navigating an education system and societal norms; developing individual assets to promote a feeling of being valued; teaching tolerance, promoting difference; working with peers to create a new society where we belong together; preparing for their future and forming hopes and goals for life.**

All of the above is enhanced through the holistic design of the provision which is underpinned by a pedagogical approach to continually have a meta-commentary about the purposes of what they are doing to help the new arrivals understand how this is an aspect of life in their new context. All of the students had work experience in different institutions in the city and for some this was life-changing as they experienced fitting into a workplace. As Eva commented, '*the work experience is the culmination of all those other bits of work that we've done. It was almost like the proof that they can do it*'.

The enrichment programme allows the students to get out into different communities in the city, to begin to feel able to build connections with others to feel part of their new place. Unlike some of the students in earlier chapters who found it difficult to make friends with their peers in their new schools, this group of students made friendships with each other, what they all had on common with this peer group was learning how to live in their new society. As new members of the class arrived, they were quickly inducted by their new peers into life at Fern. For some students, these friendships continued outside of the classroom where, like other teenagers in their city, they met up for social activities. For example, some went to the gym together, some went to worship together, two girls began to meet each Sunday at a local library to work on homework together after they went on a visit to the library with Fern. The teachers felt that a key aspect of this was to encourage individuals to have respect for their differences as well as their similarities '*to not feel like you're different whilst not losing yourself and your culture*'. Increasingly, they could see that the young people were through the provision, '*having an anchor in terms of friendship and identity*'.

For the most part, the young people were welcomed by members of the host community as they met them during their enrichment activities in the city. Gare did have a difficult experience before he was given his travel pass when a bus driver challenged his age and then made some racist remarks. He discussed this with the teachers at Fern. And James remembered how upsetting this had been. He said, '*I've got the bus with them before and there's a couple of times where you know the way people talk to them. Sometimes you can sense there is that they don't seem to see it. So obviously there's nothing really overt, I think but it's more that questioning. You know, why are you here? What are you here to get?*' But James felt that the young people generally had positive experiences. The biggest threat to belonging to the community outside of Fern was when decisions were made about an upcoming decision about their legal status or changing a young person's accommodation. Some had been moved four times in the short time they had been at Fern and James said it was really marked if they were re-housed in communities with less diversity, '*... like there's one that lived in (a multi-ethnic area) and when he moved, he got very down and part of it was he didn't have his local shop. He didn't have his local food and suddenly he's not in his community anymore. I mean he's moved to its not the worse place to be. But in terms of his culture it is. He said I can't go to the barbers or I can't get any of my food that I like from the local shops ... for him, he's lost everything else if that makes sense?*' James went onto say that two new Kurdish students had just arrived in the provision and were being housed in a different part of the city so that the other Kurdish students were planning to show them where to go to find Kurdish shops, food and the barbers.

This sense of belonging is very complex and the teachers felt that different students experienced weaker and stronger feelings of belonging with the wider society during their time at Fern. They gave the example of Gare who they felt was desperate to fit into English society. At one point during a letter-writing activity, Gare wrote that as soon as his English was good enough he was going to pretend he wasn't Kurdish. They contrasted this with another student, who was clear that he would always identify as Kurdish and that he felt he could live in England and still do that. Whereas with Gare, '*he said that he wouldn't tell people that he was*

Kurdish because he wants to be treated like a British person.' When Gare was feeling more positive about feeling valued in his interactions with the wider society outside of Fern, the teachers observed that he like many of the others wanted to *'give back to the place that has welcomed them'*. The teachers recalled one occasion when they were walking through the city centre with Gare and some of the others. Gare noticed a homeless man was struggling to hold his possessions and so went up to him, helped him with his sleeping bag and coat and gave him some change. The teachers observed that this compassion came from direct experience of being outside of society, *'When you think of how the homeless are damned by the majority of the population but those kids had been there themselves. They can't just walk by and not help.'*

Success

At the end of the previous chapter we defined succeeding as **a dynamic concept, rather than an endpoint, illustrated when individuals feel they can be authentic and have a positive sense of wellbeing, know how to make meaningful choices about next steps, can engage with opportunities for lifelong learning, are valued and able to contribute as members of society.**

The ethos of Fern College is one of nurturing positivity. Previous examples in the chapter illustrate how each of the descriptors in the definition above have been met and to avoid repetition I summarize with the observation that staff and students constantly look for ways of celebrating individual successes and that success takes a variety of forms. Students are encouraged to be proud of their identity and to develop positive self-esteem. Rewards are given at the end of each term which reflect a nuanced understanding of different markers of individual and group success. James observes, *'being collaborative. It's just as important as you know, being successful individually. And I think the students do feel that. They feel that if someone's not achieving or they're kind of struggling I think other students do ... they want them all to come through. They want them to come through as a group. It feels like that.'*

The students are proud of their achievements and those of others. In individual interviews, students were able to demonstrate that they knew how to seek support for the pathways into the next stages of their life and education in their city. They saw education as a long-term process and many had clear goals and ambitions. There were numerous examples of the ways in which they were valued by each together, by the staff at Fern, by leaders of the Trust and by all visitors to the provision.

In the evaluation meeting, the staff tried to sum up what they felt would be indicators of success:

> *I think for us or for me [success] is to see them starting to kind of I guess flourish more yes I think it is like a flower metaphor maybe I would use and starting to see them grow and blossom. And I think for them, maybe they feel that success is getting their papers or getting the status and the people get that and then realize I still don't feel maybe how I want to feel or you know...*
>
> *I think it's the success stories ... they've got a future, they've got hope, they've got something that they are aiming towards. They've got some resolution kind of with their*

past and they are independent, you know, as much as an 18 year old can be. And I think you know the student we went to an award ceremony with? He said I've got a question I need to ask you and it was about how to pay for electricity and gas online, you know how to set your account up. So I think compared to the kind of questions he was asking, you know, six months prior, it was just such a normal kind of worry.

But yes, I think I think it's trying to have that sense of wellbeing. I think it's different for every student I would think, but if the student leaves with maybe just those normal psychological kind of anchors so to speak that they feel they can start to be who they are or they can explore who they are. They can start to think about having a secure future, whatever direction that that is. They're not relying on us, you know particularly.

For some students, these experiences of safety, belonging and success seemed to be experienced in a linear fashion, whilst for others it was a more complicated process. The practitioners shared their perceptions of how Ajmal and Rasheed's stories are brief illustrations of this:

Ajmal's experiences of safety, belonging and safety during his time at Fern College

Ajmal is a good example of someone whose experience has been quite linear because he came in very shell-shocked and very nervous and he didn't say much and seemed quite scared. He was very fragile; but we wouldn't put that label on him now. He had that look people associate with pictures of World War One: that haunted look and physical shakes which he still gets at times. When he arrived we had a few students by that point and the atmosphere that existed was stable. It was very friendly and very nurturing. So he came into that and just accepted it. He began to build friendships with some of the other boys and now he has a really good friendship group. And that seems to have allowed him to be himself because he has got such a personality and a sense of humour which has started to come through. He's not your typical masculine boy and does not join the other Kurdish boys when they are at the gym and then they go to the Mosque on Friday. He has made good friends with one of the Eritreans, they play music together and see each other outside of Fern.

He's no fool and he doesn't just buy into things. He's a deep thinker and he will press us on things if he isn't sure. When he first arrived he seemed frail and fragile but now he seems to be one of the strongest. Confident with who he is. When he arrived he watched the others cooking and then he baked a cake within two weeks and he'd only just learnt to bake, it wasn't a skill that he'd brought with him. It was a fun thing really but it gave him a sense of achievement. And he'll sing. He'll sit with the girls and he's not bothered by that. He and Tao are real success stories. Part of it is not that they don't care what people think they don't get embarrassed they are strong enough to deal with it and yet they were the two most fragile kids when they arrived. They know who they are and they don't need to be someone else for anybody. It was lovely to give them both the 'student who has made most progress award' at the end of term.

He really dealt so well when his claim for leave to remain got refused initially. He was really upset, but he spoke in depth with us about it but it didn't set him back. When he arrived he struggled with sleep and headaches, which affected his mood, health and ability to focus in lessons. Towards the end of the academic year when he was refused and had the potential of all of his efforts and plans to go to college turned upside down he showed real resilience, it didn't affect how he participated or did in his exams. During his final review before he left that he said because of Fern he now felt like he was strong enough to deal with things by himself and go to college (and that was when his appeal was hanging over him). He also made friendships which we imagine will last a lifetime.

Rasheed's experiences of safety, belonging and safety during his time at Fern College

Rasheed was the first student to attend Fern College. Like many others in the group, Rasheed was forced to leave his home because of religious persecution. His village was destroyed by Isis because they were part of a minority religion. His family were killed and he lost most of his right arm. When he first arrived he was living in semi-independent accommodation but shortly afterwards because of his disability he was moved into a foster family on the opposite side of the city. He didn't feel safe in his previous accommodation and now he is physically very safe. When he first came here he settled really quickly and made incredible progress with his academic work.

His mental state has though changed completely since moving from to foster care. Whilst he has the feeling of safety it has created real confusion because he doesn't really know where he belongs. He wants to belong in his foster family but, equally, he doesn't want to lose part of himself and so he just doesn't know where he fits anymore. The big thing for him is his faith. He arrived as a member of a minority group within the Kurdish ethnic group which was very marginalised by the Muslim majority in that part of the world. He talked a lot at the beginning about his own faith but that he felt that he had to pretend almost that he was Muslim in order to conform and he didn't want us to tell people that he wasn't Muslim. The other Kurds here are all Muslim and now that he is with his foster family who are Muslim, he's decided he's a Muslim now. He's had something of an identity crisis because he just doesn't know who he is. I mean they are all struggling with who they are because they are crossing cultures and everything is up in the air. But for him it's huge and it's really difficult and that has impacted on his success.

He's had a lot of success academically especially since he arrived with little formal education. He could have got his Entry 3 but did not because his attendance dipped. He's opted out of enrichment activities because he is so conscious of his arm. He's really struggling with his prosthetic arm. We thought he felt really comfortable in his skin when he arrived as a person with one arm but now he doesn't want to draw attention to the prosthetic. So in the exam we asked him to take his coat off and he wouldn't because of his arm. It has become a big issue and he doesn't want to be called disabled and we can't point it out to anybody.

It has caused a bit of internal conflict as well because he's aware that he's not the Rasheed that he was. And he knows that. He's always on Instagram and social media and the more he's fitted in to society and made friends he's now thinking that he doesn't need us so much. There has been a real change in what he wears and he's now very fashionable. And it's not fashionable to have a prosthetic arm. He has withdrawn a lot and that has impacted on his success. He was the centre of it all at the beginning, wasn't he?

A few weeks later, Rasheed was nominated and was successfully awarded and award by the local newspaper for showing remarkable resilience. He was one of the students who met Prince Harry and seems to have found his enthusiasm for learning and being part of life at Fern. He has decided to stay for an additional year rather than move to the Further Education college. However, shortly after the publication of the news story which featured a photograph of him, his life story and the award he spoke to Louise about how the comments on social media about the story attracted affected him. *'Among lots of positive comments were some nasty anti-refugee sentiment and he couldn't understand why people felt that way.'* As Louise observes, *'It shows the cyclical nature of the process. Even at a moment of "success" there are new challenges, and issues of safety and belonging.'*

Conclusion

At the most fundamental level, the provision has been successful in meeting the aims of the Controlling Migration Funding in that at the end of the first year, each student went on to stay in education, either at Fern itself or at the local FE college. Academically, all students demonstrated accelerated progress with strong outcomes. Locally, Fern has quickly established an excellent reputation both for successful outcomes but also for its reputation for its holistic provision:

> A lot of the young people we support have had a traumatic experience travelling to the UK or find it hard to adjust to the huge changes in their environment and way of living. Fern as an educational facility caters to their specific needs, through the assessment programme each young person is aware of what level they will be starting at for each specific subject they will be learning but Fern offers more support in different areas of the young people's life. They make friends and meet people who have had similar experiences to them. The staff at Fern ensure that they communicate with all the support services, careers and stakeholders to ensure that they are meeting the needs of the young people. The support provided, especially in terms of emotional and life skills, enables the young people to improve their independence skills thereby empowering them towards future life living in the community.
>
> (Operations Manager for Care and Support Services Provider)

In many ways the work of Fern College has supported the young people arriving in the city towards resumption of an ordinary life with the education provision providing a gateway to safety, belonging and success. For the students who have attended the provision the inclusive model of holistic education has both realized their fundamental right to education in their new host society and also provided pathways to overcoming barriers to current and future participation in their new society. Whilst this chapter has highlighted a mostly positive portrait of the provision, the team are cognisant of the limitations of an inclusive model of education which physically excludes the young people from mainstream provision. However, when consideration is given to what the young people's experiences would have been without the provision it is clear that the Fern model is a successful alternative, being futures-oriented in ambition for the young people to have a longer-term route to inclusion and parity of participation in their future learning, work and social lives.

Despite these obvious markers of success and the benefits both to the young people attending the provision and those working to support young new arrivals and the city, as the project funding comes to an end, the team are finding that the same obstacles that were there two years ago to funding a post-16 provision for refugees and asylum-seeking students still exist. Without the CMF funding it is proving impossible to access alternative resources to ensure the continuity and expansion of this provision. At the time of writing, the English political context is characterized by division and media discourse is again dominated by viewpoints that consider refugees to be a threat to British life and society. In this scenario, Fraser's analysis of the barriers to a socially just response to the education of refugees and asylum-seeking children holds. Support for state funding for a school for this vulnerable group is not currently palatable and as long as there is a lack of recognition of the ways in which immigrants enhance societies, and privileged voices misrepresent the causes and impact of forced migration in dominant discourses then there will not be a fair distribution of resources to allow a provision such as Fern to continue.

The case study chapters have explored how the theoretical framework can be utilized with educational practitioners and policymakers and how it can contribute to understandings of the journeys young refugees make. We show that the act of attending school marks the beginning of transitions for children with extraordinary experiences towards resuming ordinary meaningful lives in their new context. Given the trauma and experiences they have encountered, refugee children deserve an education of value which will help them become lifelong learners able to participate and contribute to their new societies and lead meaningful lives. We suggest that the theoretical understandings we outline in this book offer a robust moral and operational approach to shape pedagogical principles for policymakers and practitioners working in resettlement communities across Europe and beyond. This is especially important at this moment in time, when issues of global importance are changing and reshaping educational policies within and across borders.

This chapter closes Section 1 and our focus on theorising best practice for an inclusive model of education for refugee and asylum-seeking children. We now turn to Section 2, where there is a shift in style to that of Fran the journalist who presents her exploration of narratives of histories of refugee education. Fran then brings us to the present day with an on-the-ground report of those working to support refugee children in a specific locality, the east of England, before concluding Section 2 with an overview of relevant policy in this field.

Note

1 Meetings of professionals supporting a Looked After Child where the child's personal educational plan is reviewed.

References

Department for Education (DfE). 2017. *Care of unaccompanied migrant children and child victims of modern slavery statutory guidance for local authorities*. Available at https://assets.publishing.service.gov.uk/government/uploads/system/uploads/attachment_data/file/656429/UASC_Statutory_Guidance_2017.pdf

Delors, J. 1996. *Learning: the treasure within; report to UNESCO of the International Commission on Education for the Twenty-first Century (highlights)*. Available at https://unesdoc.unesco.org/ark:/48223/pf0000109590.

Fraser, N. 2007. Re-framing justice in a globalizing world, *Anales de la Cátedra Francisco Suárez* (2005), 39 89-110. Available at https://www.semanticscholar.org/paper/Re-framing-justice-in-a-globalizing-world-Fraser/d2170289b4fcbd284dec04b93fb50e5a49145102.

SECTION 2
Contexts

Fran Abrams

Brief note about approach

The next three chapters draw on reviews of literature and other documentation as well as on-the-ground interviews and meetings with those working to support young refugees and asylum seekers and the young people themselves. Threaded throughout Section 2 are extracts from interviews with young people who are at different stages of their lives in England and who represent different ways in which young people experience the concepts of safety, belonging and succeeding outlined in Section 1. Throughout Section 2, in accordance with the conventions of a journalist approach, places, institutions and the adults are referred to by their real name. Those under 18, in care of local authorities or otherwise considered vulnerable are given pseudonyms unless parental permission was given. Permission was granted in the case of the girls at Iqra Academy; Hamid Khan, chair of the Refugee Support Network Youth Advisory board, is an adult and is given his real name. Throughout these chapters, rich detailed description and commentary brings past and current experiences to life.

Chapter 8 is a historical narrative illustrating various factors which have influenced educational experiences of different groups of refugees across key points in history within England. These factors are sometimes attributed to the political context at the time, sometimes to the attributes of the migrants themselves and sometimes a combination of both. In Chapter 9, the reader is brought back to the present with a deep portrait of a specific place and the ways in which young refugees and asylum seekers experience their early weeks and months in the East of England. Chapter 10 widens the lens to capture the policy environment within which those working on the ground navigate obstacles and opportunities for young refugees to thrive and aspire; throughout this chapter there are echoes of Chapter 3's analysis of policies for social justice.

Section 2 closes with an extended extract from an interview with Hamid Khan, who reflects on his interactions with education in the 14 years since he arrived in the country as a 16-year-old refugee with a dream to succeed in his new home.

Yusuf: 'A boy looking in two directions'

Yusuf is 13 and still has a round-faced, boyish look. It's lunchtime when we meet in Cambridge at the home of his learning mentor, Marie-France Faulkner, but he's just out of bed and hasn't eaten. He's hungrily eyeing a plate of chocolate biscuits.

Yusuf arrived here in December 2015 on the government's resettlement programme for Syrian families. He seems to be a boy who's looking in two directions - to a future in the UK with siblings who were born here, but also back to the Syria he remembers from his early childhood.

Our conversation drifts back often to the topics of food and football: What does he remember about school in Syria? "Cooking," he says.

"I made Arabic sweets and we tasted them, and I still love those. They're like those chocolate biscuits, but not like them. You chop them then you put chocolate on it then you mix it up and you put it in the fridge. And it turns out *sooo* nice."

He still makes those with his Mum sometimes, he says - she's a brilliant cook.

What else does he remember? He liked school, he says: "But it was not that good because if you did something not really good for teaching you would get hit by a ruler on your hand. If I was not listening, if I was playing. Not doing the work, not getting homework done - loads of stuff. I deserved it because it was my fault, I was talking. I got hit five times on my hand."

Yusuf is the oldest of four children - his younger sister is 10 now and he has two brothers, one aged 5 and one, born here, just coming up to 2. In Syria, his Dad had two businesses - a grocery shop and a recording studio. Now he's looking for work as a builder. What does Yusuf think his Syrian teachers would have said about him? "He is behaving all right, he's learning well ... not distracting and annoying people like I did a year before. I used to get some awards for being good."

And then the war started: "Basically what happened when I was six one day someone had a gun out. Because you know people are not allowed to have guns and he got his gun out and he started shooting near my house. And he was shooting people so much. Then the war started between Bashir Al Assad which is kind of the police ... the people were against the police. And that went so bad, forty thousand people died in a year."

"I was very lucky because my school got bombed when I was in it, but the bomb came down on the other class. The bomb was so hot that there were little bits of metal and when they drop on you they go through your skin. We all got hurt and we got taken to the hospital." He pulls up his sleeve to reveal the scars on his arm.

A year later, while Yusuf was playing at home with friends, his house was hit by another bomb. This time one of his friends died: "I was on the stairs. I just heard: 'Boom!' And I was crying so much. They are the friends I always trust, like they look after me, I look after them. We had to leave our house because that we are the only people left in town."

He remembers snipers, an uncle being shot while riding on a motorbike with his father: "I think about that a lot. Yeah, a lot."

"After that we moved to Lebanon. Then we had a really good caravan - a charity sent buses and we went together but my Dad had to walk from Syria."

There was a school in the camp, run by volunteers for a couple of hours each day. But much of the time Yusuf and his friends hung out together, playing marbles. "We learnt a lot but then it stopped because there are more people coming and they had to build more camps that there wasn't enough time to teach."

Yusuf and his family stayed in the camp for three years: "It was like school in Syria, but the learning was not enough. It's just two hours, and 45 minutes for our lunch. We swapped over - so we learned from one till four or from four till seven."

He has good memories of the camp in Lebanon, of fun with his friends: "Especially in Ramadan, it was so nice. We'd go to sleep and wake up at two or three, and then from about 12 we'd just play and have fun. I made really good friends. We used to play card games. The best thing we did, me and my friends used to jump on the caravans, then we'd knock down on our friend's door and he was like: 'Where are they?' It was so funny. Because it was safe, we could stay out."

"Then some charity people called my Dad - a charity that move people to different countries. We went to a meeting, then we went to another meeting after 15 days. It was so quick for us, we were so lucky. After a month they called us: 'We need your signature, we need your picture', and stuff like that. Then we went.

"And here it got better and we had schools. I made new friends. It has been good. We had CRC [Cambridge Refugee Resettlement Campaign, through which Yusuf was paired with his learning mentor].

"I met Marie-France, and she taught me more than school. I found friends, they'd say, 'You do this in here'; we played. They played football on grass and I was like: 'How do they do this?' It looked fun. So I tried and I wasn't very good. I went into a club after that. Now I just got the hang of it. Like English - I wanted to learn English so much, and I got the hang of that as well."

8 A historical narrative of refugee education in England

Fran Abrams

The historian Kevin Myers, who has done a great deal to shed light on the educational lives of refugee children in the UK, argues that their absence from most standard histories has important implications for current policymaking: "For those who are interested in how refugees settle, teach and learn in a new country, the (British) history of education will reveal nothing of interest. Even though education has long been seen as a critical experience for refugees, historians of education have resolutely ignored the presence of refugees in Britain", he writes (Myers, 2001).

The education system, he says, has learned little from its own history, regarding these children as temporary phenomena or as new ones: thus, it continues to ignore and to marginalise the needs of refugee children in school.

This chapter will attempt to redress that balance a little. What were the factors affecting past groups of refugees' progress, as Kohli puts it (Kohli 2011), from safety to belonging and then to success? Were those factors internal to those groups – did they bring with them social or cultural capital that enabled them to succeed, or which held them back? Did they come here with strong moral or political beliefs which drove them onwards? How did the attitudes and actions of others affect them? Were they welcomed by those with power or influence; if so, what were the results? Or conversely, what might have been the effects? Was there sufficient financial and practical support to facilitate their smooth entry into the education system, or were there barriers to their success? What was the role of the individual mentors and teachers they met along the way, both in their own communities and within the wider population?

Writing the history of refugees in England poses a problem – the legal definition of a refugee, set out in the United Nation's Convention and Protocol Relating to the Status of Refugees dates back only to 1951. But this chapter will apply the United Nation's simple definition of a refugee as 'a person forced to flee their country through violence or persecution' to groups of people arriving in England since the 17th Century.

This is not an attempt to write a comprehensive history; more a dive into the literature in search for examples which could prove useful or interesting to those who seek to change, implement or improve today's educational policy environment. It draws on a number of specific cases, beginning with the Huguenots not because they were the first group of refugees to arrive but because they were one of the earliest groups for whom education was key and who left behind them a rich seam of material on which historians can draw.

But where to stop? A later chapter will examine current policy and ask how it facilitates or creates barriers to success. As there are two key policy developments – the 1988 Education Reform Act and the 1989 Children Act – which date back more than 30 years, but which arguably still have huge influence on today's landscape, the late 1980s, seems as good a place to end as any.

Seventeenth century: Huguenots

According to family legend, when they fled to London in the 1680s Francis Vaillant's family were smuggled out of Paris in barrels. But the family's fortunes soon improved – John Vaillant, a bookseller, was able to set up business on the Strand and to take on his two eldest sons, Paul and Isaac, to work with him. His younger son, Francis, was apprenticed to a nearby Huguenot silversmith named David Willaume (Goodway 2001).

Francis Vaillant's career as a silversmith was not always a happy one: a few months after he began his apprenticeship a letter arrived at the Goldsmiths' Hall – headquarters of the Goldsmiths' Company, which still regulates the goldsmiths' craft today – from the Chamberlain of the City of London. There was a question over the legality of the apprenticeship, it pointed out, as Willaume himself had recently arrived in the city and had not yet been granted the Freedom of the Goldsmiths' Company. Could the situation please be regularised?

But Willaume was a well-connected man, and no less a figure than the Lord Mayor of London gave instructions he should receive the freedom which would allow him legally to trade and to take on apprentices. Francis Vaillant went on to qualify as a silversmith, though his master's connections could not protect him from the disciplinary processes of the Goldsmiths' Company: In 1709 he was fined two shillings and sixpence by its Court of Wardens for making salt cellars that were not of the required standard. Later a Francis Vaillant, silversmith, could be found living and working in St Michael's Parish in Barbados (Goodway, 2001).

The word 'refugee' entered the English language when the Huguenots, who were French Calvinist Protestants, landed here following the revocation of their civil rights by Louis XIV. Prior to that they had been legally protected by the Edict of Nantes, which gave them substantial rights in what was essentially a Catholic nation. The political climate at the time in Britain – which had its own suspicions of the motives and ambitions of Louis XIV – was largely a positive one for them and, well connected and well educated as they often were, they arrived in great numbers. It is estimated that, while a small population of Huguenots already lived in the UK, around 50,000 came in the late 1680s.

Their reception was not entirely positive. The reaction in the Spitalfields weaving community, for instance, was that this was 'an unruly and presumptuous rabble' (Swindlehurst 2001: 388). Similarly, the Worshipful Company of Clockmakers had objected that its members were 'exceedingly oppressed by the intrusion of French clockmakers'. The weavers complained that the French arrivals only employed their own, and that they should do more to share their superior skills – they tended to be broadloom silk weavers whereas the English weavers of Spitalfields were more often ribbon weavers. One correspondent described "boyes of fifteene, sixteene or eighteene years of age that come over from all parts of [foreign] countreys and here are sett at worke by many of your [foreign] congregation whether they can doe the tenth parte of their trade, yea or no." But even though the Huguenots arrived often speaking only French, and that they often worshipped in their own churches, there was a fairly integrated weaving community in Spitalfields by the end of the century – little more than a decade later.

But at just this time the Glorious Revolution of 1688–89 brought William III from Holland to power in England, and while Charles II and the Catholic James II had both been patronised by Louis XIV, William had no such allegiances. The new Huguenot migrants enjoyed the patronage of Britain's aristocracy and gentry, and not least because of their educational tradition.

Because the ability to read directly from the Bible was central to the Calvinists' beliefs, the Huguenots were usually literate and a small, but significant proportion were university graduates, having studied subjects such as law, philosophy, theology or journalism at their own academies. This educational tradition had already brought them far – they had been instrumental in translating the works of the philosopher John Locke into French, shaping their content as they did so. It has been argued that these translators had helped to set the tone and orientation of the Enlightenment debates generated by the discussion of Locke's ideas (Soulard 2012).

And as a result of their educational tradition the Huguenots had often served as tutors to the English aristocracy on its Grand Tours of Europe (Green, 2018: 405). One such tutor, Jean Gailhard, accompanied Philip Perceval, 2nd Baronet and son of the Calvinist John Perceval, who was a landowner in Ireland and had been knighted by Cromwell. Philip was in the care of his uncle, Robert Southwell, an English diplomat and Secretary of State for Ireland. On his own Grand Tour Southwell had travelled to France, Italy, the Netherlands and Central Europe, and had gained a knowledge of foreign languages as well as having "developed and exhibited a courtliness which was much admired" (ibid., 405).

As Gailhard and Perceval travelled through Italy, Hungary, Bohemia, France, Germany and Switzerland, the young man took lessons in riding, fencing, dancing, drawing landscapes, design, playing the guitar, French and Italian languages, all considered necessary for a gentleman of his era. Other subjects commonly taught by Huguenot travelling tutors included natural philosophy, Latin, history and dance.

And this tradition was to continue once the Huguenots had been forced to relocate. In London, they founded several "academies", or specific curriculum schools for nobles, teaching subjects which included military arts, mathematics, dancing, playing the lute and drawing.

The diarist John Evelyn went to visit one such establishment, kept by Solomon Foubert: "I went with Lord Cornwallis to see the young gallants do their exercise, Mr. Faubert (sic) having newly rail'd in a manage, and fitted it for the academy. There were the Dukes of Norfolk and Northumberland, Lord Newburgh, and a nephew of Earle of Feresham. The exercises were, 1. running at the ring; 2. flinging a javelin at Moor's head; 3. discharging a pistol at a mark; lastly, taking up a gauntlet with the point of a sword; all these perform'd in full speede. The D. of Northumberland hardly miss'd of succeeding in everyone, a dozen times, as I think. The D. of Norfolk did exceeding bravely. Lords Newburgh and Duras seem'd nothing so dexterous" (ibid., 397).

The training was fitted for its purpose: in addition to horse-riding, the young nobles were undertaking exercises for improving their general physical condition: the Moors had besieged Vienna a few years earlier, and they were being prepared for future roles in the army.

In addition to these establishments, by the mid-18th Century there were at least two separate French charity schools for younger children in England, one for girls and one for boys, and these too were attracting favourable comment. A contemporary historian, William Maitland, wrote: "This is a management so laudable that it well deserves to be copied after by the Trustees of our Parochial and other Charity Schools" (Barrett 2001: 376). It is worth noting that the history of refugee education in England is not a one-way street: those who have sought asylum here have also influenced the development of the system.

So the Huguenots who arrived in England in the latter part of the 17th Century were far from being mere recipients of an existing education system – they were major players in shaping educational thought and practice. And their apparently swift integration into English society – it is estimated as many as one in six people in England today are descended from Huguenots – was aided by a variety of factors, both external and internal (Tonkin 2015). The Huguenots' skills and high levels of literacy enabled them to settle easily in a new environment, but they also brought them into close contact with the wealthy, the powerful and the influential. Even more crucially, perhaps, the wider political climate of the day – with its deep-rooted suspicion of Catholicism and growing antagonism towards France – meant that the predominant rhetoric around their arrival was a positive one, and this meant a smooth transition into life in England.

Nineteenth century: Jews

At the beginning of the 18th Century the Jews, who had been banished by Edward I in the 13th Century, were readmitted to England by Oliver Cromwell. There were probably pragmatic reasons for this – the Spanish and Portuguese Jewish community, many of whom were well-to-do merchants, had recently been expelled from Spain and had relocated to Amsterdam, helping to turn it into one of the world's busiest ports. Cromwell saw that the return of the Jews to England would bring great financial benefits. And the accession of William III to the English throne had brought about a closer connection between the predominantly Sephardic communities of London and Amsterdam; enabling the major centre of European finance to transfer from Holland to England.

At around the same time a small German Ashkenazi community also settled in England, establishing its own synagogues as well as a school, the Jews' Free School. Both these communities were relatively wealthy and relatively well-integrated by the 1870s, when a wave of pogroms brought a much larger, poorer and less well-connected group of Jews to England. It is estimated that as many as 500,000 people migrated from the Russian Empire, Austro-Hungary and Romania in the half-century before World War I (Rutter 1999).

So, while these new refugees could not be said to be wealthy, well-connected or possessing of major cultural capital on their arrival in England, they did have some support – thousands of pounds were donated each year to pay for schools and hospitals, much of it from the existing Jewish population but some from other donors, including wealthy Christians.

The arrivals had support in Parliament, too: John Simon, who had been born in Jamaica in 1818 and who came to England in 1833, was a prominent lawyer and, by 1868, the MP for Dewsbury. Simon devoted himself to campaigning on behalf of Jewish people in Romania, Morocco, Russia and Serbia, and in 1882 succeeded in organising a protest from the entire

British people against their mistreatment. A meeting was called by the Lord Mayor at the Mansion House, supported by the Archbishop of Canterbury, Cardinal Manning and Charles Darwin, along with 18 members of Parliament (Jewish Encyclopedia 1906).

Yet there was nothing well connected about these refugees, and their prospects, at first glance, did not look good. Henry Mayhew described them as often desperately poor and ill-educated: "The body of the poorer, or what in other callings might be termed the working classes, are not even tolerably well educated; they are indifferent to the matter. With many, the multiplication table seems to constitute what they think the acme of all knowledge needful to a man. The great majority of Jew Boys in the street cannot read. A smaller portion can read, but so imperfectly that their ability to read detracts nothing from their ignorance. So neglectful or so necessitous (but I heard the ignorance attributed to neglect far more frequently than necessity) are the poorer Jews, and so soon do they take their children away from school 'to learn and do something for themselves' and so irregular is their attendance, on the plea that the time cannot be spared, and the boy must do something for himself, that many children leave the free-schools not only about as ignorant as when they entered them, but almost with an incentive to continued ignorance, for they knew nothing of reading, except that to acquire its rudiments is a pain" (Mayhew 1862, 129).

Despite this, Mayhew adds that the Jewish community was self-sufficient, and keen to look after its own: "The Jews' Hospital in the Mile End Road is an extensive building into which feeble old men and destitute children of both sexes are admitted. Here the boys are taught trades, and the girls qualified for respectable domestic service" (ibid., 130).

Mayhew said that at th time there were seven Jewish schools in London, four in the city and three in the West End, all supported by voluntary contributions. The biggest, Jews' Free School (JFS), was growing at what must have seemed an alarming rate: It had originally opened in 1732 as a Talmud Torah of the Ashkenazi Great Synagogue and had relocated to Bell Lane in Spitalfields in 1822. It had been set up to educate a small and relatively affluent community, but by 1900 it had no fewer than 4,250 pupils on its roll.

One of those pupils was Israel Zangwill, who was himself the son of Russian immigrants and born in London in 1864. He attended JFS from the age of nine, and describes it in his most famous novel, *Children of the Ghetto* (1895), as a hotbed of Anglicisation. His central character, Esther, is loosely based on Zangwill himself and at one point is seen in a tramp's old shoes, her father having sold the new ones given to her by the school in order to buy bread (Zangwill 1895 (2004), 62).

Zangwill's account is supported by others: According to one historian (Alderman 1998), in 1870 JFS had a staff of 70, including student teachers, and the key purpose of its head-teacher of 51 years, Moses Angel, was to anglicise. In 1905 Angel's successor, Louis Abrahams, advised parents and pupils to discard Yiddish, 'that miserable jargon which was not a language at all' (Alderman 1998, 139).

Abrahams "urged parents to 'strengthen the efforts of teachers to wipe away all evidence of foreign birth and foreign proclivities'" (ibid.). He was clearly successful: a Board of Trade report in 1894 noted with satisfaction that pupils "enter the school Russians and Poles ... and emerge from it almost indistinguishable from English children" (ibid.).

In the early years of this new population there were serious moves to set up more Jewish voluntary schools: having surveyed the situation, the then Chief Rabbi, Nathan Adler, found there were only a few Jewish schools of any substance, and that these were all to be found in the major cities.

At Adler's behest more day schools were established, and at one time as many as half the child population of British Jewry attended them. According to one historian, however, they 'suffered from an association with mediocrity, and in any case never proved attractive to the more affluent sections of the community, who employed private tutors or else despatched their children to the more select private Jewish academies' (Alderman 1998, 90). The Jewish day schools, he adds, were regarded as only fit for the 'foreign poor', and from the mid-1870s there was an observable tendency for middle-class Jewish parents to send their sons to non-Jewish fee-paying schools such as Manchester Grammar.

There was a persistent argument that the growth of a system of Jewish schools would act as a negative force against integration. And as time went on, more and more Jewish youngsters attended ordinary state schools – by 1911, it was estimated that three-quarters of Jewish children in London were in ordinary elementary schools. In some schools in Stepney, the large majority of pupils were Jewish and religious holidays were observed.

In fact, these Jewish migrants were the first group of refugees to receive a state-funded education in the UK. In 1903 school boards were wound up and responsibility for education handed to local authorities, which allowed the four Jewish voluntary schools in the provinces and eight in London to have their secular education funded by the state – a move which was welcomed, even though in London it meant the schools tended to have Christians appointed to their managing boards.

The move was largely welcomed by the Jewish community: a Reverend Levy told the Conference of Anglo-Jewish Ministers that national compulsory and free education was enabling thousands of Jewish children 'to acquire English habit of thought and character' (Alderman 1998, 141). This was reinforced by a 'battery of other devices', from free English language classes for adults, offered by the Russo-Jewish Committee, to swimming, football and cricket. There were Jewish working men's' clubs, girls' clubs, boy' clubs, including the Jewish Lads' Brigade, which aimed to 'instil into the rising generation all that is best in the English character, manly independence, honour, truth, cleanliness, love of active health-giving pursuits &c' (ibid.). The wealthy Anglo-Jewish middle classes subscribed generously to these activities.

Again, the history of the majority of Jewish refugees from Eastern Europe in the late 19th Century can be seen, in the long term at least, as an educational success story – though the growth of ultra-orthodox Haredi communities might arguably be a counterpoint to this. For the most part, as time went on more Jewish parents came to see education as a route to success, and by 1945 it was estimated that a quarter of Jewish children aged over 15 were at college or university, and a further 13 per cent were preparing to go. Most Jewish parents expected their children to remain in education until at least the age of 21 (Alderman 1998). And again, this new community was not merely a recipient or a cause of educational change – it helped to drive it. Excluded from Oxford and Cambridge, members of a burgeoning Jewish middle class were among the original council members of University College London.

None of this happened overnight. While the Huguenots appeared to have assimilated and prospered very quickly, the poorer and less well-supported Jews who arrived in the last half of the 19th Century took longer to do so. Statistics show (Prais and Schmool 1968) that the

Jewish population of the East End boroughs of Tower Hamlets, Newham and Redbridge, having grown to some 125,000 at its peak around 1900, shrank to a not insubstantial 39,000 by 1970. By 2011, it had dwindled still further, to a total of 11,055 - the large majority being in more affluent Redbridge, with just 1700 in Tower Hamlets and Newham (Tower Hamlets Borough Council 2015; QPZM Local Stats; Newham Borough Council).

1930s: Basques

During the late 1930s Ann Wolff was a pupil at Dartington Hall School in Devon. Despite the school's antecedents - it was one of a number of radical schools which had sprung up around the country in response to child-centred theories of education which were being discussed - she had not, until that time, found the place particularly political. But 1937 brought a change of atmosphere:

"We were very involved in the Spanish Civil War," she said during an interview with the author. People we knew went off there. We had refugees, one of the Spanish teachers was a refugee. There were a whole lot of children who were housed somewhere up in the hall, and we all had to knit a square which was stitched together for their blankets. Quite how they were being orphaned by the war, I don't know. Probably there were about 30 of them; quite a group and it was our duty to look after them. We weren't taught together. I don't know what happened to them eventually because they didn't stay there permanently. But that was our first introduction to war.

Those dozen children, who were apparently kept largely separate from the school's regular pupils and whose stay was not protracted, were almost certainly among the 4000 who disembarked at Southampton Harbour on Sunday 23 May 1937 (Myers 1999a) as evacuees from the fascist bombing campaigns of the Spanish Civil War. It was initially anticipated they would stay around three months, but most were here for nearly two years and around five hundred of them never returned to Spain.

The children were widely referred to as 'Basques', but were actually a diverse group, including Basque nationalists, Spanish Republicans, socialists and communists. They were a highly politicised group - to the extent that the refugee camp in North Stoneham, Hampshire that served as temporary accommodation for many of the children in the summer of 1937 had to be divided according to the contrasting political and cultural beliefs. One particularly tight-knit group consisted of 29 orphans whose parents had all been killed in the early stages of the war and who had lived together in an orphanage in Bilbao.

Although it was never intended that these children should remain in the UK permanently, it is interesting to note that - as with earlier groups of refugee children - their presence made an impression on some English educationists. Helen Grant, a lecturer in Spanish at Birmingham University, travelled to Spain in March 1937 and visited refugee 'colonies' in and around Catalonia, many of which had established schools for children in their care. "The visit to this colony was extremely interesting because the people running it seemed to me to be very simple people but with a great idea of 'educating' children, as opposed to 'instructing' them", she wrote in her travel diary. "The whole trend of education in Spain seems to be aiming at producing all round useful citizens and to provide an alternative to the intense individualism of the Spaniard" (ibid., 315).

Schools like Dartington, which ran on similar holistic principles, were rare in England at the time but thinkers like Grant were increasingly discussing their merits. After World War II, there would be a period in which those principles would be espoused very widely, and during which the notions of pupil participation, constructive activity and individual expression would become widespread in the UK. Grant, having seen them in action in Spain, wrote that they were 'the best method for producing creative, balanced and able citizens' (ibid., 315)

The English left, very deeply involved in opposition to fascism in Spain, must have been to some extent able to learn from the child-centred theories which were already being put into practice there. Not only were some of the children housed for a while at Dartington – other groups were taken up by radical organisations around the country. And many of those who got involved were educationists themselves.

In Cambridge, for example, the vice presidents of the Basque Children's Committee were Dr J. A. Ryle, a fellow of Gonville and Caius College and a distinguished medical practitioner, and the liberal academic J. B. Trend. Professor John Cornford, a classical scholar whose son was killed fighting for the Republicans' war, was treasurer.

In the case of these children there was little or no attempt to assimilate, as has already been noted. Indeed, rather than seeing them as passive recipients of aid their hosts tended to see them as free agents and as heroes. The 29 orphans who had lived together in Bilbao were taken to Pampisford, under the auspices of the Cambridge committee. 'They had been brought up', wrote Jessie Stewart, director of the Pampisford colony, 'in a very political atmosphere, and showed ... remarkable independence of thought' (Myers 1999a, 199).

There were no attempts to Anglicise these children to suppress their knowledge of home. Instead, they were actively encouraged to express themselves in their own languages, to celebrate their national heritage and to develop their political thinking.

Kevin Myers argues that these contacts had a clear influence on the direction of educational thinking in the UK: "As well as providing a discursive opportunity for the elucidation of conventional English national values, the children enabled a group of social progressives to experiment with education as a means of constructing a new kind of citizen. Their chosen means for doing so was a broadly defined child-centred pedagogy with the assumed ability to mould a new generation of children into rational, politically active and gently patriotic citizens. Cumulatively, these educational methods seemed to offer hope of moving away from narrow and exclusive nationalism towards a liberal, tolerant and open Englishness" (1999a, 325).

Not only would this influence broader educational thinking in the UK: it also affected the way later groups of refugees were treated. "The implicit pluralism of this national identity meant that the Spanish refugee children at Cambridge received an education that later became characteristic of progressive schooling for refugee children. For some refugee children at least, education for displacement has been not simply a process of assimilation but a discovery and exploration of multiple identities" (ibid., 325).

Wartime: Jews

The arrival of those 4000 Spanish refugee children was followed not long afterwards by a much larger group: Jews from Central Europe, some of them unaccompanied and some fleeing fascism with their parents.

Kevin Myers argues that attitudes struck in response to the Spanish children pertained to this group, too. While Anglicisation was seen as desirable as a means to avoid anti-Semitism, there was again a belief that these refugees would not be staying. In addition to an assumption that they might wish to return home, there was in this case the added factor of Zionism, and the intention that some of those children would go on to help found the state of Israel (Myers 1999b).

Before the war, a group named Youth Aliyah had been moving children from Germany to Palestine with the intention that their parents would join them there later. Towards the end of the 1930s, however, the political situation made it more difficult to obtain immigration certificates for Palestine, they began sending them to Britain instead. Of the 10,000 children who came with the Kindertransports, some 3500 intended to reach Palestine with Youth Aliyah when it became possible to do so.

The education they received was heavily influenced by this: "Any future state of Israel, it was argued, would need its agriculturists, mechanics and technicians as well as its doctors, lawyers and industrialists. Consequently, the Zionist youth groups set about educating and training Jewish youth in preparation for life in Palestine" (Myers 1999b, 274)

Yet there was also an equally strong body of thought which agreed that education should contribute to the children's assimilation into English society. Inspectors who visited the Yeshiva School in Stamford Hill in 1940 complained that it failed to "provide proper provision for the teaching not only of English, but also of English customs". The reason for the inspection was that Dr Bernstein, Principal of the Jews Free School, had written to express concern that refugee pupils were being moved to the school. Dr Bernstein wrote that attendance at the school would result in a "loss of moral and social sense which will stamp the boys as aliens and foreign in their adult life" (ibid., 270).

So these Jewish refugees from fascism had mixed experiences, and many among those who came believing they would go back never did so.

Hana Eardley was born in Pilsen, Czechoslovakia, in 1928 and came to England on what turned out to be the last of the Kindertransports with her twin brother, Hans. Her sister Greta never made it – some delay led to her being told she would be on a later train and she later perished with her parents and most of her wider family. Hana was interviewed by the Refugee Voices Project (2004) and I used some of that material in my book, *Songs of Innocence: The Story of British Childhood,* (Abrams 2012, 133-134):

"We have details of how some died horribly, like my uncle Arnold because he was a slight hunchback, he was one of the first. And grandpa, who never hurt a fly. Oh I don't know … Treblinka, one of these places. They were just lined up and shot. In a way I'm glad I don't know the details about Mother and Father and Greta, all we know is … that they did perish", Hana said later.

Hana was placed with the non-Jewish Crooks family in Sheffield, and her brother with another nearby. And yet despite the trauma of not knowing what had happened to their family, both flourished and assimilated – the extent that Hans was later adopted by his host family and changed his name to John Mulroy.

Both came with a great deal of social and cultural capital: their father Felix was – Hana thought later – probably an accountant in a steel firm, and she had always done well at school: "I'm pretty sure we were in an ordinary state junior school and had Jewish and non-Jewish friends. I don't remember religion being a big thing", she said.

Hana's father had written a letter, explaining that while the family would not want the children to forget their Jewish origins, he hoped they would learn English quickly: "All three children have frequented Czech schools ... you should not be concerned about the children's religious training", he wrote.

Hana was in fact taken to synagogue occasionally by a local Jewish family, but said later that she had sought spiritual solace in both churches and synagogues later in life, and in fact to some extent had blamed her Judaism for the loss of her family. Both she and Hans became part of their host families:

I was very fortunate because Mr Crooks was a headmaster and Mrs Crooks had been a teacher, and every evening Mrs Crooks used to help me with my English. I found it extremely easy, especially playing with neighbours' children during the day. What I found more difficult was the whole English mathematical system with feet and inches and yards, ... Mr Crooks used to teach me every evening for an hour and showed me the mysticism of English maths, so that helped a great deal because within six months I was able to take the exam and pass for a grammar school.

Hana later became a teacher and her brother Hans a doctor, and both became UK citizens: "I must say John and I felt more Czech than Jewish, always been very proud of being Czech ... I don't like anything said against the Czechs. I would definitely say I'm British first but I think I feel a bit like I do with religion, I'm proud of being both, but oh yes definitely British now but very proud of being Czech as well. The two families that adopted us gave us just unconditional love and opportunity for becoming part of the family and getting a good education, and I just can't say enough in praise of them."

While the circumstances of Hana and Hans' relocation to the UK could hardly have been more traumatic, they came with almost a perfect set of conditions upon which to build a sense of belonging here. Coming from, and arriving into, families which valued education and which knew how to ensure their children thrived at school, they were almost bound to succeed. They also came at a time when there was huge public sympathy and were able, partly because of their backgrounds and partly because of the circumstances in which they found themselves, to fit in quickly with other children. It seems, from seeing Hana's interview recorded 65 years later, that they barely felt 'other' for any length of time.

After the war: Poles

Throughout the war and in its immediate aftermath, around 163,000 Polish refugees came to the UK, fleeing the German invasion of 1939, escaping from occupied France, as volunteer workers, from refugee camps and later from communist post-war Poland (Rutter 1999).

According to Jill Rutter, the children of this group were the first to receive an education separate from the British mainstream (1999). In 1940, a Polish government in exile was given recognition by the British government, and during the war it ran its own schools: as with other groups such as the Belgians in World War I, their educational direction was based on an assumption that the children would be returning to Poland and would need to speak Polish. But by 1947 it had become clear that most families had not returned, and the focus was altered. Now children were being educated for a life in the UK.

Management of the schools was delegated to the Committee for Education of Poles in the UK, which included both British and Polish educationists. By 1952, however, the numbers were dwindling because Polish parents, apparently embracing the view that their children would need to assimilate, tended to take the view that for secondary education, at least, British schools were preferable. By 1954, just two Polish schools remained, and the decision was taken to transfer them to local authority control. However, a Polish supplementary school movement still exists and has seen a huge increase in demand since the accession of Poland to the European Union in 2004.

1970s: A move towards multiculturalism

The development of policy relating to the education of refugee children will be discussed in Chapter 10, but it is worth noting that the post-war period in the UK was characterised by a change in direction. Where previously refugee groups had been expected either to assimilate or to leave, those who came later were approached in rather a different way.

In May 1966, the then Home Secretary Roy Jenkins made a major speech on integration. It marked the beginnings of a new approach: "I define integration ... not as a flattening process of assimilation but as equal opportunity accompanied by cultural diversity in an atmosphere of mutual tolerance", he said (Muchowiecka, 2013).

Quite where the line is or should be drawn between assimilation and multiculturalism is open to debate, but certainly there was a sea change taking place: from the earlier belief that new arrivals must become as English as possible – in every possible respect – now it was accepted – by Jenkins, at least – that in an increasingly diverse country it would be possible to embrace many different cultures while still retaining a sense of nationhood.

In the same year, a new Local Government Act brought in specific funding to provide local authorities with supplementary funding to cope with "the presence within their areas of substantial numbers of immigrants whose language and customs are different from the rest of the community" (Lowe 1997). In fact, this funding did not apply to post-war refugee groups for the most part: it was specifically targeted at migrants arriving from Commonwealth countries, and so schools receiving refugee children had to access money from a local authority pooled funding arrangement.

The rhetoric over the next decade, according to Roy Lowe, was strongly multicultural. The 1975 Bullock Report had emphasised that 'no child should be expected to cast off the language and culture of the home as he crosses the school threshold' (DES 1975, 286). Lowe quotes Chris Mullard: "In contrast to the assimilationist's view of our society as being politically and culturally homogenous, its advocates maintain that our society consists of different groups which are culturally distinctive and separate. Therefore, within a plural society there exists a positive commitment to difference and to the preservation of group culture, traditions and history" (Lowe 1997, 122)

Ugandan Asians

One of the first groups to experience this change of attitude were the Ugandan Asians, 28,000 of whom came to Britain after being expelled by Idi Amin in 1972. Because Uganda was, and remains, a Commonwealth country, the children of these families were able to benefit from English as an Additional Language support through Section 11 of the 1966 Local

Government Act. This money funded language centres which were attended by children prior to entering mainstream schooling. "But there were doubts about the approach - withdrawal meant children missed important parts of the curriculum and also the opportunity to converse with their English-speaking peers", according to Rutter (1999, 65).

Eventually, these language centres were ruled to be discriminatory and were scrapped: in 1985-1986 the Commission for Racial Equality undertook a formal investigation into language support in Calderdale, Yorkshire, where large numbers of children had been arriving from the Indian subcontinent. These children had been required to take an English test; if they failed it, they were placed in separate classes or language centres, sometimes for years. The Conservative government agreed that separate provision was discriminatory and that the language units, including small group teaching in schools, should be closed.

Yet even in an era of multiculturalism, the newly arrived refugee groups tended to have their own take on their cultural needs and future direction.

Yasmin Alibhai-Brown, who came to Britain from Uganda as a graduate shortly before expulsion, described later how her mother's attitudes to the English shaped her migrant experience:

"My mother and those like her ... convinced themselves their babies would only thrive if they were fed "pure" English fare. Those who could afford it started buying Heinz baby food. Those who couldn't, felt guilty. To this day, my mother is convinced children should be given Cadbury's milk chocolate because each bar contains one-and-a-half glasses of wholesome milk.

"In no time at all, these women were baking cakes, biscuits and pies. They would enter these dishes in cookery competitions and proudly display pictures of themselves with rosettes next to their children's O and A level gold-framed certificates. We all agreed that these cakes and biscuits were more delectable than those being made by the domestic science teachers, because they would taste of saffron and cardamom or have wonderful toppings of carrot halva. Shepherd's pie was tarted up with spring onions, green chillies, garlic and garam masala." (Alibhai-Brown 1998)

The Ugandan Asians arrived with a good prior level of education and a strong will to succeed and have consequently been held up as a glowing example of what of migration success story can look like.

Vietnamese

And similarly the 24,500 Vietnamese who came as part of a settlement programme between 1978 and 1988, among whom more than one-third were children, have been seen as a strong example of how things can go well when a group of refugees arrives in a new country.

But in historical terms, Britain's Vietnamese community presents something of a cautionary tale, particularly for those looking to generalise about groups of refugees on the basis of their ethnicity. Since the first significant wave of refugees left Vietnam in the mid-1970s, fleeing the fall of Saigon at the end of the Vietnam War, this group has been the recipient of some easy - not to say lazy - labels.

Common tropes about the Vietnamese in England include the notion that they came in flight from Communism, that they were 'boat people' who had had links with the defeated

South Vietnamese government and that their children have been something of an educational phenomenon.

In fact, there is scant evidence to support any of this, and to regard the Vietnamese as a single, homogenous group is a mistake.

The Vietnamese have come to Britain for a huge variety of reasons, but in fact few of the South Vietnamese 'boat people' who left in small vessels at the end of the war, and who were picked up offshore by military ships, came to the UK. Most went to the countries with which Vietnam had colonial links – the USA and France – and the UK was not a popular choice for them.

According to a recent report (Barber 2018) the first significant flow of refugees to Britain was of North, not South Vietnamese origin – two communities who had, of course, recently been at war with one another. Many were ethnic Chinese, fleeing not Communism but ethnic cleansing which happened after China invaded North Vietnam in 1979. They had spent time in holding camps in Hong Kong and elsewhere and came to the UK under a quota system. And in contrast to those early South Vietnamese, who largely went elsewhere and who were often affluent and educated, these refugees tended to be from poor rural communities and to have had little formal education.

The Vietnamese 'community' now living in the UK – and they continue to arrive – includes those first-generation refugees from the late 1970s, their children and grandchildren, later undocumented migrants, asylum seekers and overseas students, each with their own set of issues and attitudes to education.

So reports that 'the Vietnamese' have been a stunning success story in educational terms are worth some closer examination. Although there is plenty of anecdotal evidence, there is little solid to go on.

The main source, much quoted elsewhere, is a small-scale research exercise dating back 15 years (Rutter, 1999 – 2006 edition). It is based on data from two London local authorities, Lambeth and Southwark, and suggests that Vietnamese and Chinese children were consistently outperforming all other ethnic groups at GCSE.

In 2001, it showed that around 47 per cent of Vietnamese pupils in Southwark had gained five Grade A*–C grades, compared with 34 per cent of white pupils. It was suggested that a strong culture of valuing educational achievement had led to a remarkable second-generation effect, in which the children of migrants who had not benefitted from much formal education themselves had taken great strides in a relatively short time.

Research by the Runnymede Trust (Sims 2007) dug deeper and unearthed some striking figures: when the results were disaggregated by gender it was revealed that girls had outperformed boys by some margin, with around 67 per cent achieving five or more A*–C GCSEs, compared to 10 per cent of boys. Similarly, in 2002, a school in Lewisham had reported that the general student body "attained well below average standards in GCSE English ... White, mixed race, and Vietnamese boys had relatively lower points scores than other ethnic groups."

There is little quantitative evidence to go on – censuses, both national and educational, do not separate Vietnamese people out as a category though around 60,000 volunteered themselves as being of Vietnamese ethnicity in the 2011 national census. But qualitative research (Sims, 2007) by the Runnymede Trust does shed some light on the issue.

Interviewees for this report said education was highly prized among all parts of the Vietnamese community, not least as a marker of social mobility:

"As [Vietnam] wasn't as 'well off' as Britain you'd tend to see that Vietnamese parents will encourage their children to study hard and use the facilities of this country, because in Vietnam not everyone was able to study up to an older age, so they see more value to it. This leads to pressuring to study and to study well. I haven't ever heard of a Vietnamese person who hasn't gone to university yet", Khanh, a 23-year-old British-born Vietnamese woman, told the author (Sims 2007, 4).

While it is hard to draw conclusions about aspiration and achievement from the experience of Vietnamese refugees in Britain, one thing is certain - it is always worth looking more closely at the most striking examples before using them as a basis for policy or practice.

Conclusion

So, what might we learn from the experiences of refugee groups throughout history? In some senses the conclusions we might draw from a gallop through the historical landscape might appear rather depressing, if predictable: those who arrive with economic, social or cultural capital tend to thrive, and thrive more quickly, than those who do not. Of course, all migrant groups, whether or not they are refugees, arrive with a range of internal baggage, if you like, which may or may not support their transition from safety to belonging and on to success, as Kohli (2011) puts it.

The classic case of social and cultural capital smoothing the path of a refugee population arriving in England must be that of the Huguenots. Not only were these migrants highly educated and skilled; they also had patronage at the highest levels of English society. This sort of patronage can bring practical support - the Lord Mayor's edict that David Willaume should receive his freedom of the Worshipful Company of Goldsmiths, for instance. But it can also help to direct the attitudes of others. Despite the initial - and understandable - concern among English artisans that the Huguenots were likely to take their business and to fail to share their skills, it seems they did come to fit into existing communities, both of artisans and educators, fairly quickly.

Positive narratives about refugee populations - certainly lacking today in the case of unaccompanied asylum seekers, but perhaps less so in the case of resettled Syrians - can make a real difference, then. They can lead to practical support being more readily available, and they can help to persuade and reassure a potentially sceptical public.

There have been positive and negative internal factors, too: many refugees have not aspired to belong, and for them a return home has been the main route to success. Some have aspired to leave but have been unable to do so. But whatever their future aspirations, a meeting of minds along the way has often been helpful. The Basque children who arrived in 1937 knew they planned to return and had a clear idea of what they needed to learn while they were here in order to rebuild the Spain to which they hoped to be repatriated. And while success, in their terms, was not for them to create and was not, in the end, forthcoming, they met with a cadre of British society which was happy to welcome and support them. Whether refugees aspire to stay or to leave, a strong sense of purpose, aspiration or direction has certainly been a positive factor for many in the past.

It is worth noting, in this context, that while assimilation is often seen by policymakers as the key to success, that may not entirely be the case for many refugee – or other migrant – communities. Louise Archer and Becky Francis (2005) reported upon one well-known migrant success story: that of the Chinese, whose exam results have outstripped those of many other ethnic groups. They conclude that the value placed on education by that community has not just been key to that perceived success, but has also allowed them to wrap a positive narrative around their migrant lives, reinforcing, in a sense, their migrant status:

> This construction of 'value of education' also becomes a strategy in the face of difficult socio-economic conditions for immigrants in Britain, by which the British–Chinese can mobilise an ethnically particular cultural capital to progress social class mobility.
>
> (Archer and Francis 2005, 106)

Archer and Francis' work underlines the fact that while refugees will carry just as many predetermined advantages and disadvantages as the next group of pupils, they will have additional external factors to wrestle with, too.

Positive external factors for refugees in the past included having sufficient financial and organisational support – the Belgians were a case in point. While the East European Jews who had arrived a few decades earlier had faced prejudice and poverty – despite charitable efforts on their behalf – the Belgian children were the beneficiaries of a huge charitable effort by some very well-connected and well-to-do people. They were hand-picked to fit in and to succeed, and so it hardly came as a surprise that their sojourn in England went smoothly.

Perhaps even more useful, in terms of modern-day policymaking, is the experience of those who had strong mentors to help them succeed. Hana Kohn's foster-father, who helped her with her maths each evening, enabled her to pass a grammar school entrance exam within a few months of arrival and helped set the course for her future life and career. In other chapters we will examine some mentoring programmes that are available now and reflect upon the difference they can make to the lives of those who benefit from them.

But still two major factors stand out: The first is internal, in the backgrounds and prior educational experiences of refugee groups, and the second is external, in the manner of their arrival and reception in the UK.

In some respects, the first is not alterable, though we will revisit the means by which negative factors might be mitigated or by which positive factors might be built upon – but history would suggest proceeding with caution when trying to draw broad messages – perhaps all that refugees have in common is the fact that they have been given the 'refugee' label. It is hard to find commonality, for instance, between the experience of a destitute and uneducated Jewish refugee from Eastern Europe arriving in London in the 1870s with little or no support from the Gentile population and amid a wave of anti-Semitic sentiment; and Hana Kohn and her brother, stepping off the Kindertransport in 1939 into the arms of a welcoming family and a school where they were very soon able to thrive. It is little wonder that the Jewish community of Stepney took a century and more to move on to more affluent districts, while Hana and Hans – despite the horrific and slow realisation that there would be no return home and that their family were dead – had every chance of success.

And the second of those two factors – the manner of their arrival here – is key, too. Hana and Hans came to England amid a wave of concern for the Jewish population of Germany and

Central Europe after the Kristallnacht attacks on Jewish businesses, homes and synagogues. But they were also arriving on a pre-arranged programme; their parents were able to write to their receiving families about them in advance and their transition into education and into life in England was a smooth one.

While refugees will always, by definition, be fleeing from persecution or violence and therefore will often have had to depart from their home countries in traumatic circumstances, it will be worth examining in more detail in the modern context how the onward educational journeys of those who benefit from planned arrivals differ from those whose entry into the UK is unplanned, traumatic and dangerous. And while there are factors that are immutable in all refugee children's lives, there is much in the history of refugee groups that can give modern educationists and policymakers both pause for thought and a sense of optimism.

References

Abrams, F. 2012. *Songs of Innocence: The Story of British Childhood*. London: Atlantic Books.

Alderman, G. 1998. *Modern British Jewry*. Oxford: Clarendon Press.

Alibhai-Brown, Y. 1998. Fish and chips like they make in Uganda? *The Independent*. (21 March). Available at https://www.independent.co.uk/life-style/food-spice-trail-1151577.html.

Barber, T. 2018. The integration of Vietnamese refugees in London and the UK: Fragmentation, complexity, and 'in/visibility. *UNU WIDER Working Paper*. 2018/2.

Barrett, E. 2001. 'Huguenot Integration in late 17th-and 18th-century London: Insights from Records of the French Church and Some Relief Agencies', in Vigne, R. & C. Littleton (Eds) *From Strangers to Citizens: The Integration of Immigrant Communities in Britain, Ireland and Colonial America*. Eastbourne: Sussex Academic Press.

Department of Education and Science (DES)s. 1975. *The Bullough Report: A language for life*. London: Her Majesty's Stationery Office

Francis, B. & Archer, L. 2005. British–Chinese pupils' and parents' constructions of the value of education, *British Educational Research Journal*, 31 (1), 89–108. DOI: https://doi.org/10.1080/0141192052000310047.

Goodway, E. 2001. The production and patronage of David Willaume, Huguenot merchant goldsmith in Vigne, R., & C. Littleton (Eds) *From Strangers to Citizens, the Integration of Immigrant Communities in Britain, Ireland and Colonial America*. Eastbourne: Sussex Academic Press.

Green, M. 2018. Bridging the English Channel: Huguenots in the educational milieu of the English upper class, *Paedagogica Historica*, 54 (4), 389–409, DOI: 10.1080/00309230.2017.1409773.

Jewish Encyclopedia. 1906. *Joseph Jacobs*. Available at http://www.jewishencyclopedia.com/articles/13742-simon-sir-john

Kohli, R. 2011. Working to Ensure Safety, Belonging and Success for Unaccompanied Asylum-Seeking Children, *Child Abuse Review* 20, 311–323.

Lowe, R. 1997. *Schooling and Social Change 1964–1990*. Abingdon: Routledge.

Mayhew, H. 1862, *London Labour and the London Poor*, 1862. Wordsworth Classics of World Literature (2008). Available online at https://www.gutenberg.org/files/60440/60440-h/60440-h.htm.

Muchowiecka, L. 2013, The End of Multiculturalism? Immigration and Integration in Germany and the United Kingdom, *Inquiries Journal/Student Pulse*, 5 (06). Retrieved from http://www.inquiriesjournal.com/a?id=735

Myers, K. 1999a National identity, citizenship and education for displacement: Spanish refugee children in Cambridge, 19371, *History of Education*, 28 (3) 313–325. DOI: 10.1080/004676099284645.

Myers, K. 1999b. Warm Beer, Cricket and faith: English national identity and refugee children in Britain, 1937-1945, *Paedagogica Historica*, 35 (1), 259–280. DOI:10.1080/00309230.1999.11434944.

Myers. K. 2001. The hidden history of refugee schooling in Britain: the case of the Belgians, 1914-18, *History of Education*, 30 (2), 153–162, DOI: 10.1080/00467600010012445.

Prais, S.J. & Schmool, M. 1968. *The Size and Structure of the Anglo-Jewish Population*, 1960-1965, *The Newham Borough Council*. https://www.newham.info/population/

QMZM Local stats. *Redbridge Census Demographics United Kingdom*. Available at http://localstats.co.uk/census-demographics/england/london/redbridge

Refugee Voices project, 2004, *Association of Jewish Refugees in Great Britain, interview no 48, conducted 8 Feb 2004 in Liverpool*. Accessed at the Weiner Library, London. Copyright of the Association of Jewish Refugees.

Rutter, J. 1999. *Refugee Children in the UK*. Maidenhead: Open University Press (2006 edition).

Sims, J. M. 2007. *The Vietnamese Community in Great Britain – Thirty Years on*. Runnymede Trust.

Soulard, D. 2012. Anglo-French cultural transmission: the case of John Locke and the Huguenots. *Historical Research*, 85, 105-132. doi:10.1111/j.1468-2281.2011.00572.x.

Swindlehurst, C. 2001. An unruly and presumptuous rabble: the reaction of the Spitalfields weaving community to the settlement of the Huguenots, 1660–90, in Vigne, R. & C. Littleton (Eds) *From Strangers to Citizens, the Integration of Immigrant Communities in Britain, Ireland and Colonial America*. Eastbourne: Sussex Academic Press.

Tonkin, B. 2015. Refugee Week: The Huguenots count among the most successful of Britain's immigrants, *The Independent*, 18 June. Available at https://www.independent.co.uk/news/uk/home-news/refugee-week-the-huguenots-count-among-the-most-successful-of-britains-immigrants-10330066.html

Tower Hamlets Borough Council. 2015. *Religion in Tower Hamlets*. Available at https://www.towerhamlets.gov.uk/Documents/Borough_statistics/Ward_profiles/Census-2011/2015-04-21-Faith-key-facts-Revised-data.pdf.

UNHCR. 2020. *What is a refugee?* https://www.unrefugees.org/refugee-facts/what-is-a-refugee/

Zangwill 1895 (2004). *Children of the Ghetto: A study of a peculiar people*. Cambridge: Black Apollo Press.

Abdul: 'I just wanted to find a safe place and find a better life, and to have equality'

Abdul is from Darfur, and he's been in England about a year. He was 17 when he arrived, and that was the first time he went to a mainstream school.

"I would like to fly, to do something amazing," he says.

"In my country it's very different. If you have dark skin you are not allowed to study. I only went to a Muslim religious school, they wouldn't let me study in a normal school. That was when I was 10 or 11. I did quite well but it was only for two years – the rest of the time I was looking after animals.

"My job was to feed the animals, but some days the Janjaweed would come and take them. And if they found you they would kill you. Every day was struggling to stay alive. It was very hard.

"I left at 15 or 16. I didn't think to come to England or Europe; I was just looking for a place to feel safe. I had no money, I had to be trafficked but when they started to put us in the transport they were asking us to pay money. If you didn't pay you couldn't continue.

"I said to them, 'I have no one to help me and my family lives in a worse place than yours'. I said: 'I can work for you', and they said OK. They had farms."

But the life in Libya was even harder than in Darfur: "They let us work for a farmer, picking vegetables and stuff like that. I worked more than I slept. They beat us without any reason. I worked there for six months without them paying me a penny.

"Then they said they would send me to Italy. I didn't know where Italy was. They said it's better than Libya. They said it's dangerous, and I said I don't care. I was dead already. I said, 'It doesn't make any difference if I am lost in the sea. I'm not scared.'

"Italy was perfect. I had my freedom. I could live freely. I was placed in a hostel but new refugees came so they said you can go. So I went with some other people, to France. We stayed in Paris under a bridge for a month, or two months. I didn't have anywhere to go. Someone said we can go to some place called Calais – there's people there who can get warm clothes and sleeping bags for us. I said OK, let's go then.

"In the jungle there were people fighting: I crossed the countries to come here but there were people fighting. I decided to take a chance, and I jumped a truck. I didn't make a difference if I stayed in Calais or came here."

When he jumped out of the lorry, he was in Luton: "I found the security in a park, and he called the police. They came and arrested me, and we went to the police station. They asked questions: 'Where do you come from, how did you get here?' They referred me to a hostel. And after that I moved to Peterborough, to a shared house. People were supporting me. The social worker helped. They said: 'We will get you an education.'"

Abdul arrived in May, and in September he started an English language course at college. He's delighted to be here:

"I am quite pleased. I got a chance to get an education. I can do whatever I want – here if you work hard, you can do whatever you want. Darfur is my home, it's my country. It's still my country. I still love my country.

"My country isn't bad. It's the government, and the people who are using the situation against the people. I would rather just stay in my home country – it's just because of conditions and circumstances that I am here. What I want is to go back and to make things better. If I have kids, I will still take them back. I'm not going to forget where I came from.

"My father was killed, but my Mum is alive in Darfur. I had an older brother and sister but one sister died."

Does his mother know he's alive?

"I'm not sure.

"The place where I was born, every day there were Tornadoes, hearing the noise of the guns and everything. Any time you can get shot. I came here and found a place that's relaxed and peaceful. To me, that's the best place to stay."

It took a year, but Abdul now has a visa to remain in the UK.

"I didn't know anything about visas and papers, they said to me they would have a lawyer, but I just entered the things that were true.

"For me the most important thing is I feel safe.

"Even if you weren't born here, you've got a chance. I still didn't decide yet – hopefully more education. I need to keep improving, developing, language and skills. I just wanted to find a safe place and find a better life, and to have equality. I feel I have those things here."

9 On the ground
The East of England

Fran Abrams

In a rather tight parking area outside a converted one-storey building on a light industrial park, a small group of girls in grey jilbabs and purple headscarves are kicking a football around in the pale spring sunshine.

This is the Iqra Academy, an independent Muslim girls' school based in a former nursery in Peterborough. Observing the impromptu match is its principal, Michael Wright. It's a typical breaktime, he says. Through the local Children of Adam charity, the school has been able to offer free places to girls arriving from Syria on the government's resettlement programme, which will ultimately lead to 20,000 refugees finding homes in the UK. And football has proved a particular passion for them. After only a couple of years in the UK – in some cases much less – they're already winning national competitions and some of them now train with the Peterborough United Academy.

Shaimaa, who's 16, says she first played football in Lebanon, where the family lived with relatives after fleeing the war in Syria.

"I came here in year nine. The Principal actually started training us … we didn't know very much. We used to go to the park and train," she says.

The first match they played, against the nearby Thomas Deacon Academy (TDA), they lost. It was seven or eight goals to one, she thinks.

"It was horrible. No-one knew how to play and stuff. So we started practicing. If we went to TDA now we would beat them."

Shaimaa and the other Syrian girls seem to have settled in quickly – there are five of them today and they're warm and chatty, laughing with one another – and they have very clear ideas about the future. Shaimaa wants to be an architect: "But I love football. I think I might do football after finishing university."

She has the route well worked out: She's now in Year 10 and expects to do GCSEs next year: two English, two science, one maths, RE, ICT. She already has Arabic and is doing a cadet GCSE.

"We have to apply for Sixth Form and get really good results", Shaimaa says – all the other girls laugh at this. "I'm supposed to be in Year 11, but I moved back a year because I thought I'd do better that way."

Down the road at the Peterborough office of the British Red Cross are another group of young people – this time, all male. They're unaccompanied refugees and asylum seekers who are being supported by a project called Surviving to Thriving – and while they would all share Shaimaa's sentiments about education, their experiences have been somewhat different.

None of these young men have been able to access mainstream secondary schools – usually because they are, or have been judged to be, over 16 on arrival – and so they have gone to college, where they hope to progress from English language courses to vocational education. The Iqra girls' route through GCSEs and A levels is effectively closed to them.

The group leader, Ruzina Begum, says that many of these young men have had long waits to get into college courses: "They have a long wait for ESOL (English for Speakers of Other Languages)."

"There's complication if there's an age dispute, they can't start school in the year they would want to, and that affects them a lot. And it's really hard to start in the middle of a year, depending on the college."

It's April now. Ruzina says one young man who arrived in November is still waiting: "Every time I phone they say he has to wait. He did start a community ESOL course, but he didn't enjoy it, and he dropped out." Even when they do get into college, they still spend much of the week kicking their heels: "The college week is 18 hours maximum. They usually have quite big gaps, most have fewer than that usually, about three hours to four on three days, so 10–12 hours."

Among some of the young men, who are eating pizza and playing Jenga, there's an air of disappointment.

Jay is 18 and from Sudan. He spends three days a week at college doing a Level 1 computing course and received his UK visa a few months ago, but he says it's been tough to get even this far.

"I have big dreams, but to get that dream you have to have status. You are studying but you are thinking about the visa. You can't study so well, it's very hard.

"I want to go to university to be a software engineer. I think next year I can start my course in Peterborough. I don't want to move but I don't really like it here."

His friend Yunas is 18; he arrived here 18 months ago from Morocco, and he radiates disappointment. His journey to this spot has been a tortuous one. He left school, home and family at the age of 12 and moved alone to Spain, where he found work in a barber shop.

"At 14 I had a nice dream, to get a good job. I left Spain for France, but in France I had problems. People wanted to kill me. So I moved to England." By the time he arrived in Peterborough, however, he was unwell and college places weren't immediately available.

"When I came here in the summer it was holidays. Then I went to hospital, I had some health problems. I waited eight months to get into education. I was applying to Peterborough Regional College for ESOL classes. I had a social worker and she told me that City College would be the best place. So I went to City College for three months, but I didn't like it. I was getting 15 per cent out of 100."

"I thought I would get a visa quickly, I thought it would be easier. In Peterborough, life is hard. There's nothing to do here. People are not nice. People aren't friendly, and we have some racism." Now he's left college, still without a visa, and is applying for a job in a warehouse.

Peterborough has become something of a hub for newly arrived refugees – both those arriving on the resettlement programme and those who find their way here alone, like Yunas, are often housed here by other local authorities because the accommodation is cheaper than in other parts of the region.

For instance, a Freedom of Information request to Lincolnshire County Council reveals that of 110 unaccompanied asylum-seeking children in the county's care, all but six are housed out of county. And while the county would not reveal how many were in Peterborough, many of them certainly are. Adeela Bainbridge, who runs the Red Cross International Family Tracing service for Cambridgeshire, Norfolk and Suffolk, provides a whistlestop guided tour. There's a sense of a multitude of communities all living shoulder to shoulder – but look closely, she says, and there are dividing lines.

At the back of the library in the centre of town there's a Kurdish café. It's used by everyone because it serves food that's palatable to lots of people – today, lentil soup is on the menu. It's run by a former Kurdish client of the Red Cross. Outside a group of young men are chatting in the street – the locals don't like this, she says, but it's home from home. Nearby there's a cheap phone shop with a Lebara mobile sign: Most people have mobiles and they often use social media to try to contact family.

Nearby is Fitzwilliam Street, where a Sudanese Community Centre has started up. The guy who runs it is a cleaner at the hospital and he works nights, she says. He comes here three times a week in the afternoon and opens up till it's time to go back to work. One of the young men we met in the Surviving to Thriving group is helping him.

Half a mile or so to the west of here, in Lincoln Road, there's a coffee shop, a shisha lounge, a food shop, cheap fast food and a halal butchers, all in a row. There's a fresh naan shop here too, along with Kurdish, Polish and Lithuanian shops. This is where newly arrived asylum seekers tend to be housed: "They are very polarised. The Eritreans don't like house sharing with Afghans. It's continued from what happened in the Jungle, if you see, they have to demarcate themselves. There's a level of drug dealing, knife crime." (The Jungle was a temporary camp set up by refugees and asylum seekers on the outskirts of Calais. In February 2018, two years after it was broken up, five people were shot in the area in a mass brawl between Eritreans and Afghans.)

"In Peterborough if you ask what's the best school it will be Kings School, Jack Hunt or Thomas Deacon." But she says that few new arrivals live in the catchment zones, even if they are the right age. Kings School is Christian, so that's another restriction.

She used to work at what's now Peterborough Regional College: "In the mid-1980s there used to be a full-time English language vocational skills course. Now there's ESOL but it's like chalk and cheese. It's very far away."

John Jordan-Hills is the Post-16 and UASC Support Manager for Cambridgeshire and works closely with the Peterborough colleges. There are pros and cons to placing young people in a place where they can find a community of people from their own countries, he says.

"Placing young people there works in a good way in that they are soon settled and have a community, particularly in the early stages before their English has developed – they can go to the shop and speak Sorani. But what we're finding is that they're not integrating. After a while it actually becomes a negative. They don't see the point of necessarily learning English because the chap that runs the Kurdish restaurant has just offered them a job."

"If we feel they're highly vulnerable we place them in Peterborough so they settle and then we look at moving them so they can develop further."

In Cambridge, there's a mentoring programme with university students volunteering, but in Peterborough it's proved harder to find mentors.

But, Jordan-Hills says, almost all the unaccompanied asylum-seeking children looked after by Cambridgeshire are in education - out of 79 who are post-16, only two are out of education and that's because they aren't engaging with any professionals.

"The problem comes when they want to move to vocational courses. We have three or four who have been here a year or two and who want to study, for example engineering or hairdressing. We have a young Eritrean woman who's good at doing Afro-Caribbean hair. But the theory involves Latin terms for types of head massage and so on - the written tests can be beyond some of them."

Jo Schofield, UASC Regional Co-ordinator for the East of England, endorses this - while there have been reports that nationally many young refugees struggle to access any form of education, in the East they are usually in classes fairly quickly, particularly if they're definitely under 16.

"I know we have had cases of kids who have been in London for a length of time then transferred to us and haven't been in education. One of the reasons for that was they didn't want kids to get settled. If you can limit that settling in initially, you have more successful transfers. But if you have a child who is transferred after six weeks or even six months, then you have got a problem."

She's referring to the National Transfer Scheme, set up to ensure local authorities across the country take their fair share of new arrivals. Because London has more new arrivals, young people tend to be transferred out from there, she explains.

In the East, they also have a rota system under which those who haven't already met their quota under the national scheme take turns to care for new arrivals. The duty authority takes any young people who arrive on the day they are in charge.

But, Jo Schofield acknowledges, the issues facing young unaccompanied asylum seekers are very different from those who arrive under the resettlement programme. Many are without papers and there's nervousness around age assessments, particularly as an Ipswich comprehensive recently made headlines after it was claimed a Year 11 asylum-seeking student was in fact much older than claimed.

"My experience of social work with schools and foster carers is anxiety around: 'Is he the age he says he is,' and 'Is he a terrorist?' The majority of these kids are desperate to learn, desperate to go to education. When I was a social worker, they used to say things like, 'Why are these UK kids playing up? I just want to learn and I want to be a doctor or a nurse or a footballer.' The teachers really like them."

Young refugees tend to get shoehorned into a sort of 'triumph or tragedy' narrative, she suggests, where there is little room left for a middle way.

"In order to be accepted by the indigenous population a refugee needs to be good, glorious and grateful. In order to get integrated and not cause offence you have to be exceptional; you have to be fantastic. People see those stories about kids playing at the Albert Hall and think: 'Those are the kind of refugees we like.'"

"We need to talk about the ones who go off because they are frustrated, they're not sure what's going on at home with mum and dad. If a kid's in school and he's plodding along and he's not going off that's a good case. But maybe he isn't thriving. Plodding along isn't OK."

Louise Gooch, who runs the Strategic Migration Partnership for the East of England, says there are many factors which give children on the resettlement programme a better chance of thriving in the education system.

"There's more parental pressure to get outcomes from schools than with UASC, because the life they had hoped for themselves has been taken away and hopes and dreams for their children remain intact", she says.

Also, by the time resettled children arrive their details have been sent ahead and arrangements made in advance: "We know when we are matching them with housing whether there's a school within reasonable travel distance that's going to be able to take them. The schools are able to prepare for them in advance of their arrival, which should make for a better service."

But, she adds, there is pressure for pupils on the resettlement programme, too, to feature in triumphant news stories in which they can be photographed outside their schools, clutching handfuls of exam certificates.

Last year the Home Office approached us and said had we got good news stories about refugees passing GCSE this Summer. We were like, 'Are you crazy? You know how long GCSE takes.' Most of our refugees arrived at the earliest in 2016, traumatised and with no English and possibly out of education for some time. We managed to find two refugee girls in Peterborough who had taken GCSE Arabic. You need English to access the exam and they had got A*. But the Home Office didn't follow that up.

10 Policy environment – England

Fran Abrams

"It would be fantastic to have a national lead. These children are having all these decisions made about them and there are pockets of people who are experts, but there's no sense of coherence. Best practice should be shared.

"We just put sticking plaster on everything. We just get on and do it. You bash out your assessment; if a kid's in school and he's plodding along and he's not going off, that's a good case. But maybe he isn't thriving. Plodding along isn't OK."

Joanne Schofield, Regional UASC co-ordinator, East of England.[1]

Introduction

The notion of analysing policy around education for young refugees and asylum seekers is oxymoronic, in that there is no clear current education policy. The Department for Education's statutory guidance on educating looked-after children has three paragraphs on this group – but, of course, it refers only to those who are unaccompanied, and therefore looked after by their local authority (DfE 2019).

And there is some sense in the lack of a coherent policy, for this is not a coherent group. Many of these children and young people are here with their families, though many are not. An increasing proportion – certainly in some ethnic groups (Gladwell et al. 2018) – have had little or no experience of formal education before arriving here, but some have had several years of formal education in their home countries. A few have a working knowledge of English, though most do not. Some have arrived alone in the backs of lorries; others – mostly Syrians coming from refugee camps in Lebanon, Jordan or Turkey – have come on a resettlement programme.

What do we know about the current population of young refugees and asylum seekers? Solid figures on how many are in our schools and FE colleges are extremely hard to come by, but the best available statistics would suggest numbers have risen in the past 15 years.

Back in 2003 Jill Rutter estimated there were 60,000 'refugee' children of compulsory school age in the UK – at the time this referred to under-16s (Rutter 2003). While it is difficult to estimate the current number, it will almost certainly be higher.

Home Office immigration statistics for the year ending June 2019 show that in the 12 months to the end of September 2019, 10,288 under-18s, including 4293 unaccompanied asylum-seeking children (UASC), applied for asylum in the UK, and a further 2706 under-18s arrived under the Vulnerable Person's Resettlement Scheme (VPRS), making a total of 12,994.

For comparison, in 2010 5139 under-18s applied for asylum and 280 people came on resettlement programmes – a total of 5419. Of those who applied for asylum, 1338 were unaccompanied.

In addition to this, between October 2016 and the end of 2018 the UK resettled 549 unaccompanied asylum-seeking children who had family in the UK in response to the clearance of camps around Calais.

Unaccompanied children are particularly vulnerable, of course, and their numbers have risen faster than those of other groups – from 1338 UK applications in 2010 (Home Office 2015) to 3058 in 2015 and 4293 in the year to September 2019 (Department for Education 2019).

Legislation affecting new arrivals

The legislative landscape is complex, and this account will not be comprehensive. But a number of pieces of key legislation affect some or all newly arrived refugee children.

-   Under Section 14 of the **Education Act 1996,** local education authorities have a legal obligation to provide education for all children ages 5–16, including children of asylum seekers or refugees, with the exception of those who are in accommodation or detention centres (in which case education would be provided by the centre.)
-   Under the **Immigration and Asylum Act 1999** the National Asylum Support Service (NASS) has a responsibility to provide asylum seekers and refugees who are waiting for a decision with accommodation and subsistence payments. In many cases, this is provided in 'dispersal areas' outside London and the South-East. This means that many young people are placed with foster families or in semi-independent living accommodation in the North and the Midlands.
-   Under the **Children Act 1989**, all children, regardless of the status of their parents, are eligible for health care, education and support from social services. Under this legislation unaccompanied children must be looked after by their local authority and are entitled to the same support as any other looked-after child. Local authorities have a duty to safeguard and promote the welfare of the children they look after. This includes a specific duty to promote children's educational achievement, wherever they live or are educated. The authority must, therefore, give particular attention to the educational implications of any decision about the welfare of those children.
-   Under **The Children and Families Act 2014** local authorities must appoint a Virtual School Head to promote the educational achievement of looked-after children.
-   Under the **Care Planning, Placement and Case Review (England) Regulations 2010**, all looked-after children should have a Personal Education Plan (PEP) which must name the officer responsible for their educational achievement – that is, the Virtual School Head.
-   Under **Statutory Guidance on Promoting the Education of Looked-After Children and Previously Looked-After Children** from the Department for Education:
    -   Appropriate education for unaccompanied children may include a period of time in a setting where their full educational needs can be assessed and integrated into the PEP.

o   Virtual School Heads, Independent Reviewing Officers, school admission officers and Special Educational Needs departments must work together to ensure that appropriate education provision is arranged.

o   The local authority should ensure robust procedures are in place to monitor educational progress. This includes securing a culture of commitment to promoting the highest possible educational outcomes for unaccompanied children.

o   All mainstream schools must give the highest priority in their oversubscription criteria to looked-after and previously looked-after children – though the guidance notes the closing dates of 31 October for secondary school applications and 15 January for primary schools. This is often an issue for migrant children who arrive in-year.

o   Local authorities must not tolerate drift and delay where looked-after children are without an education placement. This applies to those who arrive aged 16–18 as well as to younger children.

Funding

Local authorities have a legal obligation to provide education for asylum-seeker and refugee children, and under the Department for Education's funding guidance they attract Pupil Premium funding. But there is no specific funding arrangement to support the education of these children.

From 2020, according to UNESCO, the government's new funding formula for education (UNESCO 2019) will abolish specific funding for migrants and instead recognise three major disadvantages. 'Deprivation', reflecting free school meals and parental tax credits; 'Low prior attainment', reflecting the proportion of a school's pupils who do not achieve expected levels in national assessments on entry into primary and at age 10 or 11; and the proportion of pupils for whom English is an Additional Language, based on a scale which accounts for numbers who are fluent and who are new speakers of English.

Enabling factors

The factors which can facilitate or impede a refugee child's route to success are, of course, the same factors as would apply to any child. But they also face additional factors. This chapter will attempt to highlight some policy aspects of these areas. They include:

Internal factors which affect educational attainment:

- Quality of linguistic support
- Admission systems and school segregation
- Advice and guidance

External factors which affect educational attainment:

- Age assessments and their effect on access to education
- Mental health issues
- Dealing with Home Office procedures and the stress of uncertainty about immigration status

- Issues with accommodation
- The need to support other family members, including parents, particularly with language.

And refugee children also have a third set of issues to deal with. These can include:

- The ongoing effects of past trauma
- Uncertainty about the whereabouts and/or wellbeing of family and friends
- Disputes over age assessments, which can be a major barrier to educational success.

Linguistic support

"In the past I would have worked with a class teacher to produce material – you had to cut it down but it reflected what was happening in the classroom. It might be basic that child would be part of the class and the setup – there are English children who could benefit from that too. Now the class teacher is under so much pressure, they download everything off the internet. It's all on one level."

Marie-France Faulkner, former language assistant and now volunteer one-to-one teacher

For almost all refugee children, learning English is the first priority for their education providers, whether they are schools or post-16 providers, such as FE colleges or specialist centres for teaching English for Speakers of Other Languages (ESOL). But the landscape in relation to ESOL teaching has been a shifting one in recent years.

Between 1999 and 2011, local authorities had additional funding for speakers of other languages through the Ethnic Minority Achievement Grant (EMAG). This was often used to pay for a central team within the authority such as an Ethnic Minority Achievement Service.

According to the National Association for Language Development in the Curriculum (NALDIC 2020), local authority teams funded by the EMAG often worked with newly qualified teachers recruited to schools in their local authorities. They also ran professional development programmes, managed specific projects and produced guidance documents and materials. In areas with few pupils from migrant backgrounds, they would provide peripatetic support for schools and to individual pupils.

But in April 2011 this was merged into the Direct Schools Grant and schools were given much more discretion over how the money was to be used. This change coincided with austerity, and successive rounds of local authority cuts.

One year later, a survey by the NASUWT union found cost pressures had led to redundancies among both ethnic minority achievement and English as an Additional Language teachers in schools. Even though half the school leaders who responded said the pressure to meet English language needs had grown in the previous year, 19 per cent said they were aware of redundancies in their local authority area and two-thirds said resources were insufficient to meet those growing needs (NASUWT 2012).

Since then many local authority teams have ceased to exist. The website for NALDIC provides links to CPD, online resources and a service directory of weblinks to sites and resources. These are targeted at all EAL and bilingual pupils which the website emphasises is not a homogenous group. Resources and weblinks specifically aimed at supporting children from refugee backgrounds are limited (NALDIC 2020).

For young people arriving here aged 16 or older, the situation is much worse. Many report long waits to be admitted to post-16 facilities where they can begin learning English – and this applies, of course, to those who may be under 16 but whose age is in dispute and who therefore cannot gain admission to a school (see below).

Demand for ESOL services, which also cater for adults, far outstrips supply. A research report for the Department for Education (Higton et al. 2019) found waiting lists consistently stretched to more than 500 and some had more than 1000. Some of the young people interviewed for this book reported waiting many months before gaining a college place.

Once in college, young people often find themselves under-occupied. One survey for the London mayor (Stevenson et al. 2017) found that the number of hours taught on ESOL courses ranged from 1.5 to 15 per week, with the average being 5.5.

In 2016, the then Prime Minster commissioned Dame Louise Casey to undertake a review into integration and opportunity in isolated and deprived communities. The Casey Review concluded that good English skills were 'fundamental' to integrated communities. But providers of English language courses said their funding for such provision from government had reduced in recent years – under the Adult Education Budget, it had fallen 56% in real terms between 2009–10 and 2016–17, although there was an increase in 2016/17 and in 2019 the Chancellor, Sajid Javid, announced a further £10 million for ESOL in the government's 'Integration Areas'.

The Casey Review (2016) highlighted the importance of this provision for social mixing, particularly among young people, and since its publication there have been calls for the establishment of a national ESOL strategy.

Admissions systems and segregation

"I remember when I first went to college they asked me to fill in an application with my name and address. I didn't know how to use a pen to write my name. I was sixteen and a half, a child with no parents and no support in this country. I was really hoping to go to school because that teaches you the definition of education – It can help you build up from that basic level, from my understanding. I didn't get that. In college they didn't really push you in that way, it was more the language. As a young guy in the village I was always dreaming, I wanted to be an engineer because my Dad was an engineer. I'm happy about myself now because I never gave up."

Hamid Khan, Chair of the Refugee Support Network Youth Advisory Board.

"When I arrived I was 14. They put me in a foster family then they tried to enrol me into school. But some of the schools were full. They said they were not enrolling at the moment so I had to wait. I had to wait for six months, maybe more than that."

Ali, unaccompanied asylum seeker from Afghanistan.

The schools featured in this book are – almost by definition – schools which have significant populations of refugees and which have put a great deal of effort into ensuring that they are well provided for. But this is not always the case. Agencies working with young refugees report that there is resistance from some quarters to admitting pupils from this group, and that social workers looking for school places often have to work hard to place young people, particularly if they are aged over 14 or have arrived mid-year.

A recent report by Refugee Support Network for UNICEF (Gladwell et al. 2018) found that while looked-after children are supposed to be placed in school within 20 days of arrival, no one region of the UK had met that standard. Most delays happened in secondary schools and in FE colleges, where up to a quarter of children were waiting for more than three months.

The report details a survey carried out in 2016 which found among unaccompanied children, 32 per cent attended FE college while just over one quarter attended secondary school. Nine per cent were in 'other' provision, which included private tuition or simply being out of education altogether. And there was some evidence to suggest that in a small number of cases refugee and asylum-seeking children were placed in potentially inappropriate alternative provision such as Pupil Referral Units.

At school and college level, delays were caused by three key factors: "First, a lack of readily available places for children with SEN. Second, a reluctance of schools to admit students at the upper-secondary level due to fear of negatively influencing results profiles, and third, the need, in England, to undertake a lengthy process of applying for the Secretary of State for Education to direct an academy to take a child (in comparison to a Local Authority being able to direct a school themselves)."

Other barriers included the fact that children often faced long waits before being relocated under the National Transfer Scheme and were often not placed in school until this process was complete.

Catherine Gladwell, Chief Executive of the Refugee Support Network and one of the authors of the report, says there is particular nervousness in some schools about taking pupils in Years 10 and 11, in the run-up to GCSEs. She said that many schools seemed unaware of an exemption in criteria for the Department for Education's performance tables, which meant that if a pupil had been admitted to school after the start of Year 10 and did not come from a country whose official language was English, they did not have to be counted in the league tables.

"Schools are worried that if someone arrives in Year 10 or 11 it will negatively affect their GCSE results. It isn't the case", she says. "But awareness of that provision is incredibly low. We spoke to about 60 schools and only one or two were aware of it. We need to create an environment where schools want to take these children want to invest in them and are incentivised to do that."

But, she adds, there are arguments for and against school for this group of young people: they may be best served by going to college, where they can focus on language development and settle in without the pressure of exams which they are unlikely to pass.

"You have young people who say they want to do their GCSEs and there's a group of people for whom I would say school is absolutely the best environment. There tends to be better support services, it's a more manageable context to arrive in. But if the further education provision in the area is strong they may be better off there than being put into school for a year. If they don't have any English to do GCSE they fail and they have to start all over again. But there are other kids who would have done really well in the right school environment who end up in further education. For me there's no one right answer."

In policy terms, there are clear statements that English schools are expected to work to integrate newly arrived pupils and to ensure they are not placed at any additional disadvantage by the way in which the education system treats them. The English secondary education system has been categorised, with Ireland, as 'integrationist' in policy terms (Manzoni et al. 2019).

Ofsted, for example, makes a fairly unequivocal statement in a document accompanying its new inspection framework – though it does not specifically identify migrants or refugees as a potentially disadvantaged group: (Ofsted 2019b)

"The criteria make clear how important it is that high-quality education is available to all learners. This means that we will consider whether education providers offer inclusive education, for example:

- whether schools are removing some children from their rolls solely to improve published outcomes
- whether colleges and other further education providers are doing all they can to ensure that all learners are able to complete their courses
- whether the curriculum available for the most disadvantaged learners is ambitious and meets their needs."

(Missed) opportunities to aspire: the case of the Afghan refugees

"The reason I came here was because of education. If I have my education, maybe I can go back. I want to be an architect; I would like to build and design. When you see how people suffer from not getting an education, you realise how important it is to study. Obviously if you don't have education you don't get as much money and that's what happens when you move to another country and you want to start work. Education's very important. It's what makes us so, so strict about education." Shaimaa, aged 16. Iqra Academy, Peterborough

It is beyond doubt that as a group, young asylum seekers and refugees are highly aspirational. Time and again, those interviewed for this book expressed the desire to thrive, to 'fly,' to make great things of the opportunity they had been given. And yet, for some, the road to success was not a straight one.

A recent report on the experiences of young Afghan refugees who came to the UK over the past decade (Gladwell 2018) used a Freedom of Information request and focus groups with 31 care leavers to investigate their experiences and achievements.

It found plentiful aspiration among this group of young people, but also evidence that this was not being met. More than three-quarters of the Afghan care-leavers interviewed said they wanted to study at a higher level and believed this would help them to find meaningful work. In London and the South East, these aspirations were particularly high, with two-thirds hoping one day to attend university – even if they were currently only studying at a basic level.

Yet an FOI request carried out for the Afghan study revealed significant numbers of Afghan care leavers had no qualifications at all. In two local authority areas out of 11 which provided data, more than 80 per cent were without qualifications, and there were only two areas where the proportion was below 20 per cent. This compares with a figure of 8 per cent without qualifications in the UK as a whole. Among those who had achieved, most had only basic-level qualifications and few had progressed beyond GCSE level.

> *However, there was a smaller group who had exceeded expectations. The proportion of Afghan care leavers entering university, while below the national access rate of 32.5 per cent of all 18-year-olds, was significantly more than the 6 per cent national average for care leavers in general.*
>
> *There is no clear evidence on the relative attainment of all refugees when compared with the indigenous population, and they are not a homogenous group so it is hard to extrapolate from this study. But it is worth looking at some of the policy issues which have been identified by the European Commission (Gladwell and Chetwynd 2018) and others as possible barriers to success for migrants, and to consider how that applies to young refugees in England.*

The Casey Review (2016) concluded that there was broad acknowledgement of the importance of equality, a sense of belonging and access to opportunities as the means of tackling integration gaps in the UK.

However, it also noted that isolation could often begin at a young age and that some children's experience of school was 'marked by segregation from wider British communities' (ibid., 168). It recommended that the government should work with schools and local communities to encourage school provision and projects to ensure children from different communities learn alongside each other.

Yet despite this there is little clear nationwide evidence of whether refugee children find themselves segregated, though most secondary schools do have ability groupings at Key Stage 4 and it would seem likely that those arriving with language needs would find themselves in lower sets.

There is a broader debate, too, about the level of integration young refugees need in terms of the services provided for them. Adrian Matthews, a trustee of Cambridge Refugee Resettlement Campaign and a former consultant to the Children's Commissioner, expressed strong reservations about any form of segregation in schools:

> "Segregation is a form of discrimination", he says. "If it's done on the basis of race or nationality I'd be quite concerned."

Yet there's a wider debate about whether certain groups need specialist, separate services to meet their needs: "It's an interesting debate and it's also shadowed in Social Services in terms of unaccompanied children (UASC). There's a debate about whether it's better to integrate them into the general children's care system and not have any special provision, or whether it's better to have specialist UASC social care teams.

"In 2007-8, when there were large numbers, you did have big teams for UASC but then the numbers dropped off. Now you don't have the expertise that had developed in the team and I think the children get a worse deal as a result of that.

"There are issues which are specifically to do with refugees and particularly asylum seekers. They are going through a legal process and that's incredibly stressful. They are facing a different set of problems to those who came here passported and with status before they arrive."

Advice and guidance

Adara and Roberta

Adara and Roberta meet once a week in central London - Roberta works at University College, London, and Adara lives nearby and is studying and hoping to become a mid-wife. They have been paired under a mentoring scheme run by the Refugee Support Network. Adara says the programme has made a huge difference to her: "We meet once a week once a week, usually at a library, and she helps me with my coursework - with grammar and with English and maths.

"Every time I meet my mentor she asks how I'm feeling, if the place where I live is safe, if I've got things that I want. She tells me to speak out, to ask anything I want. My mentor told me how to meditate, how to breathe in and breathe out to minimize my stress. It helped me a little bit, but it did take a while.

"Back home they wouldn't have done all these things. Here, I have a good opportunity to do what I want to do in the future. If you want something, here they push you to achieve your goal."

RSN's report for UNICEF (Gladwell et al. 2018) identifies six factors the organisation believes are key to refugee and asylum-seeking children's ability to remain and thrive in education. All of them, to a greater or lesser extent, can or should involve support, advice and guidance. They are:

- a committed, caring adult who will provide support over an extended period of time
- education programmes appropriately adapted to meet their needs
- good pastoral care and mental health support at school
- on-site advice, guidance and support for refugee and asylum-seeking learners
- creative approaches to peer support, including buddy schemes and school-wide awareness raising about forced migration
- training on the educational needs of refugee and asylum-seeking children for all teachers and other school or college staff.

The report suggested central government, schools, local authorities and donors could all do more to ensure these factors were addressed:

- Central government agencies could raise awareness of existing good practice across England, Scotland and Wales through networking and information-sharing opportunities
- Local authorities could provide specialist training for those working with unaccompanied children, particularly where specialist teams have been disbanded. They could also promote broader training and dissemination of good practice, and ensure schools in their areas are resourced with resources and training on this group
- Schools should provide training in the educational support needs of refugee and asylum-seeking children for teachers at all educational levels is included as standard in

continuing professional development. They could also consider partnering with a specialist voluntary sector organisation to provide in-school/college advice and pastoral support for refugee and asylum-seeking learners, introduce peer support and consider providing for homework clubs, educational mentoring, social activities and broader holistic support.

External factors

Too old for school? The role of age and age assessments

Some of the additional factors mentioned above affect almost all asylum seekers; some only a proportion. But some, while not affecting all, can be life-changing and irreversible. The way the education system treats age is a case in point.

While the academic route through GCSEs and A Levels into university is not the right one – nor a realistic aspiration in the short term – for all, many find they are permanently cut off from it purely by dint of their age on arrival. If they are 16–18, they should still be in compulsory education – but that education rarely takes place in a school and usually consists of ESOL followed by vocational education at a low level. For those who wish to pursue an academic route and who have the ability and determination to do so, this is frustrating and potentially soul-destroying.

When I came here I went to college and started from zero, sitting in that class not knowing how to write two or three words, and still I was dreaming that I wanted to be an engineer one day. I did the ESOL and then I did a one-year IT course because I had no other options – I could do it easily and it gave me a little bit of extra help with language. Then they wouldn't take me in A-Levels so I decided to do something that included maths. I did a Level 3 qualification in medical science, which wasn't something I wanted to do. I knew it wasn't for me – I got three distinctions and one of those was starred. My tutor wanted to know what I was doing when I started applying for an engineering degree! I said, 'I'm sorry. I didn't say that I did this course because I had no other option. Now I want to change to the thing I really want to do.'

Hamid Khan, chair of RSN's Youth Advisory Board, who was sixteen and a half when he arrived here.

It is hard to avoid the sense that had Hamid Khan arrived at age 13 or 14 rather than at 16, his journey could have been a very different one. The age at which young people arrive here is not an issue that public policymakers in the UK can tackle, of course. But the inflexibilities in the system perhaps could be. Sometimes quite random and finely-tuned decisions can lead to the cut-off between a route that makes sense and leads to fulfilment and one that does not.

This is a big and perhaps intractable problem, with many complexities. Schools may have child protection concerns about taking a young person who is over 16 into Year 10 or 11. For those over the age of 19, funding must come through a very constrained adult education budget, so for those arriving at around the age of 16 there may be a sort of cut-off or restriction at the upper end, too.

And then there is the thorny issue of age assessments. When an unaccompanied child claims asylum, a social worker in the area where the claim is made is responsible for doing this assessment. As many of these children are without papers, cannot prove their age and may not even know their date of birth, the process is a complex one. There are no fixed rules, but there is guidance from the courts in a case involving Merton Council and so the assessments are supposed to be 'Merton Compliant'. Among other things the judgement suggested good practice would involve two assessors working over a period of time and involving other professionals such as residential social work staff, teachers and other young people.

As these assessments are carried out at local authority level there are no statistics on how often they take place. But interviewees for this book have pointed out that the process, which necessarily takes time, can be a bar in itself. Assessments are also undertaken by immigration officials, though young people deemed over 18 are meant to be treated as younger – that is, entitled to be looked after by their local authority – until a full age assessment is complete, unless the official has deemed their appearance to suggest 'very strongly' that they are 'significantly' over 18.

In some areas, interviewees for this book have suggested most unaccompanied young people are subject to age assessments and are barred from going to school until those are complete, even if they say they are under 16. In many cases, even if they are finally assessed as having been under 16 on arrival the passing of time means they miss the opportunity to go to school because by the time the process is complete their 16th birthday has passed.

The Refugee Council says the number of these age-disputed cases is increasing, though as a percentage of all unaccompanied young people it appears to be lower than in 2010. In that year, there were 1338 applications from unaccompanied young people, and 531 age disputes, according to Home Office statistics – though these do not include young people deemed 'significantly' over 18. In the year to September 2019 there were 4293 applications from unaccompanied young people and 886 age disputes. Yet the issue continues to be a fraught one which affects the lives of many young people.

Catherine Gladwell, Chief Executive of Refugee Support Network, believes if there is not a clear child protection issue then schools should presume in a young person's favour.

"I would say that until the age assessment is completed there should be an assumption that they are the age they claim to be until or unless they are found to be another age", she says. "That would be a huge step forward. Some social workers say it's the policy that they should be educated as the actual age they say they are until it's proven otherwise, but others say not."

Mental health issues

I used to be very smart. The teacher was explaining something to me and I already knew what she was trying to say. Now I am trying to put pressure on my head and to understand, but still it isn't working. My mind switches off and goes somewhere else. But I'm still fighting and trying my best. I will never give up. I had to go to the hospital as an emergency and then I was introduced to Baobab. I go there for group therapy and one-to-one therapy. They helped me a lot – you need support. You definitely need big support.

Ali, who arrived in the UK 12 years ago aged 14, was deported at 18, returned three years later and has just been given leave to remain after several court battles.

Mental health issues arise time and again, in various forms, in conversations with young refugees. Often their struggles are in relation to their immigration status or other practical issues. The basic and unsurprising fact is that these are young people who have gone through a great deal before coming here and who continue to do so after arriving. Their lives are not straightforward – sometimes they relive the past; sometimes they worry about the wellbeing of family members back home or elsewhere.

The research by Catherine Gladwell et al. (2018) on the experiences of young Afghans found that after immigration status, mental health was the next most frequently identified barrier to education. Young people reported their lives were 'too stressful' and talked of 'big pressure in my head.'

The two are inextricably linked. According to the report: "When they remain living in protracted limbo in the UK, with the formal labour market out of reach, this group of care leavers are, and become increasingly, vulnerable to mental health issues, exploitative work conditions, and a growing sense of powerlessness and frustration – even when they have achieved high levels of education."

Catherine Gladwell says this is the biggest bar to success for these young people: "If you ask me what's the one biggest blockage to young people progressing in education, I would say mental health. At all levels, from primary school to university. At the end of the day whatever you do and however much you advocate for the mental health of young people, it doesn't work."

There are hopeful signs, she says, but more needs to be done: "Some schools buy in therapeutic services – they are for all children who need it. That's wonderful. And there are a small number of outstanding specialist mental health providers who provide for asylum seeking children, but they tend to be provided by virtual schools and they have to compete for funding.

"One of the positive things in the last few years is a government pledge for every school to have a mental health worker. We would say that's brilliant; we would absolutely welcome that. Please make sure it actually happens. Make sure that those providing it go through training specifically on working with refugee and asylum-seeking children. I understand everyone wants their thing to be funded, but they really should make sure of these mental health workers get trauma training."

Conclusion

In this chapter, an exploration of the current policy landscape has illustrated the impact of the fragmented nature of national official policy and a range of different policies, advice and guidelines for those working to support young new arrivals and the refugee and asylum seekers themselves. This lack of coordination could be redressed by a policy shift which renders unaccompanied and asylum-seeking children more visible. One way to do this would be through the introduction of a national champion for UASC who can ensure the voices of this very marginalised group are heard across a range of issues, including education at all levels.

A major focus of the holder of this post should be to try to ensure young people are afforded every opportunity to integrate into educational settings. The post holder's office and website should become a first port of call for those seeking information and advice, including good practice and classroom resources. These should provide clear information to schools and colleges on the needs and rights of refugee children, including performance table exemptions for new arrivals. This should also include training for new and in-service teachers on the educational needs of refugee and asylum-seeking children. The national champion would ensure that the various types of information, guidance and support available to young refugees is effective and streamlined. The post holder could co-ordinate a review of the age assessment process and recommend ways to ensure age is no barrier to achievement for new arrivals. A key aspect of the work would be to ensure the government's pledge to put a mental health worker in every school is fulfilled.

The notion of a UASC champion is a key policy recommendation of this section of the book. In the final chapter, which comprises Section 3 of the book, the two authors come back together to detail further recommendations for policymakers, practitioners and researchers in the field. Before we turn to the final chapter, we present Hamid's story.

Note

1 Extract from interview with author.

References

Casey, L. 2016. The Casey Review A review into opportunity and integration. *DCLG*. Available at https://assets.publishing.service.gov.uk/government/uploads/system/uploads/attachment_data/file/575973/The_Casey_Review_Report.pdf.

Department for Education (DfE). 2019. Children Looked After in England (including adoption), year ending 31 March 2019. Available at https://assets.publishing.service.gov.uk/government/uploads/system/uploads/attachment_data/file/850306/Children_looked_after_in_England_2019_Text.pdf.

Gladwell, C. & Chetwynd, G. 2018. *Education for Refugee and Asylum Seeking Children: Access and Equality in England, Scotland and Wales*. London: Refugee Support Network. Available at https://www.unicef.org.uk/wp-content/uploads/2018/09/Access-to-Education-report-PDF.pdf.

Gladwell, C., Thomas, J., Chetwynd, G., Majeed, S., Burke, C., Stubbs, V. & Zahid, S. 2018. The impact of educational achievement on the integration and wellbeing of Afghan refugee youth in the UK. *United Nations* University WIDER Working Paper 2018/57. Available at: https://www.wider.unu.edu/publication/impact-educational-achievement-integration-and-wellbeing-afghan-refugee-youth-uk.

Higton, J., Sandhu, J., Stutz, A., Patel, R., Choudhoury, A., Richards, S & CFE Research. June 2019. English for speakers of other languages: Access and progression Research report. *DfE*. Available at https://assets.publishing.service.gov.uk/government/uploads/system/uploads/attachment_data/file/811750/English_for_speakers_of_other_languages.pdf.

Home Office. 2015. National Statistics: Asylum. Available at: https://www.gov.uk/government/publications/immigration-statistics-october-to-december-2015/asylum#data-tables.

Home Office. 2019. National Statistics: How many people do we grant asylum or protection to? Updated 22 August 2019. Available at: https://www.gov.uk/government/publications/immigration-statistics-year-ending-june-2019/how-many-people-do-we-grant-asylum-or-protection-to.

Manzoni, C. & Rolfe, H. 2019. *How Schools are Integrating New Migrant Pupils and Their Families*. London: National Institute of Economic and Social Research.

NALDIC. 2020. Available at: https://naldic.org.uk/

NASUWT. 2012. Ethnic minority achievement. Available at: https://www.naldic.org.uk/Resources/NALDIC/Research%20and%20Information/Documents/EMAG_Survey_Report.pdf.

Ofsted. 2019b. Education inspection framework: Equality, diversity and inclusion statement. Reference number 190023, May 2019. Available at: https://assets.publishing.service.gov.uk/government/uploads/system/uploads/attachment_data/file/821069/Education_inspection_framework_-_equality__diversity_and_inclusion_statement.pdf

Rutter, J. 2003. Working with Refugee Children. York: Joseph Rowntree Foundation.

Stevenson, A., Kings, P. & Sterland, L. May 2017. *Mapping ESOL Provision in Greater*. London: Learning and Work Institute.

UNESCO. 2019. Global education monitoring report 2019: Migration, displacement and education: building bridges, not walls. Available at: https://unesdoc.unesco.org/ark:/48223/pf0000265996.

Hamid Khan: 'Education is the light that brightens your mind'

Hamid Khan is 30 and has the air of a man emerging from a very long tunnel. At the end of our interview he produces his phone to display a picture of his 4-month-old son. Having lost his parents in an air strike he is delighted now to have married and begun a new family, he says.

"I came aged 16 and a half from Afghanistan – from Helmand. I didn't have any education when I came, just some basic education from local people.

"I remember when I first went to college in North West London, they asked me to fill in an application with my name, my age and address. I didn't know how to use a pen to write my name. That was the beginning of my journey into education."

The barriers Khan faced are worth enumerating. The first was his age – he was over 16 and therefore too old to go to secondary school.

"I was really hoping to go to school," he says, "Because that teaches you the definition of education. It can help you build up that basic level, from my understanding. In college it's a bit different, they don't really push you. It was more just language, not really focusing on my future career. In college, they don't have very much information about refugee rights and how to build them. That's why a lot of people stop education and go into basic work – they don't know how to go further ahead. They lose their dreams."

Even at the age of 16, Khan had big ambitions – like so many of the other refugees interviewed for this book.

"When I was a young kid I had no education, but I knew what I wanted to be. As a young guy in the village I wanted to be an engineer because my dad was an engineer. I always looked at his books and thought how nicely they were drawn.

"When I came here I was thinking about it. I went to college starting from zero, sitting in that class not knowing how to write two or three words. Still I was dreaming that I wanted to be an engineer one day."

Unlike many Khan had some clear ideas – or gained them – on what he needed to do to succeed. But despite his hard work and determination, doors remained closed.

Language was a major barrier, he says. At many points along the way it held him back, not least from progressing on to A-Levels, which would have helped him to access university.

"I did the ESOL and then I had one year on an IT course because I had no other option. It was something I could get into easily and it gave me a little bit of extra help with language. They wouldn't take me in A-Levels because of my language so then I decided to do something that included maths. I did a Level 3 qualification in medical science, which wasn't something I wanted to do. I knew it wasn't for me – I got three distinctions and one of those was starred. My tutor wanted to know what I was doing when I started applying for an engineering degree! I said, 'I'm sorry. I didn't say that I did this course because I had no other option. Now I want to change to the thing I really want to do.'"

"One day, sitting in college and they said: 'No way, you can't go to university because of your status. I felt I would never succeed and nobody could understand the feeling I was going through', he says.

"If you have discretionary leave you can get an education because you can get a loan. My local authority supported me till I was 25, but I still had an issue which was the law. The law wasn't in the hands of the local authorities. It's one of my dreams that the law can change.

"It doesn't make sense to me – if someone is going to school or college they can achieve their dreams and become an engineer or a doctor. They want to study here. They want to stay here and to contribute and you are stopping that person just because they don't have five years here?

"RSN had to negotiate with my local authority – it was a long conversation. In the end Brighton University said I could pay half fee, but it was still £12,000. And my local authority agreed to pay my housing and in the meantime pay the 50 per cent till I got my status. Luckily, when I was in my first year, in December, my documents came through.

"I had to apply again as a home student and change course but my tutor found a way for me, then I could get a loan.

"Eighteen months ago I graduated in aerospace engineering. I want to do a masters and I have applied to Brunel. I hope to start next year."

Yet all the way through, he says, he has had to struggle. More specialist support would have helped:

"When I was doing IT, those born here knew how to use all this stuff. So I could sit with them and get help from them. But I was thinking if only there was a class support for us where we could get extra help with language. These other guys, they could write their reports so quickly.

"That was my struggle during my degree as well. Everyone was struggling with the practical work. But for me it was writing the reports that was a struggle.

"I think if I didn't have the language issues, nobody would have beat me in the class. It was hard for my teachers to understand these things.

"I felt colleges and universities need someone who knows how to explain these things to refugees and people who come from outside the country. Staff training is very important.

"Many of the universities told me I didn't have the right qualification. They said, 'We can't take you.' If I hadn't been pushing I would have given up.

"Then I called Brighton University and I said, 'This is my case. I'm a refugee. I don't have the right qualification.' There was this guy, his name was Chris. And he told me, 'You have three weeks before the class starts. You need 5.5 IELTS points – it's an international language test.'

"I went to an independent college and I paid £450 – I don't know how I made the money; I ate less, spent less on me. I took that money and I got those 5.5 IELTS points, and they said: 'OK.'

"I was there for four years and I never met this man Chris. Before, I only spoke to him on the phone. But one day in my final year I passed his door and I thought, 'Let's knock.' He was busy but I told him: 'I spoke to you on the phone three or four years ago.'

"He said: 'You're Hamid!'

"I told him: 'I am graduating in the next few months. One small mistake could have meant me not being here today. You are a great person. You gave me the option and because of that luck I am here. I touched him and he understood the importance of that.

"I had my graduation and he was there.

"I am happy about myself personally because I never gave up.

"Education is the light that brightens your mind. It tells you the difference between good and bad. Those younger kids who came from countries like Afghanistan, they are bright people and they can contribute to this country. If they go back they can also contribute: they won't be misled by those warmongers and those bad elements.

"If we stop them from education, they go into the wrong ways, walking on the streets causing trouble to other citizens.

"So education should not be a struggle for them. There should not be barriers, you know, especially when they have a desire to go into higher education and be someone.

"I am a citizen now, but I'm not happy deep inside because I know there's a lot of people who are still struggling like I was back in those years. I have status. It's like a ticket in the train station: when you don't have it, you can't pass through those barriers.

"If someone wants to educate themselves, there shouldn't be those difficult rules.

"If I could say one thing to those politicians, I would tell them: 'Please, just this one thing: don't stop people from education. They will stay in this country. They will contribute to you – nurses, doctors. We need those people.'"

SECTION 3
Ways forward

In this final section Jo and Fran come together to reflect on what we have learnt from history, from those working on the ground to support refugee children to access education and on the dilemmas faced by school leaders and practitioners who work to include refugee pupils in what has been an increasingly hostile landscape for new arrivals. What has emerged from Sections 1 and 2 are narratives of optimism and hope which we have drawn upon to design pedagogical principles for policymaking and future practice prioritising the rights and needs of refugee children. We have gained much from our dialogues and encounters with children from refugee backgrounds and from those working with them. The practical theorising approach underpins our recommendations for policy, practice and future research. We end with a call for action which is explicitly about hope for the future.

11 Concluding thoughts

Joanna McIntyre and Fran Abrams

We began this book with an account of the numbers of child refugees crossing Europe: the highest recorded since World War II. We planned the research for our different sections knowing that, across Europe, there was a shift towards populist governments that took a more hostile stance towards the plight of refugees. In our own context, nationalistic discourse was increasingly prominent and unchallenged in the post-Brexit landscape. As we articulate in Chapter 2, the discourse around government's political attitudes towards immigration has a knock-on effect on policy and practice for the inclusion of refugee children in schools and colleges.

Now, as we write the concluding chapter to the book, we are in the grip of a global pandemic: societies are in lockdown and countries are closing their borders. Schools are closed in line with social distancing policies and teaching and learning has moved to online platforms. For the children who have featured in this book, now physically isolated from the places and communities of which they had been supported to feel a part, the experiences of safety and belonging are shifting. Most have access to online learning only through mobile phones and so their early experiences of succeeding are becoming less frequent as they struggle to access materials and support in meaningful ways. As with other vulnerable and disadvantaged groups, for refugees social injustice is felt most keenly when participatory parity is dependent upon material and human resources to which marginalized groups have limited access. Inevitably, we are thinking about what the positions of young refugees and asylum seekers will be in the versions of society that emerge once the global crisis has passed. For this reason, we present in this final chapter concluding thoughts, during this unprecedented period in our lives, a process by which we hope to contribute to a dialogue about what schooling and society could look like in a post-pandemic world.

Inclusive schooling for all matters in any reconceptualisation of society, at local, national and global levels. A central feature of the book has been the bringing together of researchers and practitioners in a rich and reciprocal dialogue to learn about an inclusive approach to the education of refugee and asylum-seeking children. Ravi Kholi's theory of the 'resumption of ordinary life', and Nancy Fraser's 'participatory parity', have been fundamental to these conversations. The theoretical framings have provided a language and vocabulary for making sense of existing (good) practice within the case study sites and to identify areas where this could be strengthened even further. In this way, we have come together in a community of school leaders, practitioners and academics to develop a theorised practice for inclusive refugee education which we believe should inform refugee education policy and practice in other school contexts. It is clear that the two theoretical frames work in tandem – that safety, belonging and succeeding are concepts that characterise aspects of practice which are dependent upon a socially just moral framing that foregrounds parity of distribution of resource and recognition of the needs and potential contributions of all within a policy landscape that is able to represent the views of those most usually disregarded by mainstream educational policy.

What has emerged is a focus on activities and pedagogies that foreground opportunities for new arrivals to engage in 'place-making'. Whilst these primarily emerged in discussions around the concept of belonging it became evident that place-making is also an important element of safety and success. Place-making is a concept utilised in some (mainly) urban planning strategies, where the links between attachment and bonds to a place and community and wellbeing, community building and civic engagement have been long established (cf. Lefebvre 1968). Importantly, place-making is recognised as a process and one that is ground-up rather than top-down. This is to recognise that communities and societies are always changing and that people living in specific locations contribute towards building a sense of that place. Doreen Massey talks of the importance of social relations in the make-up of spaces and refers to the 'thrown-togetherness' as spaces are turned into meaningful places by and for those who inhabit them (2005, 302). There is insufficient space to detail Massey's argument here but, to summarise, she argues against the idea of locations being fixed static concepts, seeing them instead as continually in flux, remade though people's engagement in and with those spaces over time. In this way, places are seen as 'a product of routes rather than roots' (Creswell 2004, 53).

Clearly, in areas where refugee and asylum seekers are provided with housing, new arrivals can contribute to this evolving sense of place identity and, in turn, can find points of connection and meaning in their new contexts. For Massey, places are profoundly political: newcomers to those places need to be supported to make sense of a locality's stories, histories and connections for different people. In educational contexts, place-making pedagogies, such as those described in Chapters 4–7, allow students to engage with activities that make sense of these different layers of meaning about a place whilst also allowing opportunities for them to create their own meaningful engagements with that place (for example, Comber 2011, Hall and Thomson 2017).

What has also emerged through working with the case study schools is a clear sense of education as process. This is despite the shift in most of high-income, refugee-receiving countries in the Global North to an endpoint, test-orientated school system. Throughout Section 1, the practitioners' sense-making about each of the concepts – of safety, belonging and particularly success – showcases the enduring nature of education as an encounter between human beings (Biesta 2013, 1) rather than an abstract set of learning outcomes and performance data. The school leaders and practitioners in Section 1 and those working with young refugees as they arrive into our communities in Section 2 have an orientation towards viewing each new arrival in terms of what they bring, as well as what they need:

> Such an orientation, therefore, is not just about how we can get the world into our children and students; it is also – and perhaps first of all – about how we can help our children and students to engage with, and thus come into, the world.
>
> (ibid., 5)

This asset-based view of the potential of each new arrival works alongside a commitment to viewing education as requiring something beyond test-led pedagogies. In this way inclusive models of education for new arrivals are distinguished from the currently dominant model of schooling. The practitioners, and those supporting them into education, recognise that an inclusive school's role is foundational in helping shape the experiences of the refugee teenager who arrives in their classrooms too late to be able to achieve in ways that have currency for peers in the host community (examination results tied to specific school years: GCSEs and 'A' levels in the English context). Instead they focus on the here and now – establishing pedagogies which foster small, but significant experiences of safety, of belonging and of succeeding – whilst also imbuing in their students a sense of confidence and optimism that they will be able to continue once they have moved on to the next stage. So these pedagogies are also future-focused, fostering in the new arrival an attitude towards lifelong learning, continuing to experience safety, belonging and successes as they develop ways of leading lives they and others can value, alongside others in their new context. It is in these ways that our dialogues recognise that education is always a process. Refugee children, who have experienced turbulence and instability in their pasts, need an experience of education which is predicated upon an optimistic future. The concept of success needs to be focused on feeling valued in the here and now, feeling confidence that they can make meaningful choices about next steps that might well be asynchronous with those of others of the same age in the host community. This means the learning outcomes for recent new arrivals in the upper ages of school will look very different from their peers' outcomes and might not contribute to the currency of performance league tables.

Schools which work in these ways are dependent upon senior leaders who are willing to exhibit what is described in Section 1 as 'brave' leadership or in the wider literature as 'ethical leadership' (for example, Strike 2007). Each interview with school leadership teams made it clear that leaders continually balance risks to their school performance data with their moral and inclusive stance. In one example, this conversation continued well beyond the interview, through email exchange between Jo and Jayne, the CEO from Jasmine Gardens. Jayne described her motivations for engaging with the Framework for Ethical Leadership pathways (ASCL 2019), explaining that the ethical leadership framework accorded with her commitment to the most vulnerable and marginalised so that her inclusive approach to refugees across the academy chain was an integral part of her personal professional ethos. In turn this gave Amy, who had oversight for new arrivals across the academy, the confidence to prioritise and meet the specific needs of refugee students in her work. This pattern was repeated across the case study sites.

Though this book has worked to articulate an inclusive model for education of refugee and asylum-seeking pupils in mainstream settings, the final case study, Fern College in Chapter 7, is of a holistic full-time and separate provision for post-16 students. Our argument here is that it is the bespoke nature of this provision, otherwise not available for refugee students aged 16-18 in the mainstream, that makes this an appropriately inclusive model for this group of learners. The alternative, to wait for months for a place, was untenable (following Slee 2018).

In the sustained interactions with practitioners described throughout Section 1, important work, which is often rendered unseen and unvalued in performance metrics, is made visible. This work continues in spite of the policy vacuum around the education of new arrivals. In part, it depends upon what is referred to in Chapter 5 as 'policy memory' of resources, peda-gogies and documentation that support culturally responsive approaches to diverse class-rooms. This brave leadership and reliance on shared policy memory accords with Fraser's reminder that participatory parity can only be achieved if marginalised groups such as refu-gee children are represented within strategies for redistribution of resource and recognitive policy directives.

The application of Kohli's and Fraser's ideas to refugee education practice has been illumi-nating. Whilst the theories of each have much to offer to debates about refugee education, we have utilised their ideas interdependently and it is when they are applied in confluence as here that the real potential is realised. As barriers to operationalising aspects of safety, belonging and succeeding for all students are identified, the lenses of redistribution, recogni-tion and representation shed light on the causes or sources of these barriers. Inevitably, localised experiences are shaped by national and global policy contexts. The absence of spe-cifically targeted policy for the education of refugee and asylum-seeking students in English schools is felt keenly by those trying to offer models of inclusive education. Where there is a vacuum, other policy fills the void. At the national level, the educational policy void is filled with immigration policies, such as control of movement through dispersal strategies and management of risks to national security. These have implications for the work of schools. British values, the Prevent agenda and other similar policy moves lead to configurations of new arrivals as threats, within a refugee crisis narrative that appeals to the populist 'fear of the other' discourses referred to above and in Chapter 2. At the same time, international poli-cies promoting global comparisons of test performance such as PISA tables prioritise the need for national governments to develop educational policies that are focused on school performance data. When this is the case, as in the English school-led improvement system, local accountability for fair distribution of high- and lower-attaining pupils diminishes. Thus, in the competitive school choice landscape, schools serving economically disadvantaged communities, where most housing for new arrivals is located, have higher concentrations of lower-attaining pupils and consequently do not perform well in the league tables and/or pri-oritise a reduced curriculum that is almost entirely focused on teaching to test pedagogies (cf. Reay 2017). Whilst the interviews with the case study school leaders demonstrate bravery, compassion and moral purpose, the impact of (inter)national policies which create an immi-gration–education policy nexus is a daily dilemma for all headteachers working in communi-ties with refugee populations (McIntyre and Hall 2018).

Whilst we have been able to engage with senior leaders and practitioners in education who shape policy at an institutional level and with local advocates working on the ground with young refugee and asylum seekers, we are acutely aware that what has been missing are the voices of Policymakers (with an intentional capitalised 'P'). To our knowledge, there is no schools-focused agency within the Government's Department for Education with a responsi-bility for the development of policy for the education of new arrivals, though there is over-sight within the Department's Children's Services Safeguarding team who monitor the progress of those children who are unaccompanied and thus fall within the label of 'looked after children' within the care of the state. However, as we have stated elsewhere, there has been no policy development around educational best practice for these vulnerable groups of learners for more than a decade.

In Section 2, the narrative of the history of different groups of refugees, their experiences and expectations illustrate that these are shaped by a recognition of what the refugee brings and by the level of political will to develop strategies to foster a welcome for immigrants. Dryden-Peterson et al. (2019) outline how educational policy for refugees is heavily influenced by how far national governments view the refugee as a temporary visitor or a future permanent citizen. Those who have contributed to this book share the view that education is a public good and that the refugee student is a future citizen. As such, it is to the benefit of all society that we have high-quality models of inclusive education for all.

Principles for policy and practice

Before we outline the implications of our work for practice, policy and future research, we share some underlying principles for future policymaking. These principles are derived from the practitioners who contributed to this book. The practitioners worked on them during the focus group meetings and through follow-up emails until they agreed the following:

1. The child and their potential contribution to society should be at the heart of all educational policymaking.
2. Policy at (inter)national and local school and classroom level should promote the **safety, belonging** and **success** of each child.
3. Every school, every stakeholder and each member of staff should be responsible for ensuring that the policy is enacted, with appropriate training.
4. This policy is underpinned by:
   - an awareness of the social, cultural and political issues leading to migration
   - an understanding that we are **all are** affected by migration and that immigration can be beneficial for all society
   - an awareness of what young people need to know and understand in order to experience safety, belonging and success
   - a recognition that schools need to know where to be flexible and where there is a need for consistency about expectations for new arrivals
   - respectful sharing of information about an individual's circumstances and prior experiences and the knowledge and training to offer appropriate support
   - a recognition of the assets that each young person brings with them
   - an appreciation of success as a multifaceted concept, experienced when potential is fulfilled, and manifested in different ways.
5. This all requires a commitment to **ongoing, recursive questioning** about how individuals, groups and organisations promote safety, belonging and success for each child**.**

Implications for practice, policy and future research

In Chapter 2, we underlined the importance of finding a language to use with policymakers, language that makes clear what those working in the field of refugee education stand for and a narrative that illustrates what is possible. The experiences of young refugees and asylum seekers and those working to support them, detailed throughout Section 1, have illustrated what is possible and the values of those working in this field of education. Section 1 also argues that the concepts of 'safety', 'belonging' and 'success' resonate with practitioners as a frame for developing an inclusive model of education for all, and that barriers and facilitating factors for enacting this model are bound up within choices made about the redistribution of material and human resources, recognition of the assets and the rights of refugee children and representation of these in policy spheres. The two conceptual frames provide a language underpinning a model of inclusive education for all children in our schools and colleges, especially for marginalised groups such as refugee and asylum-seeking children. The examples of pedagogies and approaches in the case study chapters showcase how practitioners and schools can embed safety (Chapter 4), belonging (Chapter 5) and success (Chapter 6), in their own contexts. **The frameworks, and particularly the concepts of safety, belonging and succeeding, should be utilised to generate a language for practice and for policymaking,** noting the ways in which success within education has been reconceptualised for the benefit of individuals and society.

Throughout the book, practitioners have communicated their belief that refugee and asylum-seeking students have much to bring and that this is more quickly realised if they are viewed in terms **of an asset-based pedagogy which aims to enable all students to realise their potential contributions to society,** supported by an initial holistic assessment of their knowledges, skills and attributes. **In addition to a positive attitude towards fostering multilingualism with support for the acquisition of English, schools should also be encouraged to adapt place-making and culturally responsive pedagogies in recognition of the needs of newly arrived pupils.** This is significantly supported by markers of inclusion where children can see people like them represented amongst the adults that shape their experiences of life in their new society. Schools should be encouraged to work with representatives of diverse communities both inside and outside of the school gates.

In Section 2, narrative descriptions of the histories and lived experiences of young refugees within one place need to be shared so that lessons from history and the recent past are understood. **We argue that curriculum content should include teaching about narratives of immigration, not only in terms of the benefits that refugees and other migrants bring to host societies but also in order to educate future citizens about the causes of forced migration. By these means we can better understand how our actions have consequences for lives lived thousands of miles away.**

In both sections of the book, the invisibility of data and policy about refugee education causes difficulties for those trying to support young new arrivals to access and then thrive in schools and colleges. **There is a need for a named body/agency which can act as a champion to ensure that the rights of refugee children to a high-quality, inclusive education are realised.** This agency should have representatives from refugee communities so that their voices are able to be heard. Within the English context, this body could be an additional arm of the Children's Commissioner Board and support its work in ensuring that the rights of the most vulnerable are considered by policy initiatives and developments.

Throughout the book, we have queried whether accountability systems for schools and school leaders have privileged the things that society most needs from an education system. We argue for **a recalibration so that moral responsibility and the public good drive curriculum and pedagogy in schools, so that school leaders can be encouraged to**

foreground quality, equity and inclusion for all. This should be underpinned by a more equitable distribution of resource for schools in areas of economic deprivation so that those schools can play a role in supporting communities to grow and flourish. Such an investment would mean that young people in those communities are more likely to be able to have equal access to participation in the future jobs market and in society. This would be **an investment of resource into a holistic future-focused model of education rather than a series of interventions based on test-driven pedagogies and outcomes**. Significantly, a recognition of the specific needs of young people who have experienced significant crises that caused them to flee from their homes and set out on journeys to places of refuge thousands of miles distant means ensuring some flexibility in education provision, flexibility that will eventually allow them to flourish. **The inclusive model of safety, belonging and succeeding will also need to incorporate trauma-informed approaches.** Refugee students are not a homogenous group, they come with different experiences but usually with a sense of optimism about the role of education in helping them to build lives of meaning in their new context. We would welcome **policy initiatives that take account of interruptions to schooling and ensure that the age of the student on arrival is not a barrier to achievement**.

Whilst we have tried to include interviews with young refugees, Fraser's lens of representation was identified as an area of weakness by the practitioners as they reflected on their work in schools. **There is a need for future research that engages directly with the voices of refugee and asylum-seeking young people to better recognise different strands of experience.** This might take the form of research that explores the life journeys of refugee pupils currently or recently educated in their resettlement contexts, to look back at those who arrived since 2015 and look at what happened, what were the barriers and what were the facilitating factors for them.

Whilst the book has focused on local responses to the needs of refugee students within specific schools, colleges and places the issues are framed within a significant global policy response to forced migration. **We need to understand what reciprocal learning can be acquired through study of policy and practice for refugee education from different contexts across Europe and other international endpoints of forced migration journeys.** This book has focused on teenage refugee and asylum seekers; we now need to look at their next steps, whether this be in formal or informal learning contexts, to understand how different policies and societal pressures affect each stage.

Fundamentally, the suggestions in this section and in our final call to action reclaim and reimagine the role of education for public good and its role in responding to, and shaping, local, national and global societies. **Future research is needed to measure educational policy and reform through a sociological lens: to see how it impacts differentially across societies and to understand if we are shifting towards an inclusive model with social justice at its core for all our pupils.**

Call to action

In the face of a pandemic that has affected all populations across the world and in which the health of every individual is dependent upon that of the most vulnerable, it is inconceivable that societies emerge without asking questions about what is important and what should be valued. Whilst this unprecedented global emergency provides opportunities for considering alternative ways of living and being, the messages in this book about meaningful inclusion of disenfranchised groups such as refugees within education systems should remain a priority for all as this book is fundamentally about hope for the future, for agency and change.

We end this book with a call to action for (inter)national policymakers and individual citizens of the world to demand a more equitable set of principles to guide the ways in which societies are reconceptualised. Aiming for all children and members of society to experience feelings of safety, belonging and succeeding seems like a good place to start, as the long-term economic and health effects of international lockdowns will be felt for generations to come. The alternative is a shift back to what was before: a vision of addressing inequality through models of social mobility based on a false notion of meritocracy ostensibly based on an individual's talents, but actually skewed towards those who have economic and social capital and resources to be able to succeed. Inevitably, refugees and those most disadvantaged feel this inequality most keenly.

Models of success based on economic measures of productivity lead to inequality and social injustice.

We call for future social models to be underpinned by policies across all areas of governance which prioritise wellbeing for all. An education for wellbeing policy would require different measures of success for individuals, for schools and, ultimately, for societies. School leaders would be required to evidence curricula and pedagogies that prioritise moral and ethical equity. For refugee and asylum-seeking children this would incorporate their rights to a high-quality, inclusive education on a par with peers in their new communities, and a commitment by the state to providing lifelong learning and training (United Nations 2015). Measures of success would be predicated upon the numbers of people who felt that they were able to live lives they and others in society valued.

Writing in the post-war years, as she reflected on her own and others' experiences of life as refugees in far-flung destinations, Hannah Arendt described writing her seminal text, *The Origins of Totalitarianism*, 'against a background of both relentless optimism and relentless despair' (1951 (2007), x). The same can be said of the background for the writing of this book. However, what dominates is the optimism of the young refugees and asylum seekers and the people working with them that we met along the way. For them, we urge policymakers, educational leaders and practitioners, and all who strive for an inclusive and fair world, to take action to ensure we shift from despair to hope. To call for policies – and especially educational polices – which ensure that those families who have made the despairing, yet also optimistic decision to entrust their most precious assets, their children, to countries vast distances away do so in the secure knowledge that they will to be able to live ordinary lives, participating in all aspects of life on a par with others, and contributing towards a better world for all.

References

Arendt, H. 1951 (2017 edition). *The Origins of Totalitarianism*. Harmondsworth: Penguin.

ASCL. 2019. Framework for Ethical Leadership in Education. Available at https://www.ascl.org.uk/Help-and-Advice/Leadership-and-governance/Strategic-planning/Framework-for-ethical-leadership-in-education. Accessed 20 January 2020

Biesta, G. 2013. *The Beautiful Risk of Education*. Boulder: Paradigm.

Comber, B. 2011. Making Space for Place-Making Pedagogies: Stretching Normative Mandated Literacy Curriculum. *Contemporary Issues in Early Childhood*, 12(4), 343–348. https://doi.org/10.2304/ciec.2011.12.4.343

Creswell, T. 2004. *Place: A Short Introduction*. Oxford: Blackwell.

Dryden-Peterson, S. Adelman, E. Bellino, M.J. and Chopra, V. 2019. The Purposes of Refugee Education: Policy and Practice of Including Refugees in National Education Systems, *Sociology of Education*, 92(4), 346–366.

Hall, C. and Thomson, P. 2017 *Inspiring School Change: Transforming Education through the Creative Arts*. Abingdon: Routledge.

Lefebvre, H. 1968. *Le Droit à la ville* [The Right to the City] (2nd ed.). Paris: Anthropos.

Massey, D. 2005. *For Space*. London: Sage Publications.

McIntyre, J. and Hall, C. 2018 Barriers to the inclusion of refugee and asylum-seeking children in schools in England. *Educational Review*, DOI: 10.1080/00131911.2018.1544115.

Reay, D. 2017. *Miseducation: Inequality, Education and the Working Classes*. Bristol: Policy Press.

Slee, R. 2018. *Inclusive Education Isn't Dead, It Just Smells Funny*. Abingdon: Routledge.

Strike, K. 2007. *Ethical Leadership in Schools: Creating Community in an Environment of Accountability*. Thousand Oaks: Corwin Press.

United Nations. 2015. 2030 Agenda for Sustainable Development. Available at https://www.un.org/sustainabledevelopment/education/ Accessed 20 January 2020.

INDEX

Page numbers in *italics* refer to figures.

Printed in Great Britain
by Amazon